Fulfilling the Contract

Fulfilling the Contract

The First 100 Days

James G. Gimpel
University of Maryland

Allyn and Bacon
Boston • London • Toronto • Sydney • Tokyo • Singapore

Vice President Publisher, Social Sciences: Susan Badger
Executive Editor, Social Sciences: Sean Wakely
Senior Editor: Stephen Hull
Editorial Assistant: Susan Hutchinson
Marketing Manager: Karon Bowers
Senior Production Administrator: Marjorie Payne
Manufacturing Buyer: Aloka Rathnam
Cover Administrator: Suzanne Harbison

A Simon & Schuster Company
Needham Heights, MA 02194

Library of Congress Cataloging-in-Publication Data

Gimpel, James G.
Fulfilling the contract : the first 100 days / James G. Gimpel.
p. cm.
Includes index.
ISBN: 0-205-18887-7 (alk. paper)
1. Republican Party (U.S. : 1854–) 2. United States. Congress.
House—Elections, 1994. 3. United States—Politics and
government—1993– 4. United States—Economic policy—1993–
5. United States—Social policy—1993– I. Title.
JK2356.G55 1995
324.2734'09'049—dc20 95-38907
CIP

Printed in the United States of America

10 9 8 7 6 5 4 3 2 1 00 99 98 97 96 95

For Ana M. Brooks and Rosa de Yacobucci Lapaitis

Contents

Preface

Much of the recent literature on the U.S. Congress has failed to distinguish that institution from the Democrats who ran it for forty years. Now that the Republicans are in power, many established "truths" may have to be revised. Basing their evaluations on the volumes of research on Congress drawn from forty years of Democratic rule, many political scientists and pundits would have insisted that something like the first 100 days in the 104th Congress could never happen. Now it appears that Congress is not just individuals, although there is still room for member autonomy. Political parties are not mere phantoms, although they are still not as strong in Congress as in most parliaments. Congressional party leadership has been dismissed to such an extent by the existing body of work that no serious scholar in 1994 would have imagined in mid-July 1995 that *The Washington Post* would run a front page story by David Broder titled, "AT 6 MONTHS, HOUSE GOP JUGGERNAUT STILL COHESIVE."[1]

Few would have predicted the redirection in the policy debate either. Who would have thought five years ago that the Washington policy community would be discussing a flat tax? Two years ago, no one would have predicted that Congress would take serious steps toward giving the president line-item veto authority, end a sixty-year-old federal welfare entitlement system, and restrict the capacity of the federal government to dictate state government policy. Who would have expected President Clinton to devise his own plan to balance the budget in ten years? And who would have guessed that the U.S. House of Representatives would enact the sweeping internal reforms adopted on opening day of the 104th Congress?

Reform-oriented proposals on welfare, crime, foreign policy, product liability, term limits, tax reform—ideas that the previous majority had kept off the agenda—suddenly surfaced in the first 100 days of the 104th Congress. Although they complained about their diminution of power, even many Democrats welcomed the high level of the policy debate. In the words of one senior Democrat, "[T]here is something to be gained institutionally by shifts in power. It's cleansing for our system."[2]

---

[1]*The Washington Post,* July 17, 1995, p. A1.

[2]Interview with Congressman Paul Kanjorski (D-PA), 3/29/95.

Some Democratic staff interviewed for this book welcomed the new challenges of preparing their bosses to play the opposition role that Republicans had mastered after forty years in the minority.

The support of Senate Republicans (and a Democratic President) would be crucial for quick passage of the items in the "Contract with America," but the discussion of these measures has had a lasting impact on the policy debate regardless of whether they become law in this Congress. House leaders knew full well that little of the Contract would have become law at the end of their 100 day deadline. But to dismiss the first 100 days as irrelevant simply because some of the bills would either be ignored by the Senate or vetoed by the President is to suggest that the greater part of the complicated congressional policy-making process can be ignored. As Congressional Quarterly's Ronald Elving has pointed out in his recent work, *Conflict and Compromise* (Simon and Schuster, 1995), it took family leave legislation first introduced in 1984 a full nine years to generate the momentum to pass the U.S. House and Senate. But few would argue that the initial House passage of family leave was a trivial and insignificant event simply because it took the Senate several years to catch up. Only a fraction of the bills passed in one chamber ever make it to a vote in the other. But nothing becomes law if it is not passed in one chamber first.

The research for this book is based largely on over seventy personal interviews with members of the U.S. House of Representatives and their staffs during the spring and summer of 1995. I spoke with fifty-two members of Congress from both parties and twenty staff members. All but one of the members of Congress agreed to speak on the record. About half of the staffers agreed to speak on the record. The interviews were semi-structured. Certain general questions were asked of every member, and more specific questions were tailored according to the member's party, position in the leadership, areas of interest, and committee assignments.

The names of those interviewed who were willing to be identified for the sake of this very grateful acknowledgement are as follows:

Members of Congress: *Rick White (WA); Bob Ehrlich (MD); Charles Canady (FL); Mark Souder (IN); Lincoln Diaz-Balart (FL); Jerry Weller (IL) Floyd Spence (SC); Enid Waldholtz (UT); Carlos Moorhead (CA); Dick Chrysler (MI); Ray LaHood (IL); Sue Myrick (NC); Ileana Ros-Lehtinen (FL); Bob Ney (OH); Lynn Rivers (MI); Amo Houghton (NY); Steny Hoyer (MD); Albert Wynn (MD); Ben Cardin (MD); Peter Hoekstra (MI); Owen Pickett (VA); David Dreier (CA); Barney Frank (MA); Bill Emerson (MO); Jim Bunn (OR); Phil Crane (IL); Joel Hefley (CO); Barbara Cubin (WY); Paul Kanjorski (PA); Rosa DeLauro (CT); Chris Cox (CA); Andrew Jacobs (IN); Dana Rohrabacher (CA); Ron Coleman (TX); Dan Frisa (NY); John Boehner (OH); Tillie Fowler (FL); Bill Goodling (PA); Bob Inglis (SC); John Tanner (TN); Christopher Shays (CT); Bob Livingston (LA); Mike Parker (MS); Dave Camp (MI); E. Clay Shaw (FL);*

Scotty Baesler (KY); Jim Talent (MO); John Hostettler (IN); Roger Wicker (MS); Tim Hutchinson (AR); Bill Luther (MN); and Glen Browder (AL).

Staff and others: *Tony Blankley (Speaker Gingrich); Dan Meyer (Speaker Gingrich); Scott Reed (Republican National Committee); Kerry Knott (Majority Leader Armey); Ed Gillespie (Majority Leader Armey); Brian Gaston (Conference Chairman John Boehner); Barry Jackson (Conference Chairman John Boehner); Chuck Greener (Republican National Committee); Paul McNulty (House Judiciary Subcommittee on Crime); Katherine Hazeem (House Judiciary Subcommittee on the Constitution); Frank Luntz (Pollster); Daniel Mitchell (Heritage Foundation); Elizabeth Humphrey (Lincoln Diaz-Balart); Robert Woodson, Jr. (Bob Inglis).*

The idea of writing a book on the Republican takeover of Congress was originally that of David Mason, the Director of the Heritage Foundation's *Congress Assessment Project.* I owe a weighty debt of gratitude to Mason and the research support provided by the Heritage Foundation during the spring and summer of 1995. My research assistants at Heritage, Jennifer Hagen from Claremont McKenna College, Richard Moha from Hillsdale College, and Hans Nichols from Cornell University, ran errands and pulled together hundreds-of-pages-worth of information under my high-pressure deadlines and in spite of my occasionally sour disposition. My research assistants at Maryland, Aparna Srinivasan and Brian Crane, cheerfully undertook the tedious task of collecting and entering data. Two former Capitol Hill colleagues, Mike Boisvenue and Holly Harle, collected valuable insider information that found its way into the book.

I also thank my academic colleagues at the University of Maryland and elsewhere who read major sections of the manuscript and provided helpful comments. These include Robin M. Wolpert, Roger H. Davidson, Paul Herrnson, George Quester, John J. Pitney, William Connelly, Eric Uslaner, and Mark Graber. Intermittent discussions with my graduate school mentor, Mark Hansen, and my good friends, Robert Eisinger and Thomas Pavkov, clarified my thinking and redirected the project at key points. Thanks also to Allyn and Bacon's reviewers: Richard Hardy, University of Missouri; Clyde Wilcox, Georgetown University; Michael Malbin, State University of New York at Albany; and Michael Johnston, Colgate University for their part in improving the book. Steve Hull, Marjorie Payne and Sue Hutchinson made dealing with Allyn and Bacon a very pleasant experience.

Veronica deserves praise for loyally supporting me through one of the busiest times in our ten-year marriage. After a full day of her own work, and a long day of interviews on the Hill that sometimes ran late into the evening, she always made it feel so good to come home. Finally, but most important, the kind of cooperation I had in securing the interviews during such an intense period in the history of our national legislature can be explained only by divine intervention, for which I express my praise and thanks.

Fulfilling the Contract

1

Republicans Ascendant: The 1994 Elections in the U.S. House

November 8, 1994, was a landmark in American electoral history. Republicans walked away with their most spectacular gains since 1948. When network election coverage began that evening, well before polls had closed in most of the country, the surprised and sometimes somber tones of those anchoring election coverage suggested that something was up. Network pollsters had been collecting data throughout the day, and their research showed that a major electoral earthquake was underway. It wouldn't even be a long night in most places. Republicans were winning decisive victories almost everywhere.

One of the most stunning turnabouts came in Washington state where five established Democratic incumbents in the House of Representatives were defeated, including Speaker of the House Tom Foley. Another Democrat lost an open-seat race. Suddenly, the Washington state delegation had changed from nine Democrats and one Republican to eight Republicans and two Democrats.

Overall, Republican pick-ups across the states were remarkably even. A few seats here, a few seats there, totalling 52 new seats in all for a total of 230.[1] Not a single Republican incumbent was defeated. Democrats saw their majority drop from 256 to a minority of 204 seats. Thirty-four Democratic incumbents lost, the most since 1966. More important, Republicans would now control the House for the first time since the election of 1952.

In the weeks before the election, many had predicted a Republican takeover of the U.S. Senate. The Senate was more evenly divided, with Republicans holding forty-four seats. Democrats were defending twenty-one seats, compared with just eleven for Republicans. Knowing that the president's party almost always loses some seats in midterm congressional elections, a Republican gain of six or seven Senate seats was not wildly implausible. By contrast, a Republican pick-up of the forty seats necessary for a House majority simply seemed beyond reach. Traditional models of midterm seat loss predicted that Democrats would lose only half that many seats.

EXPLANATIONS FOR THE ELECTORAL QUAKE

President Clinton's Performance

Several explanations account for the staggering Democratic defeats. Perhaps the most obvious is the public's dim view of President Clinton's performance. Although the president had not won a majority of the popular vote in 1992, his approval ratings were high at the beginning of his presidency (59% among men, 57% among women).[2] Just six months into his term, Clinton began to sag in the court of public opinion. For much of his second year in office, his approval ratings remained below 50 percent. Moderate Republican John Porter (IL) could say without much exaggeration that "If Ronald Reagan was the Teflon president, this president is the Brillo president..."[3]. Everything sticks to him.

President Clinton's record in passing legislation was solid. Year-end figures suggested that Congress went along with the president about 86 percent of the time—the best legislative record since Lyndon Johnson's nearly thirty years ago.[4] Of course, there were some significant and highly publicized defeats. The president put enormous effort into health care reform, only to see it flounder and die by August, 1994. At about the same time, a major piece of crime legislation was delayed when a large number of House Democrats sided with Republicans on a procedural vote.[5] Crime legislation eventually passed, but the set-backs overshadowed the victories on many smaller issues.

Then there were the lingering questions about the Clintons' partnership in the Whitewater land deal, kept alive by the flame-fanning of Senator Alfonse D'Amato (NY) and Congressman Jim Leach (IA), the ranking members of Senate and House Banking committees. This attack challenged the president's honesty and character as well as the integrity of certain highly visible administration officials. In the end, several key administration appointees were forced to resign.

The president's woes generated doubts among voters. Many had doubts about his character and competence to begin with and the troubles of 1994 only seemed to firm up these earlier assessments. Poll after poll showed the public's declining confidence in and respect for the president. Complaints surfaced about the president's appearing unpresidential—so much so that people were said to be ignoring him as he was passing through airports. By mid-October of 1994, the president's approval ratings had sagged to 38 percent among men and 44 percent among women.[6] All of this portended bad things for the president's party in November.

Voter Hostility toward Washington

A second factor underlying the electoral quake of the 1994 elections would have to be the voters' dwindling confidence in the institutions of national government.[7] Criticism of Congress had been particularly harsh and in March 1994, surveys by the Gallup organization showed that the percentage of citizens expressing "a great deal" of confidence in Congress was at a mere 18 percent, compared with 39 percent in 1985 and 42 percent in 1973.[8] The public's attitude was accurately described in President Clinton's post-election news conference, in which he claimed that the message sent in the election was that "We [the voters] don't think government can solve all the problems. And we don't want the Democrats telling us from Washington that they know what is right about everything."[9] The message, according to Democrats, was that the voters were expressing general unhappiness about those in control. The White House denied, however, that the election was a mandate for a shift to the right. The president voiced his conviction that the American people were simply upset with the pace of change in Washington.[10]

Republicans emphasized that the message was more specific: the people wanted less government intrusion and lower taxes. As a sophomore lawmaker saw it, "The elections reflect voters' basic disgust with Washington. The attitude of my voters is that government is burdensome and that people in Washington aren't serious about change."[11]

The truth varies by Congressional district and is probably somewhere in between these partisan assessments. Many of the highly attentive voters were casting a protest vote specifically against President Clinton's record and in favor of a Republican alternative. Voters who base their judgments on general impressions of government performance, on the other hand, were simply angry at whoever happened to be in the White House. Two years earlier, many of these same voters had supported Ross Perot.

The connection between Perot voters and Democratic losses in 1994 is probably not coincidental. Republicans had deliberately crafted their campaign appeals to attract the independent voters who wanted change. Table 1-1 presents some evidence of the influence of the Perot vote on Democratic defeats in the 1994 House races. These figures show the difference in Perot's 1992 vote share between the congressional districts Democrats won in 1994 compared with those where Democratic incumbents went down. In those districts where Democrats lost their seats to Republican challengers, Ross Perot ran substantially better in 1992 than he did in the districts of Democratic winners. Similarly, the seats the Democrats lost were much more marginally Democratic in the 1992 presidential election than were the remaining seats. Bill Clinton won an average of 40 percent in the congressional districts where his party's incumbents lost, compared with a much higher 51 percent in the winning Democrats' districts. In other words, the president was not very popular to begin with in the losing Democrats' districts. His performance in the interim did nothing to help convince Perot voters that the Democrats were the ticket in 1994.

Table 1-1 Differences in 1992 Perot and Clinton Support between Districts Where Democrats Lost and Those Where Democrats Won

Seat status	Perot % 1992	Clinton % 1992
Incumbents won	16.1 (n = 192)	51.4 (n = 192)
Incumbents lost	20.4 (n = 34)	39.6 (n = 34)
T-test	T-value = 4.40	T-value = –8.69
Significance	$p < .001$	$p < .001$
Cases	226	226

N reflects the Democratic Districts from the 103rd Congress where incumbents were defending their seats. Figures for incumbents who won include Vermont Independent Bernard Sanders who affiliates with Democrats on matters of House organization.
Source: Almanac of American Politics, 1994 and author's calculations.

Republican Opportunism with the "Contract"

Issues are important in democratic politics because they give voters an idea of what program of action a political party will pursue if its members are elected. If this program fails, incumbents supporting that program can be held accountable at the next election.[12] This is the classical statement of the party responsibility model of good government. In American politics party responsibility rarely exists in this form because candidates can rarely agree on a coherent program.[13] Constituencies and their interests vary widely from place to place. Popular issues in one area are unattractive in other areas.[14] Consequently, the American political system is highly decentralized and candidate-centered compared with other democratic systems. In cases in which the party platform and constituency preferences are at odds, members of Congress have a strong incentive to ignore the party. When the national parties do provide issue guidance, candidates freely ignore it. For these reasons, congressional elections are said to be local (rather than national) contests and party government is correspondingly weak.

In the context of a highly decentralized American political system, it was risky to attempt to nationalize the 1994 congressional elections on a set of themes that would bind all candidates. Perhaps the effort would have failed miserably had there not been such widespread unhappiness about government's size and ineffectiveness. Public opinion was unusually homogeneous on this issue. Little insight was needed to spot the prevailing dissatisfaction with government that was evident in polls throughout 1993. At the direction of two aggressive House Republican leaders, Newt Gingrich (GA), the Minority Whip, and Richard K. Armey (TX), the Conference Chair (*Conference* is the official name of the Republican party in Congress), House staff put together a package of legislative proposals calling it the "Contract with America". The Contract was designed to attract the attention of the increasing majority of Americans who were unhappy with Congress, unhappy with the president, and dissatisfied with government. Many of these citizens were Perot voters who repudiated business as usual with their protest votes in 1992.[15] Key to the sales pitch was that Republicans would promise to place these agenda items at the top of their legislative calendars during the first 100 days of a Republican-led 104th Congress. Republican leaders were quick to point out that there was no explicit promise that these agenda items would *pass* in a Republican Congress, only that they would be debated and brought up for a vote. This would be an important qualification many Republicans would later call attention to as elements of the Contract ran into opposition and delay in the U.S. Senate. But even though House Republicans realized there was no guarantee their Contract would become law in this Congress, the successful effort to bring House candidates and incumbents on board a common agenda was a step away from the every-person-for-him/herself character of American politics.

Substantively, the Contract was a collection of ten bills and three resolutions dealing with a variety of issues (see Table 1-2 and Chapter 2) from term limits to

Table 1-2 Elements in the Republican "Contract with America"

Title	Bill	Focus of legislation
Congressional Accountability Act	H.R. 1	Apply anti-discrimination laws to Congress
Line-Item Veto Act	H.R. 2	Enhance president's recision authority
Taking Back Our Streets Act	H.R. 3	Crime control
Personal Responsibility Act	H.R. 4	Welfare reform
Unfunded Mandate Reform Act	H.R. 5	Reducing burden of federal mandates on states
American Dream Restoration Act	H.R. 6	Tax code reform
National Security Restoration Act	H.R. 7	Defense/military procurement
Senior Citizens' Equity Act	H.R. 8	Social Security reform
Job Creation/Wage Enhancement Act	H.R. 9	Deregulation/tax code reform
Common Sense Legal Reforms Act	H.R. 10	Product liability/tort reform
Family Reinforcement Act	H.R. 11	Child support/adoption
Balanced Budget Amendment	H.J. Res 1	Balanced budget
Citizen Legislature Act	H.J. Res 2	Term limits, 12 years for House members
Citizen Legislature Act	H.J. Res 3	Term limits, 6 years for House members

crime to welfare reform, deregulation and deficit reduction. Republican leaders deliberately stayed away from divisive social issues such as school prayer and abortion. They realized that it would be difficult enough to hold the party together without generating internal divisions on such controversial themes. If the Contract were to serve as a platform for all Republican House contenders, it must consist of proposals that would be overwhelmingly popular.

Contrary to popular myth, there was no public opinion polling conducted on the Contract before it was assembled by the Republican leadership. Gingrich and Armey were generally aware that specific items were popular, including term limits and the balanced budget amendment. But the legislation forming the core of the Contract was selected primarily because it was consistent with themes the Republicans had been emphasizing for years. All of the legislation had been introduced in the 103rd Congress in one form or another. The Republican National Committee (RNC) did commission focus-group research and polls once the Contract had been assembled to determine how best to describe the legislation.

Focus group research, or "concept testing" as pollsters describe it, is designed to probe more deeply into citizen responsiveness to political themes and issues than a public opinion poll does. Typically, a focus group is assembled by recruiting twenty-five to thirty people at random to come to a designated location to participate in a discussion about the issues of interest. Each participant is paid $30 to $40 for a two-hour discussion session. In the case of the Contract, focus groups were assembled in several locations around the country. The participants were given copies of the Contract in different forms and asked for their reactions. Pollster Frank Luntz was especially interested in the responses of the Perot voters. "The point was to ask them how they felt about the issues in the Contract. We allowed them to argue with each other. We wanted to know what stirred them up."[16] According to Luntz, focus groups are superior to ordinary polls because they allow people to express justifications for the positions they take. Luntz emphasized that the value of focus-group research is to tap into people's emotions and basic commitments. Polls do not reveal deep seated values and commitments because the format of a poll, conducted over a telephone at a rapid-fire pace, does not permit reflection and interaction.

Luntz's surveys were influential in helping to describe the Contract by asking people why they liked certain provisions. For example, respondents to opinion polls would be asked why they wanted term limits. "Is it because we need a citizen legislature?" or "Is it because professional politicians eventually forget who they represent?" In testing phrases such as these, Republican leaders were able to select the descriptions that had popular appeal. In this case, they chose the former, titling the Contract's term limits measure, "The Citizen Legislature Act."

In addition to the legislative thrust, the majority-to-be promised to pass ambitious internal reforms aimed at restoring the "faith and trust of the American people in their government."[17] These reforms included what was to be the first bill to pass both the House and Senate in the 104th, H. R. 1, to require all laws that apply to the rest of the country also apply equally to the Congress, including the 1964 Civil

Rights Act and the Americans with Disabilities Act. Other internal reforms that would pass as rules changes in the House included procedures to implement an audit of Congress to ferret out waste, fraud and abuse; to cut the number of House committees and cut committee staffs by one-third; to limit the terms of all committee chairs; to ban the casting of proxy votes in committee; and to require committee meetings to be open to the public. In the end, the legislative initiatives promised in the Contract would have both widespread public support and the support of 367 Republicans running for House seats.

None of the proposals in the Contract was truly brand new. Many ideas, such as term limitations and the balanced budget amendment had a long history extending decades into the past. Others, such as welfare reform, had generated momentum in recent years. As in most arenas of life, new ideas on Capitol Hill require acclimation as they compete for acceptance. Through the 1980s, Republicans repeatedly introduced such legislation, only to have it ignored by the Democratic leadership. By the 1990s, however, these ideas had gained substantial momentum and the sponsorship lists had grown quite long. H. J. Res. 1 (to require a balanced budget) had 170 Republican cosponsors and eight Democratic cosponsors at the time of its House passage.

Through the Contract, the Republicans sought to inject a strong measure of party responsibility into the campaign, actually inviting voters to "throw them out" if they failed to deliver on their Contract promises. The move was bold given the conventional wisdom that House races are local, not national. "There were many nay-sayers who thought the Contract strategy would fail," said Scott Reed, the RNC's executive director.[18] "Many Republicans in the consulting community were concerned that it wouldn't help their candidates. The conventional wisdom was that House elections are won on local themes." This was clearly the message from academic political scientists also: "It has become increasingly difficult to speak of House elections as national elections in any meaningful sense," wrote three prominent scholars in a 1992 article.[19]

In political circles, the debate about whether the party should emphasize national or local themes had been raging since the late 1980s.[20] But as early as 1990, most Republican elites were at least willing to concede that a mix of national and local themes was optimal.[21] It took the leadership of Gingrich and Armey to put together a coherent package. What the Contract provided both incumbent and novice candidates was a ready-made platform that the Republican leadership sensed would be a no-fail vote getter. "It gave those who were new to politics something to talk about," Reed reported. Candidates did not have to flounder about, casting here and there for popular messages and issues as they often do.[22] Republicans were not compelled to campaign on all aspects of the Contract and few voters on election day knew much about it as a document, much less its background. But they did know something about the issues associated with it. Most candidates chose the items in the Contract that they thought would resonate with their constituencies and tailored their messages to focus on specific items rather than on the document itself.

In a carefully orchestrated national media event, leadership staff, together with staff from the RNC and the National Republican Congressional Committee (NRCC) organized a forum to highlight the Contract as a national campaign theme. The vast majority of Republican House candidates convened on the Capitol steps on September 27th to sign the Contract. This event generated national publicity for the party as a whole, but locally the Contract generated free publicity for challengers and incumbents alike. The public response in some areas was overwhelmingly favorable. Campaigns reported being deluged with telephone calls from voters requesting copies of the Contract. Two-hundred twenty-four of the 367 signatories to the Contract (61 percent) went on to win on November 8th. Notably, several Republican nonsignatories also won in November: Don Young (AK), Ileana Ros-Lehtinen (FL), Lincoln Diaz-Balart (FL), Ray LaHood (IL), Sam Brownback (KS), Jim Bunn (OR), Jim Longley (ME) and Tom Coburn (OK). In Chapter 2, I will deal more extensively with the background of the Contract and how it was used in congressional campaigns.

Marginal Seats

A marginal seat is one subject to frequent changes in party control. The seats most vulnerable to takeover by the opposition are those for which the incumbent won less than 55 percent of the vote in the previous election. In 1994, there were seventy-nine such seats, forty-five of them were in Democratic hands. One upshot of the comparisons presented in Table 1-1 is that Republicans won many of their upset victories by fiercely pursuing seats that were marginal for President Clinton and the Democrats in the 1992 election. Consider the closeness of the races between Republican challengers and Democratic incumbents who lost in 1994. Republicans who defeated incumbent Democrats did so with an average 54 percent of the vote. The remaining seats that were either left open by retirements or occupied by incumbent Democratic victors were much less marginal, with Democrats winning 66 percent (t-value = –7.35, $p < .001$). The success of Republicans in these competitive districts reflected the targeting strategy of party and interest group donors who tend to aim the bulk of their contributions toward viable candidates.[23]

Candidate Quality

Deficits in candidate quality have been considered a Republican scourge for several years now.[24] The notion is that Republicans have not done well in House elections because they have been unable to field credible challengers. Of course, there is no unanimity about what it means to be a "quality candidate," but most studies define the term to include political experience.[25] Previous experience is associated with the ability to field a better-managed and better-funded campaign as well as the capacity to draw upon established coalitions.

While the 1994 Republican class is notable for the number of freshmen without political experience, many of the new members do have some. Indeed, almost half (47 percent) had held prior elected office at some level. Several more had held appointed positions or had served as political aides. Only twenty had no previous political experience of any kind. The victories of amateur politicians such as Fred Heineman (NC) over experienced Democratic veterans such as David Price suggests that political experience was a liability in some districts. In areas where voters were most dissatisfied with government performance, political experience was something to run from and conveyed no advantage in a year in which outsiders were preferred.[26]

The Republican Challengers' Financial Advantage

The relationship between dollars spent and seats won is not simple. For challengers and for those competing for an open seat, the effect is most direct: the more you spend, the more likely you are to win.[27] For incumbents, the relationship between money and votes is more complicated since they spend in direct proportion to the threat they face (Figure 1-1).[28] The stronger party in a given election should find its incumbents spending less and its challengers spending more than the opposing party. If this is our criterion, the role of improved campaign finance cannot be overlooked in the Republican victories. Although extensive campaign expenditure data were unavailable at the time of this writing, the finances of Republican challengers were up some 42 percent over 1992 and were significantly higher than the funds Democratic challengers were able to raise (see Figure 1-2). This is an important difference,

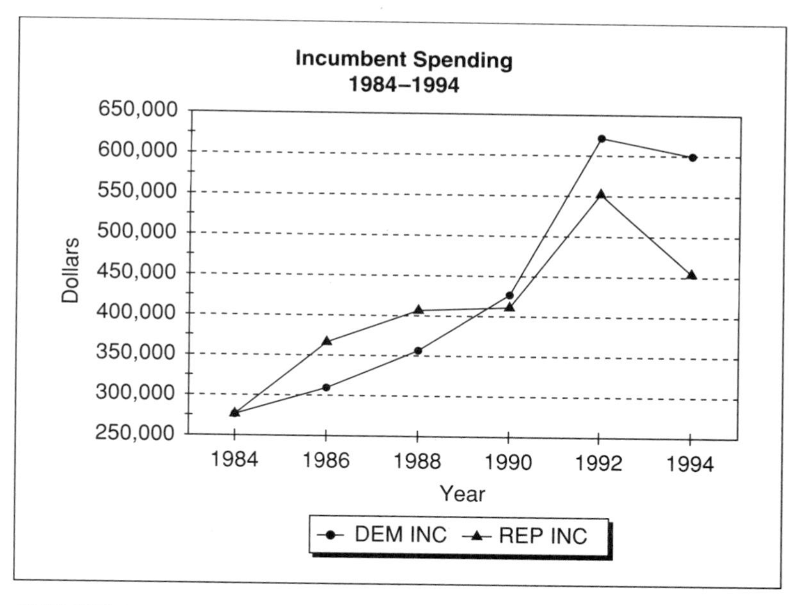

FIGURE 1-1 **Incumbent Spending in Congressional Campaigns, 1984–1994**

Source: Norman Ornstein, Thomas E. Mann and Michael Malbin, eds., *Vital Statistics on Congress 1995–1996,* Washington, D.C.: American Enterprise Institute, 1995.

since challengers are ordinarily disadvantaged and what they do spend clearly pays off.[29] The Republican average for dollars spent on open seat races was also slightly higher than Democratic spending, for the first time since 1988.

The average spent by Democratic incumbents was about 30 percent greater than the Republican average. This is not a trivial difference since incumbents tend to spend more when they have tough races. The bottom line is that Republican candidates were in a stronger financial position in 1994 than Democrats. They forced Democrats to spend more defending incumbents while launching a highly competitive bid for open seats. The success of Republican fundraising has much to do with Newt Gingrich. Together with Congressman Bill Paxon (NY) who headed the NRCC (National Republican Congressional Committee), Gingrich overhauled Republican fundraising efforts by involving each incumbent. He established a formula for voluntary contributions by each member. Unless they were in financial dire straits for their own campaign, they were expected to contribute. Teams went around to each member to solicit their fundraising capacity. Gingrich's press secretary, Tony Blankley, explained:

> *Many had never raised money before, except for their own campaigns. One member said, "I don't know how to do that." Newt said, "I'll teach you."*

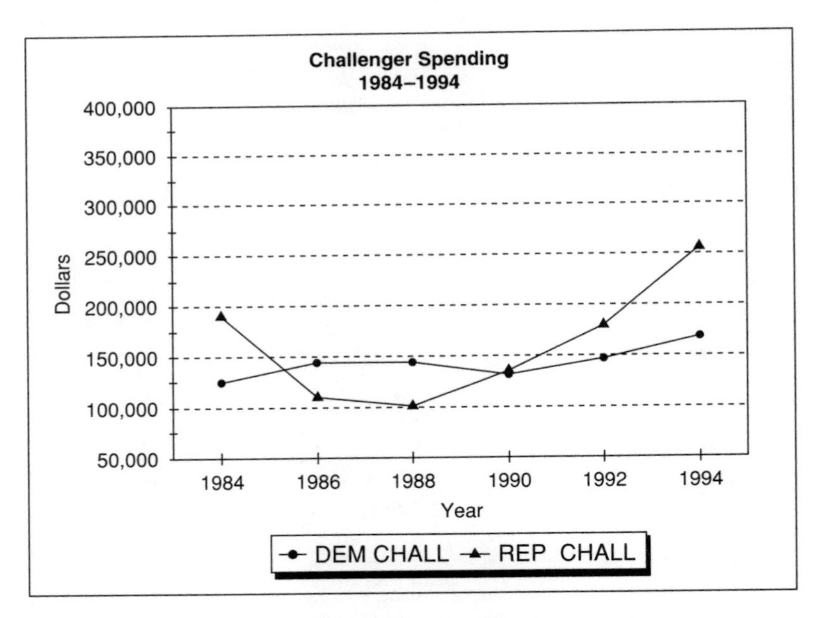

FIGURE 1-2 **Challenger Spending in Congressional Campaigns, 1984–1994**

Source: Norman J. Ornstein, Thomas E. Mann and Michael Malbin, eds., *Vital Statistics on Congress,* Washington, D.C.: American Enterprise Institute, 1995.

And they sent him over to the RNC. The member came back a while later and excitedly said, "I just raised $50,000 over at the RNC!" As more members saw we had a chance of winning [the majority] more of them pitched in on the fundraising effort.[30]

With the focus on the Contract's message, the story of the 1994 fundraising effort is usually overlooked. "Gingrich took a standard practice of helping out other candidates with money and turned it into a money making machine," explained conservative California Republican Dana Rohrabacher.[31] Several members raised hundreds of thousands of dollars for other campaigns. Two of the leading fundraisers were Jennifer Dunn (WA), who raised about $300,000 and John Boehner (OH) who raised $250,000 in part by calling on Washington-based PACs allied with Republican causes. Others, like Bob Inglis (SC) made smaller but still significant contributions drawing mostly on small donations from home, while aggressively campaigning for Republican challengers:

I went to my own donors to raise money for other candidates. I don't accept PAC money so I wasn't comfortable soliciting it for others. But I raised about $40,000 for other campaigns. I also went into [Democratic incumbent] John Spratt's [neighboring] district and toured around with our candidate. This violated a long-standing rule of comity in South Carolina politics but this rule needed to be broken so we broke it.[32]

In previous years, the effort to raise funds and to campaign for other Republicans was usually half-hearted. According to John Boehner, in 1992, only twelve Republican incumbents campaigned for the NRCC and they raised about $50,000. In 1994, 130 members were involved with the NRCC's campaign effort and they raised $1.2 million just to protect incumbents, and another $5 million to help the Republican challengers.[33] The 1994 campaign signalled the coming of a Republican revolution both in terms of message and money.

Other Factors in the 1994 Campaign

With 435 separate House campaigns around the country, one cannot boil down the 1994 election results to the simple formula of President Clinton's performance, Republican opportunism, dissatisfaction with Washington, Republican money and marginal seats. Ordinarily, campaigns are won and lost on the basis of a complex combination of themes and events. In 1994, as in other years, there were many local and idiosyncratic elements. Among the most important was the incumbent's record on controversial issues.[34] Several entrenched Democrats, including Jack Brooks (TX), the chair of the Judiciary Committee, lost because of controversial votes they cast—in Brooks' case in favor of gun control. Many Democrats were tarred for other votes in support of President Clinton's agenda. A second factor contributing to victory is the favorable image a local campaign creates on behalf of its candidate. Mark

Souder (IN) upset two-term incumbent Jill Long in part by emphasizing his small-town upbringing and his Amish heritage. Although Souder had been a congressional staffer for the eight years prior to his election, he successfully shook off the image of Washington insider by stressing his local roots.

A third idiosyncratic factor relevant in some races was scandal.[35] Dan Rostenkowski (IL), chair of the Ways and Means Committee, was felled by the growing corruption charges that had swallowed up his distinguished career and forced him to give up the powerful committee post well before the election.

Some credited the impact of conservative talk radio, such as the popular talk-show host Rush Limbaugh, for energizing right-wing activists and saturating the airwaves with anti-Clinton sentiment. Finally, the out-parties in American politics have a tradition of innovation.[36] The Republican party apparatus in Washington, under the direction of Republican National Committee (RNC) Chair Haley Barbour, underwent a massive reorganization. Barbour streamlined the operation by eliminating bureaucracy and paying off debt, then moved to channel more money directly to GOP challengers.

Accounting for the totality of elements figuring into the unexpected Republican takeover of 1994 is probably impossible given existing data. Suffice it to say that being tied too closely to an unpopular president in an election year in which the opposition was fully mobilized to exploit citizen dissatisfaction with government explains much of the resulting Republican earthquake.[37] The effort to win reelection was all the more difficult for Democrats who were in marginal districts. The combined weight of these influences would provide the Republicans with the occasion to push a new agenda in 1995.

The New Congress

The results for the 1994 elections strongly suggested that the new Congress would likely be more polarized in partisan and ideological terms than previous congresses. Not surprisingly, given what we have learned about the weaker support for candidate Clinton in the districts where Democrats lost, we find that many of the members who were defeated were of conservative stripe. The Democratic party is more homogeneously liberal than perhaps it has ever been. For evidence of this we can look to the conservative coalition score, calculated from the votes in which the conservative coalition between northern Republicans and southern Democrats appears.[38] The higher the score, the more likely the member is to vote with the coalition. A comparison of the scores of the defeated Democrats with the scores of the winning Democrats in the 103rd Congress appears in Table 1-3. A second measure of ideology, the *National Journal* economic liberalism score, also illustrates the difference. Higher scores on the *National Journal* rating indicate stronger liberal tendencies. Defeated Democrats were more likely to vote conservatively than the Democrats who remain in office. This means that the group that was voted out of office leaned toward the Republicans, with their much lower liberalism scores.

Insofar as the U.S. Congress is electorally responsive, these ideology ratings reflect the lawmakers' constituencies. Differences between Democratic winners and losers in the type of constituency represented are also reported in Table 1-3. The winning Democrats' districts contained an average of 18 percent African Americans, compared with just 7 percent for those who lost. Similarly, the winners, on average, had twice the percentage of Hispanics residing in their districts. Not surprisingly, the median income of constituencies who lost a Democratic incumbent were slightly higher than those who elected someone new. The winners' districts also had a significantly higher percentage of citizens on welfare and public assistance programs (Table 1-3).

Of course there were thirteen new Democrats elected in 1994 and their ideological tendencies will not be clear for a year or more. Still, only four of these thirteen emerged out of southern districts where we might expect conservative sympathies; and one of those, Sheila Jackson-Lee, was elected to a seat that is the most liberal and Democratic in Texas (TX-18th, in Houston).

For several years, observers have noted that the congressional parties are growing increasingly homogeneous.[39] This trend has continued in the 1994 congressional elections for the implications of the simple comparisons presented in this chapter are

Table 1-3 Comparison of Ideology and Constituency Characteristics of Incumbent Democrats Losing in the 1994 House Elections Compared with Democrats Who Won

Seat status	Conservative Coalition Rating	National Journal Economic Liberalism Rating	% on Public Assistance	% African American	% Hispanic	Median Family Income
Incumbents won	43.7 (n = 192)	66.6 (n = 190)	9.5 (n = 192)	17.9 (n = 192)	11.6 (n = 192)	28,494 (n = 192)
Incumbents lost	57.1 (n = 34)	56.2 (n = 33)	6.5 (n = 34)	6.7 (n = 34)	5.7 (n = 34)	31,337 (n = 34)
T-test	2.95	–4.03	–5.12	–5.84	–3.53	2.12
Significance	$p < .005$	$p < .001$	$p < .001$	$p < .001$	$p < .001$	$p < .04$
Cases	226	223	226	226	226	226

Sources: Congressional Quarterly Weekly Report, 12/31/94; *National Journal,* 1/14/95; *Almanac of American Politics, 1994;* and author's calculations. Demographic and public assistance data are from the 1990 Census. Public assistance refers to the percentage of people receiving benefits from the Federal Supplemental Security Income Program (SSI), Aid to Families with Dependent Children (AFDC), and general assistance. Figures for incumbents who won include Vermont Independent Bernard Sanders who affiliates with Democrats on matters of House organization.

clear. Democrats have been shorn of a large bloc of moderate-to-conservative votes. The incumbents who remain, coming from safer districts with a higher proportion of minority and low-income voters, have decidedly liberal records.

On the Republican side, the election strongly favored the conservative wing, with some saying that the new bloc of Republican freshmen were even more stridently conservative than the veterans in the leadership were.[40] Political scientists have long noted the tendency for the amateur to be more ideological than the experienced politician. Amateurs are more likely to get involved in politics to advance ideas rather than interests.[41] If this remains true today, the 1994 freshman Republicans promise to have an ideological bent.

Much of the work on the history of Congress has emphasized the declining role of partisanship in House politics since the turn of the century.[42] Certainly there are more safe seats on the liberal left and the conservative right than in previous years—witness the emergence of the majority minority districts—most of which are not competitive. But the kind of redistricting that has made for less-competitive House elections may make for a highly ideological and highly partisan Congress. The stage would appear to be set for a very confrontational and ideological debate. In the wake of the partisan bickering of the last ten years, it is difficult to imagine a more unfriendly Congress.[43] The kind of conflict we would expect for the 104th, though, could make previous congresses look tame.

Plan of the Book

Having outlined the explanations behind the Republican victories in November, I will deal with the background and formation of the new majority's agenda, the Contract with America in the next chapter. Few members or candidates shared the optimism of the party leadership and most were surprised to find themselves in a position to act on the 100-day plan. Chapter 3 highlights details of the transition in the interim between election-day and the opening gavel, including the election of the leadership and the appointment of committee chairs.

The subsequent chapters, 4 through 9, will tell the story behind the passage of the individual items in the Contract. Beginning with the Balanced Budget Amendment and moving to the story behind Tax Cuts, I will highlight the background of the issue, the committee and floor activity and finally the vote. Each of these chapters will then conclude with reflections about how the Contract version of the legislation weathered the legislative process.

Finally, the concluding chapter will summarize the themes and points of conflict that emerged during the first 100 days. The Republicans brought a renewed measure of party discipline to the Congress and framed a new policy agenda in Washington. But the goal of the Republican agenda was not just to change the public policy debate. Even Republican leaders would admit that this is too easy a test. The more ambitious aim was to restore the bond of trust between electors and the elected. This is a lofty goal but it is, after all, the one the new leadership set for itself.

▶ 2

The Contract and the Campaign

Many people went to bed on November 8th, 1994, surprised by the results, including many incumbent and newly elected members of Congress. A veteran Republican described his reaction on election night as one of complete astonishment:

> *I didn't believe it on election night. I had no remote belief or hope that we would make gains like that. On election night, when I saw 25 I was surprised; then 30; then 35 and my heart skipped a beat; then we were at 40, the magic number, I rubbed my eyes, and I told people that I wouldn't believe it until I got up the next morning and read it in black and white.*[1]

Others echoed this amazement: "I was absolutely floored!" exclaimed Colorado Republican Joel Hefley. "At an election day lunch, my prediction was a thirty-seat gain. I could hardly believe it!"[2]

And from a committee chair who had grown accustomed to the wolf-wolf cry of previous NRCC head and former representative Guy Vander Jagt (MI):

> *If there is anyone who said they thought this was going to happen, they are the best prevaricators around. I used to hear the Vander Jagt speech before every election—how this was the year we were going to take the majority. Year after year, same old thing.*[3]

Even optimistic freshmen doubted they had much of a chance to be serving in the majority:

> *I never dreamed I would serve in the majority. I expected a 20-seat gain but was actually looking forward to serving in the minority. I had been in the majority in the Wyoming legislature. I don't care what those leaders say,*

they didn't know we were going to win either. If they had, they would have known what to teach us at orientation.[4]

The Republicans were serious about the provisions of the Contract, but few rank-and-file members thought they would have the opportunity to bring them to a vote. "I figured it was just a great showboat piece, for a couple of reasons: one, the public wouldn't bother to examine it, and, two, only a few people would have heard of it by election day."[5]

The most optimistic locales on the Hill were the offices of the Minority Whip, Newt Gingrich (GA), the Conference Chair, Richard K. Armey (TX), and Gingrich insider and party leader, John Boehner (OH). "Armey was so confident of victory that he sent letters to all of the Republican members in September soliciting support for his election as majority leader," said Ed Gillespie, Armey's press secretary.[6] "He was to the point that had we not won the majority, it would have been a crushing emotional defeat." Boehner explained that he sensed big gains as early as August while he was out campaigning for other candidates:

I was absolutely convinced we would be in the majority. I'd been out in the West and Midwest and it was clear that something was burning in America. Health care framed the mindset of the people about this Administration. But the last straw was the crime bill. This was the first time I really saw public opinion race right by the majority in Congress. People were saying, "here they go again on the crime legislation, enacting more big social welfare programs." At that point, the smoldering fire became a raging fire.[7]

Armey, Gingrich, Boehner and a tiny handful of others[8] were the exceptions. Most of the challengers were stunned to find themselves part of the new majority. Now the sobering thought of going to work to fulfill the Contract set in. But the leaders' optimistic planning had laid a firm foundation. The Contract event on September 27th guaranteed nearly unanimous support for the agenda within the Conference. Only seven of the Republicans elected had not signed the document. A few liberal members of the party who had signed probably secretly hoped that at least some of the provisions would never be voted on, but a majority had incorporated elements of the Contract into their campaigns. On November 9th, the task ahead was still daunting. The majority-elect was suddenly reminded of the old religious adage, "Be careful about what you pray for, 'cause you just might get it." While few Americans could actually identify the specific provisions in the Contract, the Republicans would have to deliver what they promised or pay in 1996.

BACKGROUND ON THE CONTRACT WITH AMERICA

Before November 8th, the Contract with America was a campaign document, much like a presidential platform except that it was being offered in a nonpresidential year and was simpler. The Contract's promise to bring sweeping policy changes to a floor vote could easily be ignored once individual Republicans took their place in the "permanent minority." After all, the fulfillment of the Contract was promised only in the unlikely event that Republicans would win the seats needed to take over the U.S. House for the first time since 1952. In retrospect, it is not surprising that so many doubted this would happen. The Republicans needed forty seats to take the majority. Such a margin would require nothing less than a major electoral landslide.

One week from the election, the Contract had already served many members well by tapping into the prevailing anti-government, anti-Clinton sentiment. But the Contract did more. It provided the Republicans with something positive to run on. Instead of being tagged as the party that says no to everything, the Contract gave candidates a program to counter the Clinton Administration's agenda. Voters did not have to understand all of the Contract's initiatives to sense that the Republicans stood for change. Once it was apparent that there would be a new congressional majority, however, the Contract suddenly took on a much more significant status. Now the proposals were the core of the most ambitious legislative agenda in recent years.

Origin and Making of the Contract

On Capitol Hill, where ideas bounce around between many members and staffs often evolving over months or years, it is often impossible to identify and credit the parent of a particular notion. Add to this the fact that members seek to take credit for ideas, whether the ideas are theirs or not, and attributing credit where credit is due is next to impossible. Staff understand this, of course, and are paid to accept it. The Contract is apparently one of those odd exceptions, though, because everyone credits Newt Gingrich with the idea and apparently it was his alone.

The general notion of a "Contract" had been circulating in political circles at least since the 1992 election when there was much talk of contracts, compacts, and covenants by both sides. In his 1995 State of the Union address, President Clinton returned to a 1992 campaign theme in his discussion of a "social compact" and a week later his radio address emphasized a "new covenant."

But Gingrich had something more definitive in mind. He pushed the idea for crafting a national platform in a February, 1994, conference Republicans had held in Salisbury, Maryland. Candidates that came to Washington to attend campaign schools sponsored by the RNC and NRCC were hearing about the Contract as early as that very month. From the February conference, a mission statement was drafted that summarized the Republicans' basic "philosophy of American Civilization." That vision comprised these five tenets:[9]

1. Individual liberty
2. Economic opportunity
3. Limited government
4. Personal responsibility
5. Security at home and abroad

Early into the year, Gingrich also decided that the Contract should involve a "Capitol steps event" with all of the members and candidates convening at some critical point right before the election. In 1980, having just been elected two years before, Gingrich was involved in organizing "Governing Team Day," an event in which Republican congressional candidates gathered on the Capitol steps with presidential contender Ronald Reagan. His plan was to duplicate this effort in 1994 and use it as a platform for unveiling a legislative plan. Insiders reported that Gingrich had even consulted a weather forecaster friend months ahead of time about what the weather would be like on September 27th—a date that was about six weeks before the election. It is reported that the weather forecaster told Gingrich that the 27th would be a sunny day, perfect for the occasion. That settled it. September 27th was marked on the calendar.

Once the date was set, the hard work began: deciding what legislation would be included. A brief background on the legislation contained in the Contract, the list of sponsors and those most closely involved can be found elsewhere.[10] The legislative work on the Contract was delegated by Gingrich to the House Republican Conference Committee under the direction of Congressman Richard K. Armey (TX) and his staff director, Kerry Knott.

With the help of pollster Frank Luntz, the Conference designed a questionnaire to be sent to candidates and members on which issues would be relevant to the fall campaign. Not all of the Contract items were taken from the surveys, but the leadership wanted to be sure that the members and candidates had some say. Contrary to popular belief, there were no public opinion polls conducted prior to the selection of the issues that formed the Contract's core. The RNC's Chuck Greener explained:

> *Consultants and pollsters had no role in the policies that were formed. Kerry (Knott) and the Conference were down the pike before any survey research was done. One of the myths that has developed around the Contract was that it was based on polling. That's silliness. If they [had] waited around to do polling, it would have never gone forward. These were Newt's ideas and the ideas of the Republicans in the House.*[11]

Independently, the leadership decided that certain items would be sure bets. For years Republicans had advocated the line-item veto and the balanced budget amendment. Other items were more controversial but the House Republicans were mostly unified. Conference staff reported that 70–30 support from the Republican members was adequate. After all, if there was unanimity on an issue it was probably too trivial to include anyway.

The next step was to draft the legislation. Gingrich wanted to be sure that there was legislative language ready to go in order to make good on the 100-day deadline. Drafting the legislation was a major effort. From June to August, the Conference staff organized a series of working groups consisting of a heterogeneous mix of younger members, more senior members and members of the relevant committees.

"One of the big challenges was to get the members out of the minority mindset," said one Conference staffer who ran a working group. "Our members are conditioned to think like a minority and float modest proposals that could attract some members from the other side. We had to push them to accept bold, courageous proposals."[12] The most contentious working group was on welfare reform. The leadership wanted a welfare reform bill because it was one of the highest-ranking issues listed on the surveys Frank Luntz had sent to candidates and members. Task force members Dave Camp (MI), Rick Santorum (PA) and Nancy Johnson (CT) pushed for a bill that had been introduced in the Ways and Means Committee in 1993. Several more conservative members, including Jim Talent (MO) and Tim Hutchinson (AR), wanted a more ambitious proposal. "In the end, we had to lock them in a room and make them work it out. We wound up with a nice compromise where they took the best components of each measure and melded them together" (see Chapter 7).[13]

"The legislation was difficult to draft because members were eager to put a lot of stuff into it," said Kerry Knott, Armey's staff director. "We stressed that the bills had to be "doable." That meant that we had to remove many controversial provisions." The proposals left out of the Contract are about as important as what was included. For instance, the original Contract did not include a repeal of the Democratic-passed assault weapons ban. Armey's own flat tax proposal was removed because it was thought to be too controversial to pass within the 100-day deadline. "Newt's single most important decision, once Armey took over the legislative effort, was to keep school prayer out of the Contract," said Gingrich spokesman Tony Blankley.[14] In addition, the Conference staff decided to scrap health care and campaign finance proposals because by late spring it appeared that President Clinton might still pass a health care and campaign finance bill. Had he succeeded it would have made those proposals obsolete.

The formation of the Contract was quite inclusive in principle. Full member participation was invited at many points along the way. There were several policy forums and formal Policy Committee meetings for the explicit purpose of seeking responses from the members. "For the most part, though, these meetings were not well attended," Knott reported. "A large percentage of the membership simply didn't take the project seriously. Few people thought we would ever be in a position to do anything about it."

Did some members feel left out anyway? Apparently some of the moderates did. Congressman Amo Houghton (NY) reported that he hadn't been invited to participate, saying,

> *I'm a northeastern Republican. This thing was driven by Texas and the South. The party that I am associated with is in the tradition of Dewey, Rockefeller, Eisenhower. I am from a long family tradition of party moderates.*
>
> *. . . The support of the moderates for Newt has been passive. They really haven't been in the inner circles creating the policies. Northeasterners have not been invited into the inner sanctum. I really don't think the*

others have been included, people like Chris Shays (CT) or Nancy Johnson (CT). People fantasize about having included certain members. They want certain things to be possible. Anecdotally, they have a report or two of someone being included.[15]

Another moderate, Bill Goodling (PA), the chair of the Education and Economic Opportunities Committee echoed this sentiment about the centralization of the project in the hands of a few:

No. I didn't participate. This was done by the Speaker and Mr. Armey, period. There wasn't that much input from anybody. They didn't have any idea any more than the rest of us that we would be in control.[16]

But moderate Republican Christopher Shays (CT) defended the way the Contract was framed,

At one point when the project was quite advanced, I went to Newt and said, "I would have liked to have been part of this process [of framing the legislation]." Newt said, "I gave this to Dick Armey because he had the staff and resources to do it. The door was never shut to the input of others." And he was right. One thing you have to remember about Newt. He recognizes that every member of Congress has a talent. He tries to utilize those talents.[17]

Other members reported that they were aware of the project but trusted Gingrich and Armey to put it together. The members had other concerns running their own campaigns, "I didn't go to that many meetings because we had our own work to do. But they were very open and had widespread support."[18] One senior Republican explained, "We didn't pay that much attention to it until it finally came together and they had in it what they wanted. People considered it just another part of the campaign."[19]

For the Conference, this attitude was an unexpected blessing of sorts. Had more members taken the project seriously, it would have undoubtedly been much more difficult to assemble. As it was, the drafting of the Contract was left to Gingrich, Armey, their staff, and the working groups they had assembled.

As the end of September approached, Republicans began to sense that momentum was on their side. Others who were less enthusiastic decided they needed to go along to learn what was included in case they would have to defend it in their campaigns. But many of the ideas in the Contract had caught on. Most of the new candidates were campaigning on them even prior to the signing ceremony. The main item of contention in the Conference was over the cost. The Democrats would surely try to stir up public concern about how the Republicans were going to gut Social Security, education, farm subsidies and veterans programs. In addition to the balanced budget amendment, the Contract's tax cut provision was estimated at $150 billion over five years. In the end, however, leadership convinced fence-sitting members that the people were willing to bear the costs for the sake of change.

On the morning of September 27th, the members gathered in the Cannon Caucus Room for the signing ceremony. Meanwhile, the candidates challenging Democratic incumbents were gathering in front of the Capitol for a dramatically staged, well-organized ceremony put on by the RNC's special "Contract Office." The event was carefully orchestrated so that all of the speeches were brief and to the point. The national press corps was in attendance along with many local television stations. The members joined the candidates in front of the Capitol in a display of party unity the likes of which had never been seen in a nonpresidential election year.

Campaigning with the Contract

Much of the campaign is waged in the last month. Voters do not begin to focus on the race until late so consultants wait to launch major advertising efforts in the waning days. Once the Contract had been signed, the Democrats figured they had a major campaign theme. For strategists, members and candidates alike, the Contract threatened many popular programs. Clinton aide Leon Panetta derided the Contract as "a fraud" and "a flim-flam." Democratic National Committee Chair Tony Coehlo claimed that the Contract was a "godsend for Democrats." He tarred the Contract as a gimmick and stressed that the Republicans favored rich yuppies with their promise to cut the capital gains tax cut and pass a balanced budget amendment. Democratic campaign material poured into districts stressing how bad the Contract would be for average Americans. "There is not a night that I don't thank God for the Contract," said Democratic consultant Paul Begala.[20] Indeed, many Republicans claimed that the public heard more about the Contract from the Democrats than from their own campaigns:

> *I didn't use the Contract that much. I made very limited reference to it and the voters didn't know much about it. What I did have to do was respond to accusations about it. My Democratic opponent made it the number one issue. The basic thrust of his message was that the Contract would threaten Social Security and other programs. As for my campaign, I did talk about things that were in the Contract, but that's not the same as using the Contract per se. I talked mostly about term limits and the balanced budget amendment because these things were popular with my voters.*[21]

Mark Souder, an Indiana freshman who managed to unseat an incumbent echoed these remarks in pointing out that most of the advertising on the Contract was done by his Democratic opponent who zeroed in on the Social Security issue.[22] Jerry Weller, running for an open seat in Illinois' 11th District, experienced the same deluge of negative advertising about the Contract, "We weren't quite prepared for how fiercely the Democrats were going to attack us on it. In fact, the Democratic attacks drew greater attention to it."[23]

But elsewhere in the Democratic party, there were worries. For southern Democrats, many of the Contract items were popular issues that they had championed in years past. They were in no position to attack. "I remember thinking that the Contract was a good political maneuver," said conservative Tennessee Democrat John Tanner.[24] "I took it very seriously," said Alabama Democrat Glen Browder.[25] "I knew its value because I supported many of the things in it: the balanced budget amendment, unfunded mandates, welfare reform, strong defense." "I knew it would be more effective politically than the Democratic leadership gave it credit for," said Scotty Baesler (KY).[26] The Democratic party remained insensitive to the sensibilities of its conservative wing as President Clinton launched his own full-scale assault on the Republican proposals.

Candidate use of the Contract varied widely. By the time the proposals were ready to go public in late summer, many candidates had been running for several months. Republican leaders couldn't be so presumptuous as to throw the Contract in everyone's lap as if to say "Here, here's a new campaign!"[27] So the practical effect of the Contract was to underscore some of the themes that candidates had already been emphasizing. "We had to incorporate it into the campaign we already had going."[28] Mark Souder's campaign made heavy use of the Contract in publicity efforts but he didn't credit it as the main theme of the campaign, saying "If we were to replay the campaign without the Contract I would guess we might be at 52 percent rather than 55. So obviously the Contract made a difference. It gave me a platform that emphasized my accountability. It told people that I was conservative and sincere enough to sign a pledge. But there were other issues that drove this election."

Several candidates had run before and emphasized the same themes that were now in the Contract. "Almost everything in the Contract we had discussed in our campaign in 1992: job creation, welfare reform, balanced budget, line-item veto. In 1994 we stressed the same themes. That made it easy for me to sign onto the Contract when it came out."[29] "The Contract provided a coherent framework in which to fit a set of issues that I had discussed in my [unsuccessful] 1992 campaign," said Enid Waldholtz, who upset freshman Karen Sheppard in Utah's second district.[30] Waldholtz pointed out that when her voters learned that people everywhere had the same vision for government, it generated a kind of momentum:

> *I sought to explain that my support for this legislation was part of a national movement. The Contract bolstered my argument that these themes were national. And people could see that everyone was concerned about the same issues that they were. . . . The Contract showed everyone that I was not a lone voice. I was part of a team.*
>
> *When I would talk to a crowd about these themes that were on their minds locally and then they realized that other people around the country were thinking the same thing, that generated even more enthusiasm. People realized that this was a national movement.*[31]

Enthusiasts, Supporters, Passives

As the accounts above begin to show, some candidates enthusiastically campaigned on the Contract while others were more reserved in their support. From this, one gathers the impression that Republican use of the Contract ran along a continuum. At one end there were the Contract *enthusiasts.* These were members who campaigned most heavily on the Contract. They are members such as Dick Chrysler (MI) and Enid Waldholtz (UT), freshmen who are ideologically very conservative. Incumbent members who were part of Newt Gingrich's inner circle also fit here. These include members such as Deborah Pryce (OH), Chris Cox (CA) and Peter Hoekstra (MI). Hoekstra not only mentioned the Contract in his stump speeches, he handed out 10–15,000 of the *TV Guide* inserts listing the items in the Contract.[32] South Carolina incumbent Bob Inglis could also be classified as a Contract enthusiast:

> *The Contract fits my district like a glove. BBA [balanced budget amendment], term limits, line-item veto, regulatory reform, tax reform, troops not under U.N. control. This fits America. This is what people have wanted for years. When I tell people back home what we're doing, they cock their heads at me and say, "Why didn't you do that before?"*[33]

A second style of Contract campaigning was that exhibited by the *supporter.* This person signed the legislation and occasionally mentioned it, but it was not a centerpiece of the campaign. These members had no trouble signing the Contract, but for various reasons campaigned on other issues. One of these was Wyoming's Barbara Cubin:

> *It was mostly ignored in my campaign. It is infinitely important but it didn't address the immediate problems my state was facing. People in Wyoming are concerned about the federal ownership of land... The government blocks the use of land for timbering, recreation, grazing and water usage. My campaign was on states' rights, individual rights and access to public lands for exploration, agriculture and recreation.*

Contract supporters include the many Republican incumbents who were conservative and would wind up voting for almost everything in the Contract but who played no active role in its formation. Members such as Carlos Moorhead (CA), Charles Canady (FL), Philip Crane (IL) and Dana Rohrabacher (CA) fit here. Moderate members such as Christopher Shays (CT) and Nancy Johnson (CT) found themselves in strong support of the Contract although they did not center their campaigns around it. Freshmen who signed but did not mention the Contract, such as Bob Ney (OH) and Dan Frisa (NY), could be classified as supporters but not enthusiasts.

At the other end of the continuum were the Contract *passives.* These were the members and candidates who were not only silent on the Contract, they played no role in the Contract's formation and may have expressed strong reservations about parts of it. These include the freshmen and incumbents who refused to sign (see below) as well as those who signed, such as Amo Houghton (NY) and Bill Goodling (PA), but who had little reason to run an innovative campaign because of the absence of strong opposition.

In summary, incumbents, and the challengers with previous political experience, tended to emphasize it less than did challengers who were new to politics. This was to be expected. Incumbents, after all, had their own records. Conservatives spoke about it more often than moderates. Those running successfully in marginal and heavily Democratic districts hardly mentioned it. One of these was Bob Ney. Ney's eastern Ohio district is only 16 percent Republican and Bill Clinton's approval rating was quite high throughout the fall. Even though he signed the Contract, Ney ran a campaign emphasizing his record as a state legislator. Happily, he could talk about the balanced budget amendment and the line-item veto because those were issues he felt strongly about from his 13 years of experience in Columbus. But the focus of his campaign was on constituency service.

> *In none of our ads or speeches did the Contract ever come up. My opponent didn't even bring it up. We did campaign on some of the issues in the Contract. But nothing ever came up about the Contract per se. I didn't camp on it because I had a set theme. I vaguely remember on the day before the election that one reporter mentioned it.*[34]

Picking and Choosing Contract Themes

While the Contract provided a national platform, most Republicans tailored their message to their local audience by selectively choosing issues from the list. In districts where members could sense the most disgust with government, candidates emphasized issues such as the line-item veto and the balanced budget amendment as means of bringing government under control. Tax cuts were popular and in certain districts regulatory reform as a means of reducing the burden of government on small business played well. Few of the candidates emphasized the entire Contract. Bob Ehrlich, the freshman Republican who replaced Republican Helen Bentley in Maryland's Democratic leaning 2nd District put it this way:

> *Certainly my constituents didn't know what was in the Contract. They were in touch with the "spirit" of limited government behind it. I actually ran against term limits. For that reason, I was a little worried about my constituents' understanding of the Contract. We agreed to bring these issues to a vote, to have them discussed. We didn't sign it to pass all of these items. Some of them I may oppose.*[35]

The Contract was a risky, unproved strategy, after all. Many Republican consultants were wary and instructed their candidates to avoid it. "In the closing days of the race, I received word from the Indiana Republican party and from Washington consultants at the RNC and NRCC to go negative and simply bash Clinton and not mention any positives. I didn't buy that, but that's the advice we got."[36] Members and candidates alike were instructed that they could make great gains simply by capitalizing on Clinton's unpopularity that was nearly universal in some quarters. Sources working inside the RNC at the time confirmed the claim that the RNC was a house divided:

> *There were field staff within the RNC who were telling campaigns to ignore the Contract. If Scott [Reed] and Haley [Barbour] [had] known the extent of that, they would have been furious. These people were schooled that negative works. Don't give the opposition anything positive to shoot at. They didn't understand that the Contract was carefully targeted toward people we wanted to bring back into the fold—Perot voters that had been alienated and would respond to a positive message.*[37]

The RNC's Chuck Greener summed up the pre-election uncertainty and the state of thinking within the party apparatus:

> *In any campaign, when you undertake bold strategies that carry risk, people question and reflect on what they are doing. I can remember there being some very upset people right here in the last weeks before the election who were really unsure. Later most of them said, "brilliant strategy."*[38]

The uncertainty was compounded by the fact that in most areas the press simply ignored the Republicans' positive message. In places where it was scrutinized, such as in the Seattle press, it was also heavily criticized, steering candidates such as Rick White (WA) toward themes of his own that only coincidentally overlapped with the Contract's message. Like Bob Ney, he underscored his independence from the Contract while adapting his campaign to some of its themes:

> *I had a poster of the Contract in my office and before I signed I thought I would really take it on the road but we didn't make as much use of it as we could have. The '94 election really wasn't about the Contract specifically. This was a vote against the status quo, against the way things were being done in Washington. That was the sentiment. The election results reflect a spontaneous movement that arose against Democrats. The election was nationalized but this was not because of the Contract.*[39]

Successful candidates are serious students of their opponents. White comes from a marginal district in the north Seattle suburbs. In speaking of his victory over freshman incumbent Maria Cantwell, White pointed out that Cantwell had been hobbled by her party leadership. In addition, her association with President Clinton was a major liability. Establishing independence from party leadership and conveying to constituents the message that they can think for themselves is important for members of Congress, especially those in highly competitive districts. Perhaps the comments of newly elected members such as White reflect the need to stake out their independence quickly after taking office. Such independence was often a tool of political survival for John Miller, a Republican who had occupied Rick White's seat during the 1980s prior to Cantwell's election.[40]

Like Bob Ehrlich (MD), most Republicans were quick to point out that their pledge when signing the Contract was to bring the measures to a vote, not necessarily to vote yes on every measure. In limiting the role that the Contract played in their campaigns, some members may have been reserving the right to vote against certain provisions they found questionable.

There may be other explanations for the tendency to minimize the role the Contract played in nationalizing the election. Political scientists have pointed out that members of Congress usually attribute their successes to their own unique leadership capacity and presence.[41] Most of us prefer to think that our role in the places where we work is critical and that things would fall apart without us. In this sense, winning candidates sometimes overestimate the extent to which they ran a smart campaign.[42] And while they may downplay the significance of the Contract in their individual races, most members would readily acknowledge that it did play a role in nationalizing the election and regaining the majority. The Speaker's Chief-of-Staff, Dan Meyer, provided a modest and levelheaded assessment:

> *It was a marginal thing. If we hadn't done the Contract what might have happened? How many seats would we have won? The Contract played some marginal role. If you're a candidate out there, nationalizing the election had an impact, but just a marginal one. It was certainly not the sum total of the campaign. National trends generally come very late in the campaign cycle.*

Congressman Ehrlich's (MD) observation that his constituents were in touch with the "spirit" of the Contract's message seems apt. The Republican leadership was careful to frame the Contract around themes that were popular with both the candidates and the public. This ensured the substantial overlap of candidates' personal themes and the national message of smaller government conveyed in the ten-item platform.

The Nonsigners

The story about the fall election would not be complete without mentioning several members of the new majority who did not show up on the steps of the Capitol on September 27th. There were only seven of them. Three of these stayed away on the basis of their philosophical objections to pieces of the legislation. The other four did not attend the official signing ceremony but were generally behind the leadership's effort.

Two of the nonsigners were Floridians already in office: Lincoln Diaz-Balart and Ileana Ros-Lehtinen, both Cuban Americans, both with large Cuban constituencies, both running unopposed in the general election. Their opposition was principally due to the provision in the welfare reform legislation that would deny certain program benefits to legal residents. In fact, they were applauded throughout the Miami area for their refusal to sign. Interestingly, this was the only measure in the Contract they strongly opposed. But the intensity of their feeling and the valence of the issue among constituents dictated opposition to the entire package. Diaz-Balart (FL) explained:

> *This [welfare] provision is blatantly unfair. It should have never been mixed in with the Contract.*
>
> *To me, this provision is like a cockroach in a bowl of soup. When you see a cockroach floating in a bowl of soup, you don't eat the soup.*[43]

For Ros-Lehtinen, the decision came down to both the morality of the measure and the impact it would have on her constituency:

> *When I saw the welfare reform package, with its denial of assistance to permanent U.S. residents, I couldn't sign on. They call these people "aliens" but they fully comply with U.S. laws, they pay taxes, they fight in wars. This would have had a severe impact in my congressional district.*[44]

The cases of Diaz-Balart and Ros-Lehtinen are noteworthy because they add substantial credence to R. Douglas Arnold's theory about how members think not just about issues, but about potential issues.[45] Neither of these members were threatened by defeat in the 1994 election since neither had opponents. But Diaz-Balart's legislative director, Elizabeth Humphrey, explained that the refusal to sign was partly due to the probability that it would become an issue in future races.

A third dissident was Ray LaHood, running for an open seat in Illinois. LaHood was no less than the chief-of-staff for Congressman Robert Michel (IL), the outgoing Republican leader. LaHood's principal concern was that his race looked very close and his opponent was running against Washington. Having been the Republican leader's "eyes and ears" for twelve years, LaHood could not easily shake the image of Washington insider. "The last thing I wanted to do was align myself with Washington, D.C."[46] As a deficit hawk, LaHood also opposed the tax reductions in the Contract. When asked what advice he received from Michel, LaHood explained,

> *I expressed my reservations. He agreed with my thinking on it. He thought I was thinking clearly. He never pressured me to come out and sign. . . . I didn't put that much stock in the Contract. We had talked about being in the majority for so long. I had been through this every two years for the entire*

time I'd worked for Bob Michel. To me, the Contract was just another campaign appeal, variations of which we heard every two years.[47]

Jim Bunn, a candidate from Oregon running in a dead-heat race, also refused to sign. His objection concerned the cutting of welfare benefits to teenage mothers. A strong pro-lifer, Bunn was concerned that cutting welfare benefits would encourage abortion:

I first heard about the Contract when we received a fax sometime late in the summer. Immediately when I saw the language about teen moms I was worried. I mean, what are they supposed to do when welfare funds are cut off?

. . . I understand why some people signed on in spite of their opposition to an item or two. I respect them for that. I felt that it would have caused more confusion for me to sign, then oppose the welfare plank, than for me simply not to sign on at all.[48]

The natural next question is whether these members faced any pressure or discipline for their refusal to sign. After all, they were in a tiny minority. The answer is no. The leadership has been tolerant of their views. There have been no serious attempts to retaliate. After all, members are often applauded by constituents for being independent minded. LaHood did express the concern that his refusal to sign may have kept him from securing a coveted seat on the Appropriations Committee. He also said that his freshmen classmates have not looked favorably upon his refusal to sign. "They see me as part of the 'old guard,' whereas they are part of the 'new breed'."[49] Similarly, Ros-Lehtinen described the sanctions as quiet and informal:

There was no pressure for me to sign. Newt knew I wouldn't sign. And I'm a subcommittee chair and haven't been treated any differently. . .

I do think that the rank-and-file are resentful that I didn't sign. Just today, I went down to the floor to give a one-minute heralding the 50th day. I overheard some people say, "But she didn't even sign it. She shouldn't talk about it if she didn't sign it."[50]

Barbara Sinclair has pointed out that leadership in the post-reform Congress has very little disciplinary capacity.[51] This may still be true in spite of the Republican effort to recentralize the House. The most commonly used tool of party discipline in Congress is persuasion, "the carrot is more effective than the stick."[52] As it turns out, the nonsigning members voted for almost all of the bills in the Contract. In addition, the pace of legislating in Congress is quite fast and coalitions of various shapes and sizes are constantly dissolving and reforming from issue to issue. Given such a slim majority in the 104th, Republican leaders cannot afford to hold their grudges for very long as new issues arise.

100 Days with Open Rules?

The story of how the Contract came together would not be complete without dealing with the idea of bringing the legislation to a vote in 100 days. Why 100 days? Why not 85? Why not 150? The concept suggested "honeymoon" periods ordinarily attributed to presidents. President Roosevelt set about to push through major components of his economic recovery program within the first 100 days of his presidency in 1933. President Kennedy's administration had been associated with the idea of accomplishing certain goals within the first 100 days,[53] but never before had the idea been applied to a congressional majority. The House Republican Research Committee did issue a 100-day agenda in 1985 but no one paid much attention to it.[54] There is, of course, some arbitrariness in 100 days. But there was a familiar ring to the number. When the Contract was unveiled on September 27th, it made the majority-to-be appear serious and purposeful about their reform agenda. Ultimately, there is no real reason for 100 days, except that it sounded as if the Republicans were serious about change.

The goal of fulfilling the Contract by mid-April was complicated by the simultaneous promise to open up House rules. Republicans had complained for years about the restrictive rules that had prevented them from debating alternatives and offering amendments to Democratic initiatives.[55] But it was also clear from the beginning that promising to open up House rules and promising to complete an ambitious legislative agenda in 100 days were at odds. Freshman-to-be Rick White (WA) reportedly asked Gingrich about the aggressive schedule at the time of the September signing. "Gingrich replied that the 100-day schedule was reasonable since public opinion would be on our side," White recalled.[56] Apparently, to Gingrich, the momentum provided by a 40-seat gain in the U.S. House would be sufficient to force the Republican agenda to a vote, even with unrestrictive rules. Republicans also dealt with the conflict between the 100-day deadline and the promise to open up the rules by claiming that their promise was for a "more open" debate, not a totally open debate. This would prove to be an important qualification as rules had to be increasingly limited to ensure that the 100-day goal would be reached.

Conclusions: The Contract and the Campaign

For a variety of reasons, many members emphasize the local component to the 1994 House elections. For some, it may simply be their natural reluctance to attribute their election to a national tide. Even Contract enthusiasts, generally from safe, conservative districts, gave the strategy only limited credit. For others, it may be that the election was truly local. Almost all of the members admitted that few voters, aside from a few "C-SPAN groupies,"[57] could recognize what the Contract was by election day. So one is left wondering whether the Contract is anything more than the sum of its parts. For many candidates, the Contract could be reduced to just a few of its parts, usually the balanced budget amendment, the line-item veto and congressional reform, or some similar constellation. One could argue, though, that those items are not the Contract, but just part of the Contract.

For all the talk about the Contract's influence in the election, one is left asking, Where was it influential? Clearly some candidates give it credit for adding weight, credibility and momentum to their message. Others say that the pledge underscored their sincerity about the issues they were campaigning on.

The Contract's principal influence may be on future elections. If the candidates who were elected had campaigned on many of its themes even without the formal pledge, the Contract's influence in the 1994 race would be exaggerated and mythologized. Once the election results were in, however, it was plain that the Contract would now bind the newly elected majority. That placed Republican reelection prospects in 1996 and beyond squarely atop the ten-point agenda.

3

Taking Control

Once the campaign was over and Gingrich and Armey's daring prophecy had been fulfilled, an entirely new set of tasks had to be undertaken. Capturing the House after forty years was an astonishing surprise and novelty—far more so than in the Senate, where Republicans had held the majority as recently as 1986. House Republicans were so often described as the permanent minority that many of the members had grown used to their underdog status. What could it possibly mean to run the place? Not a single House Republican had ever served in the majority.

Newt Gingrich wasted no time putting transition plans in place. There were four major reorganizational tasks to accomplish during the transition period. First, the Republican Conference had to vote on party leadership positions. Second, committee leadership posts had to be filled. Third, committees had to be reorganized to reflect the goals of the new leadership and the partisan balance of the new Congress. And finally, the Republicans would propose some sweeping rules changes to be enacted on opening day. All of these tasks, if carried out as planned, would dramatically improve the Republicans' control of the chamber.

THE SOUTH RISES AGAIN: REPUBLICAN LEADERS EMERGE

The transition to Republican rule saw the reemergence of the South at the congressional helm. Thirty years ago, southerners held a majority of the leadership posts but within the ranks of the Democratic Party. These leaders were displaced from their influential positions through a series of reforms in the 1970s that undercut the seniority system.[1] At the same time, the South began its long-term electoral shift toward the Republican party.[2] This shift was first observable in the 1964 presidential election as Barry Goldwater won four southern states against Texan Lyndon B. Johnson. Republican presidential candidates have done well there since.

Even in 1992, George Bush won a majority of southern states, including Texas, Florida, Alabama, and Mississippi. In Congress, Republican takeover has come much more slowly because the party did not fully capitalize on its strength at the top of the ticket.[3] As Figure 3-1 shows, the 1994 election is noteworthy for being the first in which Republicans captured a majority of southern House seats. The Republican percentage of the House vote in the southern states has also been steadily on the rise, moving from 34.5 percent in 1964 to 52 percent 30 years later (Figure 3-1).

In Congressional leadership, the rise of the Republican South would not be observable until the 1980s, with the election of Trent Lott (MI) as the Minority Whip in December 1980. The Republican leadership became even more southern with the steady exit of prominent northern members such as Dick Cheney (WY), Jack Kemp (NY), Silvio Conte (MA) (died in office), Guy Vander Jagt (MI), Bill Frenzel (MN), Tom Tauke (IA), Vin Weber (MN), Barber Conable (NY), Edward Madigan (IL), and Robert Michel (IL). Moreover, many of the southern seats now in Republican hands are safe, owing to the increasingly conservative tenor of the electorate there and the movement of the national Democratic party toward the left.

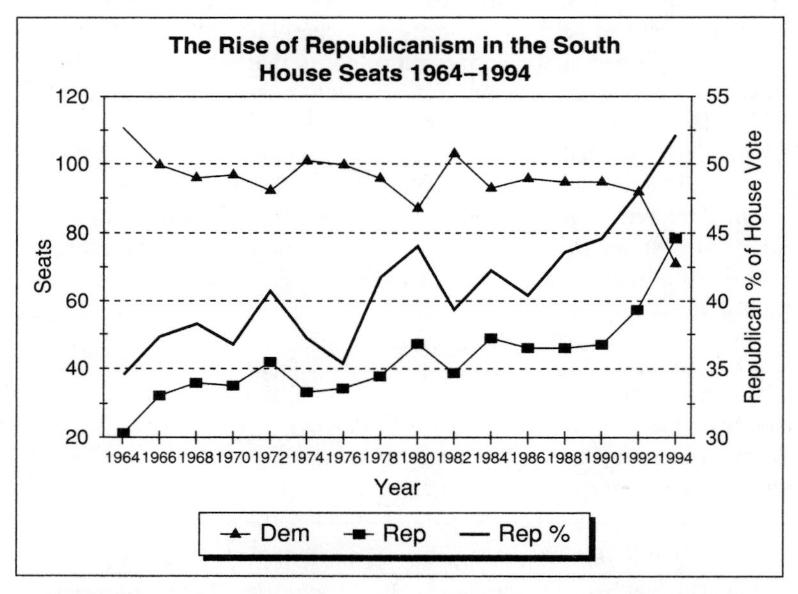

FIGURE 3-1 **Republican Seat Gains and Percentage of the Two-Party House Vote, 1964–1994.** Following the definition of the U.S. Census Bureau, southern states are: AL, AR, DE, FL, GA, KY, LA, MD, MS, NC, OK, SC, TN, TX, VA, and WV.

Source: U.S. Department of Commerce, Bureau of the Census, *Statistical Abstract of the United States,* annual.

Leadership Elections

As the Republican Whip, Newt Gingrich was the natural heir to Republican leader Michel when the latter decided to retire at the close of the 103rd Congress. Since his election in 1978, Gingrich had worked to put himself in position to be Speaker. Initially, he was no more a favorite of the old guard Republican leadership than he was of the Democrats.[4] But through sheer persistence, will, and his torment of the Democratic majority, he attracted enough attention to be elected Whip in 1989 over leadership favorite Edward Madigan (IL). In spite of two, close, general-election victories in 1990 and 1992, there was little thought of a challenge from anyone else in the Conference. Similarly, there was no doubt that Richard K. Armey, the head of the Conference Committee, would step up as Majority Leader. Armey's rise was even faster than Gingrich's. Elected to his Arlington, TX, district only in 1984, he won reelection by sizable margins in every election since, including his overwhelming 76 percent vote share in 1994.

Below these top positions, much less was clear. The position of Majority Whip was contested by three senior Republicans: Tom DeLay (TX), Bill McCollum (FL) and Robert Walker (PA). DeLay, another ambitious Texan elected in 1984, used a behind-the-scenes style to become Secretary of the Republican Conference Committee in the 103rd Congress. Walker is a Gingrich ally and was Chief Deputy Whip in the 103rd. His strength has been in parliamentary procedure and he specializes in the same confrontational tactics as Gingrich. McCollum also had a leadership position in the 103rd Congress, as Vice Chair of the Republican Conference. McCollum's strength was in the area of crime legislation where he has led opposition to gun-control legislation. These strong contenders all had very conservative credentials. After the balloting, DeLay emerged with 119 votes to Walker's 80 and McCollum's 28.

With the top three Republican leadership posts going to southern conservatives, one has to move to the fourth position to find a northerner, John Boehner (OH), a conservative young member who had served only two terms. He won the position of Republican Conference Chair over a much more senior Republican, Duncan Hunter from San Diego. The only moderate in the Republican leadership ranks is Susan Molinari (NY), the wife of NRCC Chair Bill Paxon (NY). Molinari won the Conference Vice Chair position in spite of the efforts of pro-life groups to defeat her.[5]

What this leadership team has in common is youth and, except for Molinari, conservatism. They represent a departure from former Republican leader Bob Michel's (IL) more pragmatic inclinations. Boehner and Molinari also reflect Gingrich's preference for active, articulate and energetic members.

FILLING COMMITTEE SLOTS: SOUTHERNERS AND CONSERVATIVES

Committees are the "policy workshops" of Congress.[6] Much recent research has heralded the strength of committees as the central feature of a decentralized, even fragmented Congress. Because each element of the Contract with America would have to wind its way through committee before reaching the floor, party leaders knew that the committee chairs needed careful consideration. Gaining control over committee activity, then, would be one of the the most important of all leadership strategies in the 104th Congress. Committee chair selection was at Gingrich's discretion but his slate was ratified overwhelmingly by a vote of Republican party members. From the start, the Speaker-to-be's goal was to render committee output more predictable by selecting chairs who shared his basic philosophy. In naming the candidates, the new Speaker did not ignore seniority for ideology entirely. As Table 3-1 shows, the seniority system was bypassed in three instances. A majority of the committee chairs

Table 3-1 Committee Chairs in the 104th Congress

Committee	Chair (state)	Year elected
Agriculture	Pat Roberts (KS)	1980
Appropriations*	Robert Livingston (LA)	1977
Banking	Jim Leach (IA)	1976
Budget	John Kasich (OH)	1982
Commerce*	Thomas Bliley (VA)	1980
Economic & Educational Opportunities	Bill Goodling (PA)	1974
Government Reform	William Clinger (PA)	1978
House Oversight	Bill Thomas (CA)	1978
International Relations	Benjamin Gilman (NY)	1972
Judiciary*	Henry Hyde (IL)	1974
National Security	Floyd Spence (SC)	1970
Natural Resources	Don Young (AK)	1973
Rules**	Gerald Solomon (NY)	1978
Science	Robert Walker (PA)	1976
Select Intelligence	Larry Combest (TX)	1984
Small Business	Jan Meyers (KS)	1984
Standards of Official Conduct	Nancy Johnson (CT)	1982
Transportation & Infrastructure	Bud Shuster (PA)	1972
Veterans Affairs	Bob Stump (AZ)	1976
Ways & Means	Bill Archer (TX)	1970

*indicates more senior committee members passed over in appointing the chair in the 104th Congress.
**indicates more senior member passed over in the 103rd Congress.

have been in office since 1980. The average term of service for these chairs is about 9.7 terms. In addition, several of the chairs are not staunch conservatives: Jim Leach (IA) and Ben Gilman (NY) come readily to mind as party moderates. The new party leaders apparently had the presence of mind to recognize the diversity within Republican ranks. Resources were distributed so as to placate influential moderates.

Insiders suggested that Gingrich's judgment was based on a combination of factors including ideological loyalty, seniority, his assessment of each candidate's management skill and the energy each could bring to the committee. He was not looking simply for conformity. "The committees needed chairs who were activists. [Jim] Leach (IA) is an example of someone who may be moderate, but is very energetic."[7] Southerners, once again, fared well under the Gingrich formula. Another Texan, Bill Archer, assumed the chair of Ways and Means. Robert Livingston (LA) was selected to head Appropriations. Floyd Spence (SC) became the chair of the National Security Committee (formerly Armed Services), and Thomas Bliley (VA) was awarded the chair of the Commerce Committee. Several senior Republicans were bypassed in Gingrich's selection, including John Myers (IN), Carlos Moorhead (CA), Joe McDade (PA), C. W. Young (FL) and Ralph Regula (OH). As consolation prizes, each was awarded a major subcommittee post. McDade was passed over due to a pending federal indictment. Moorhead and Myers were passed over because they were thought to be too friendly with Democratic committee members. Tony Blankley described these decisions as extremely difficult for the Speaker:

> *We went through the campaign to accomplish certain things if we won. Newt and the leaders wanted to put the right people in charge. The most painful decision was not giving a full chairmanship to Carlos Moorhead (CA). He is a very loyal, hard-working member.*
>
> *Basically, Newt thought that Carlos was too nice and amiable a person to fight at the level we would have to fight. The Judiciary Committee has the likes of Chuck Schumer (NY) and Barney Frank (MA). The chair would have to fend off those people on a daily basis. He wasn't sure that Carlos was up to that.*
>
> *Similarly, on Appropriations, Newt understood that the big fight beyond the first 100 days would be over money. He reached way down the seniority ladder to get [Robert] Livingston. Newt wants to change the culture and mentality of that committee. He wants it to go from being a spending committee to a cutting committee. So he overthrew the seniority system and asked the committee members to write a mission statement that would conform to party goals. The fun of being on Appropriations is over. It will now be the hardest committee to serve on.*[8]

Livingston did not know ahead of time that he would be chosen to head Appropriations. He had been planning to run for Conference Chair, the position that John Boehner (OH) ultimately won. Livingston explained that just after the election, "Boehner called me and said he wanted to be Conference Chair and asked if there was some other position I wanted. I told him that I would like to be chair of Appropriations but that I couldn't campaign for it."[9] Boehner then stepped in and pushed for Livingston with the leadership and with the junior members on the Appropriations Committee. "Newt would not have picked me had it not been all right with the other Appropriations members," Livingston explained.[10]

Chris Cox (CA), a quick-minded, aggressive Republican who heads the Policy Committee put Gingrich's committee choices in a far different light. He emphasized the importance of choosing aggressive chairmen who would heed the Speaker's call:

> *Here in the House, this is a one man show. Gingrich went around the seniority system to get around people like the ones who are running the Senate. He tapped Livingston and what a difference that has made. If he hadn't done that, we would look just like the Senate.*
>
> *. . . You don't have to change the head of every committee when you change just a few. Gingrich has given them a renewed sense that chairs serve at the Speaker's pleasure.*[11]

Where southerners were not chosen, Gingrich selected strong conservatives, such as Solomon (NY) for Rules, Walker (PA) for Science, and Kasich (OH) for Budget. In this manner, leadership sought to ensure that the key elements of the legislative program would not be compromised before they reached the floor.

A comparison of ideology and district characteristics of twenty-six Republicans in top leadership slots with the remaining Republican incumbents from the 103rd Congress appears in Table 3-2. (Freshman have been excluded since they have no ideological rating yet). The figures show that leaders are slightly more conservative than other returning incumbents when measured by their tendency to vote with the conservative coalition. Using the *National Journal*'s 1994 social liberalism rating, similar results obtain. The leadership is about ten points less socially liberal than the other returning Republicans. But Table 3-2 also shows that the districts supplying the leaders were less likely to vote for Bill Clinton and had slightly fewer elderly voters who might be threatened by Social Security cuts. Fortuitously, the differences between the leadership and the rank-and-file is not as great on the economic issues measured by the *National Journal* for the 103rd Congress (Table 3-2). Since the Contract focuses on economic issues, the relative homogeneity of the party on economic concerns was a happy fact. Previous research has shown that the Republican party in the House tends to be more homogeneous than the Democratic side.[12] The simple comparisons here suggest that the Republican leadership in the 104th appears to be more homogeneous still. Once again, maintaining a certain ideological cohesion in the leadership reflects the foresight of Republican party bosses. Heterogeneity at the top is a recipe for disagreement.

The upshot is that after 40 years as the out-party, Republicans had anticipated many of the problems of fulfilling the Contract and decided to cede to Gingrich sweeping power. These developments are certainly consistent with David Brady's

Table 3-2 Comparison of Ideology and District Characteristics of Republican Leadership to All Republican Incumbents Returning to the 104th Congress

Leadership Status	Conservative Coalition Rating	National Journal Economic Liberalism Rating	National Journal Social Liberalism Rating	% for Clinton	% Over Age 65
Leadership	90.5 (n = 26)	14.7 (n = 26)	14.3 (n = 26)	32.5 (n = 26)	11.4 (n = 26)
Nonleadership	86.3 (n = 132)	17.3 (n = 130)	23.0 (n = 130)	37.0 (n = 132)	13.2 (n = 132)
T-test	2.06	.69	2.33	3.19	2.05
Significance	$p < .009$	$p < .49$	$p < .03$	$p < .003$	$p < .05$
Cases	158	156	156	158	158

Sources: Congressional Quarterly Weekly Report, 12/31/94; *National Journal,* 1/14/95; *Almanac of American Politics,* 1994; and author's calculations. Demographic data are from the 1990 Census. The 26 leadership posts include 19 standing committee chairs and seven offices in party leadership. Freshmen members and their districts are excluded from these calculations.

prediction that electoral groundswells can lead to major changes in House organization and policy.[13] Observers claimed that Gingrich had successfully "recentralized" power in the House. But Republican compliance with leadership was mostly a function of having been a minority for so long. While the leadership was careful in its selection of committee members, Republican unity would come at a rather low cost given the unique opportunity the party now had to take the reins. Still, the leadership was not about to take anything for granted. With the aid of the Steering Committee (formerly called the Committee on Committees), the remaining committee assignments were approved in a process that weighted the votes of Gingrich and Armey more heavily than any of the others voting.[14] Each slot was considered carefully. Many freshmen were put on the major committees because they were known to be committed to the issues in the Contract. The party leadership also screened the staff directors for each of the major committees and ensured that all subcommittee staff slots would be hired by the chair of the full committee, and not by subcommittee chairs. Given how much of the work is performed by staff, this was another way of ensuring that everyone was on the same team.

In addition, the sizes of committees were adjusted to provide Republicans with a solid, but not overwhelming partisan edge. This was consistent with the promise to reduce the size of committees. As a result, many Democrats lost plum posts. However, the leadership did not go so far as to inflict 60–40 ratios (60 percent Republican members, 40 percent Democratic members). There is no reason why they could not have divided the committees in this manner. House rules do not prohibit such a division. According to Gingrich staff members, the leadership did not think it would be fair to divide up the committees so lopsidedly given the ratios in the House as a whole (53 percent Republican, 47 percent Democratic). This decision was also in accord with precedent. Most committees have reflected the ratios in the chamber. Exceptions have been in the Rules Committee, and Ways and Means, where secure majorities were deemed essential for policy purposes.

Three standing committees were eliminated in opening-day rules changes: Merchant Marine, District of Columbia, and Post Office and Civil Service. From now on the issues arising in these areas would be considered by other panels. Originally, Small Business was also on the chopping block, but a strong lobbying effort by Republican committee members and interest groups kept it alive. In addition, it was chaired by Jan Meyers (KS), the only female to hold a top committee post.

Many of these reforms were welcomed by Democrats. "The institution needs updating from time to time," said Paul Kanjorski, a senior Democrat from Pennsylvania.[15] Kanjorski wasn't even sorry to see the Post Office and Civil Service Committee eliminated, a committee on which he served, "We won't reconstitute either the D.C. or the Postal committees when we win again. We may strive for better committee alignment with the executive branch. But I didn't mind seeing some change. Even changing the names of the committees was useful."[16] Other Democrats complained that the Republicans did not go far enough in their reform effort, "Gingrich missed a once-in-a-lifetime opportunity. He could have been really generous and changed more things," said Ben Cardin (MD), who headed the Democratic transition.[17] Cardin also complained that the Republicans had not fulfilled their campaign promise to be open, fair, and inclusive, "The Republicans didn't share any information with me. They were not at all inclusive. They catered to special interests. The structural changes they made were all partisan and designed to their advantage."[18] The idea that the Republicans went back on their word would be a persistent Democratic drum beat throughout the first 100 days.

REWRITING THE RULES ON OPENING DAY

"I am very proud of the changes we made on the first day," said Rick White, newly elected from Washington's first district. "I will definitely talk about them in my 1996 campaign because they have changed the way Congress does business."[19] Republicans made good on their promises to pass sweeping institutional reforms. In addition to the elimination of three standing committees, committee staff were cut by one-third from the level of the 103rd Congress.[20] As an accountability measure, committees must now publish the votes of committee members for all bills and amendments. Also abolished was the long-standing practice of referring bills to multiple committees jointly. Bills may still be divided up for consideration by separate committees, or may be considered sequentially.[21]

As far as the official reorganization of the House was concerned, one move by the new leadership proved to be one of the most galling to Democrats. This was the defunding of the caucuses. Until they were eliminated in the Republican rules changes, caucuses were legislative service organizations (LSOs) that functioned in a research and advisory capacity for participating members. Members belonging to the larger caucuses would pay dues from their budget allocation to support caucus staff and operations. Twenty-eight of these caucuses received office space and equipment from the House budget governing internal operations. The elimination of the caucuses brought about a rather modest reduction in House staff of ninety-six positions and saved about $4 million.[22] Many caucuses had a bipartisan membership so this was not necessarily a partisan slap. Democrats did use two of these organizations quite extensively for information, research, and organization: the Congressional Black Caucus and the Democratic Study Group (DSG). The Black Caucus continues to exist as an association of forty African-American members in the new Congress, thirty-nine of whom are Democrats, but it no longer has staff or offices.

The elimination of the DSG was an even more serious matter. Democrats used the DSG as a homegrown think-tank and independent source of information on House schedules and bill briefings. Once eliminated, Democrats would have to scramble to replace it or forgo valuable information about committee and floor activity. Without institutional support, the DSG is in the process of setting up operations off the Hill but it has struggled to raise funds from Democratic offices.[23] In late January, Democrats were set back in their attempt to take the DSG and several other LSOs private. Republicans in the House Oversight Committee enacted regulations barring members from using their office allowances to pay for services from organizations that cannot prove they can support themselves without congressional subscriptions.[24] Once the DSG collects sufficient funds from private sector sources, it will probably make a comeback as the Democrats' leading information source. Reform-minded Republicans threw as many obstacles in the way of congressional funding for such entities as they possibly could. Democrats charged that Republicans were playing partisan politics, and that the rules changes were designed simply to "get at the Democratic organizations that had clout."[25] Republicans pointed out that the LSOs were corrupt, opened the Congress to inordinate interest group pressures, and mishandled some $7 million in unaccounted-for funds.[26]

Several of the institutional reforms were not designed to smooth the flow of legislative business and may well have the opposite effect. Republicans eliminated proxy voting—the system whereby committee chairs and ranking minority members were allowed to cast votes for absent members. With proxy votes it was often possible for the chair to control the outcome of committee votes even though he was the only majority member in the room. By eliminating proxy voting, members of the committee will have to be present in order to vote. With the intense pace of the first 100 days, members complained about having to be present at the committee markup all the time, but members adjusted to the new rule without missing many votes.

A reform long advocated by Congress-watchers and critics is the rotation of committee and subcommittee chairs.[27] With this rule change, committee chairs serve limited terms of six years. The idea is to prevent the entrenchment of special interests around certain members. Coupled with the reduction in the size of committee staff, Republican leaders hope to prohibit the kingdom building typical in the Energy and Commerce Committee under Democratic Chair John Dingell (MI). Republicans went further, however, in adopting a term limit for the Speakership of eight years. This may be only symbolic, however, as no Speaker in recent memory has served that long.

Members have grown accustomed to editing their remarks before they were printed in the *Congressional Record.* In this manner, they could always manage to make themselves sound better than the way they actually sounded. They could strike gaffes from the official record and even change the meaning of what they said on the floor. This practice ended with the adoption of a rule requiring verbatim accounts and allowing only technical and grammatical corrections. Finally, roll-call votes are to be recorded for all conference reports that make appropriations and raise taxes. This reform is an accountability measure to ensure that taxing and spending policies are easily traceable to action taken by members.[28]

House Republicans enacted a new rule to strip delegates from the District of Columbia, Guam, the Virgin Islands, American Samoa, and Puerto Rico of their voting privileges in the Committee of the Whole. While these delegates were never allowed to cast a deciding vote on bills and amendments, their vote had substantial symbolic significance. Delegates have long served on committees and in 1993 the Democrats had changed the House rules to permit them to vote during floor deliberations, largely to offset Republican gains from the 1992 elections. With this reversal, the Republicans eliminated the 1993 rule. It is not clear what the Republicans might gain from this move, except to perhaps dampen the ambition of D.C. statehood advocates. As it happens, all of the delegates are Democrats and have what could be described as typical Democratic constituencies, including substantial numbers of lower-income, non-white residents. This rule change was most likely designed to dilute Democratic strength. As expected, the Republican action met with howls of protest from the delegates themselves as well as from their Democratic allies.

CONCLUSION: A SUCCESSFUL TRANSITION

Considering that the Republicans had been out of the majority for forty years, the transition went remarkably well. There were a few missteps, mostly by way of controversies generated by Newt Gingrich's new ideas, a book deal that included a $4.5 million advance, and his penchant for shooting from the hip in interviews and press conferences. People were getting used to Gingrich's openness, however, and his gaffes didn't appear to stick for long. He was also quick to handle the problems that did arise, turning down the advance for the book and firing a controversial appointee as House Historian.*

With these bumps aside, the transition went better than expected. By allowing the leadership to centralize decisions in the offices of the Speaker and Majority Leader, the Republican members benefitted from a smooth transfer of power and opening day of business. Forty years of out-party status ensured a strong degree of unity behind the new leadership. In addition, Gingrich and Armey had spent much of the 1994 election season building support for the Contract, bringing on board partisans of every stripe and hue. By deliberately keeping issues such as abortion and school prayer out of the Contract, even liberals in the party such as Constance Morella (MD) and Jim Leach (IA) were solidly in the Gingrich camp.

Historical trends and circumstances beyond the control of any one individual also deserve some measure of credit for the smooth transition. The increasing homogeneity of the parties has created less room for dissent within Republican ranks. Increasing southern seniority has ensured that many key committee posts could be filled by members with solidly conservative credentials—true believers and Gingrich allies. The electoral changes in the South helped bring in a class of freshmen who only added to the conservative tenor of the new majority, while making the Democrats more homogeneously liberal than ever before. Finally, the anti-government sentiment that has welled up in the public, culminating in the changes of November 8, provided the Republicans with the argument that the American people had given them a mandate. Whenever opposition might arise, the Republicans could always criticize the "obstruction-mongers" for standing in the way of the popular demand for change. Democrats and Republicans had switched roles almost overnight.

*The appointment controversy erupted over the naming of Christina Jeffrey as House historian. In the mid-80s, Jeffrey had criticized a history curriculum on the Holocaust, under review by the Department of Education, for not including the viewpoints of Nazis and Ku Klux Klan members. Upon hearing of her controversial remarks, Gingrich withdrew the nomination saying he had not been aware of Jeffrey's comments. (*Roll Call,* 1/19/95, pp. A1, A15.)

4

The Balanced Budget and Line-Item Veto

Some problems loom so large and politically intractable that Congress has found it difficult to resolve them. One of these problems is that of deficit spending. Simply put, the problem lawmakers confront is that citizens make demands for government services but are unwilling to bear the costs of those services in increased taxes. When asked, solid majorities of Americans favor a balanced budget amendment to the U.S. Constitution. From a January, 1994, poll came a report stating, "There is a broad consensus in favor of the [balanced budget] amendment of a sort rarely seen in American politics."[1] Budget balancing is deeply rooted in American culture.[2] But the public also wants its representatives to protect government spending on health, education, Social Security, student loans, Medicare, space research, drug eradication, and the homeless.[3] Everyone wants a balanced budget but no one wants to bear the costs. Costs, after all, are what inspire people to oppose legislation.[4] A balanced budget is a collective good, but, as in all collective goods problems, individuals want to avoid the costs associated with obtaining that good.[5]

In the face of contradictory mandates, members of Congress have been unwilling and/or unable to attack the problem of rising deficits. Legislators understandably shun policies that would impose high costs on their constituents.[6] But legislators are not oblivious to the problem of out-of-control deficits. What is that problem? Briefly, deficits matter because covering the gap between revenue and spending through borrowing takes capital that could go to other, more productive sectors of the economy.[7] The more money government borrows, the less money is available for savings and investment by private citizens engaged in, say, business enterprises. This is why economists say that the deficit is a "tax on capital." By permitting government to engage in deficit spending, Congress and the president have allowed government to make spending decisions that commit a large share of anticipated future income to debt repayment. The result, according to a General Accounting Office (GAO) report is that "The federal deficit has absorbed half or more of the resources available to promote long term growth."[8] A substantial share of our future income has been precommitted.[9] Perhaps government borrowing to finance deficit spending would not be so painful if it were interest free. But as indebtedness rises, so do the interest payments. As interest payments have increased, they have put pressure on existing uses of government money for valued programs such as defense, entitlements and crime control.[10] In other words, the level of government service is threatened not just by the deficit, but by the high interest payments needed to finance it.

This difficult quandary has led many congressional leaders to search for ways of reducing the deficit that are less politically threatening than wholesale cuts in entitlements and defense spending. Enacting a balanced budget amendment to the U.S. Constitution is one means to this end. Giving the president line-item veto authority is another. These measures are designed to address the deficit problem by moving the political burden of budget cuts elsewhere. For years, politicians from both parties have considered more conventional remedies, but clear majorities in Congress could not be found either for tax increases or spending cuts. Meanwhile, the deficit continues to mount. Several scholars have pointed out that, when Congress cannot muster the will to resolve a problem, it kicks the ball elsewhere. By delegating difficult spending cuts to others, members avoid being held responsible for actions adversely affecting constituents.[11] While critics of these measures believe that proponents of the balanced budget amendment and the line-item veto would have Congress shirk its responsibility, proponents recognize the difficulty the legislative branch has had in exercising that responsibility. In their view, the responsibility for balancing the budget should be kicked elsewhere.

The Contract with America placed a high priority on deficit reduction. The balanced budget amendment and the line-item veto are right up front both in the book that was mass marketed[12] and on the Congressional agenda. Originally incorporated into a single bill, "The Fiscal Responsibility Act," the two measures were split into two separate bills upon introduction in January. Although I will address both in this chapter, the two pieces of legislation developed quite separate lives.

BACKGROUND ON THE BALANCED BUDGET AMENDMENT

Amendments to the U.S. Constitution can be brought up in one of two ways: (1) a proposed amendment must pass the House and Senate by a two-thirds majority vote and then be submitted for ratification by three-fourths (38) of the states; or (2) two-thirds of the states (34) can call for a constitutional convention to consider an amendment. This second method has never been used.

The idea of placing a constitutional constraint on fiscal policy is not new. Thomas Jefferson was hostile to government borrowing and wrote of denying the government this power as a means of protecting states rights.[13] The first balanced budget amendment, however, wasn't proposed in Congress until 1936. The amendment wasn't taken seriously, and it died in committee. In 1956 and again in 1980 and 1981, hearings were held in the Senate Judiciary Committee on proposed amendments, but no proposal made it past the committee vote. In 1982, a balanced budget amendment passed the Senate by the required two-thirds majority but failed to pass the House by 47 votes.[14]

In the mid-1980s, momentum for the amendment subsided as lawmakers enacted the Gramm-Rudman-Hollings deficit reduction measure. This legislation set specific deficit reduction targets that were designed to eliminate the gap between revenues and expenditures by 1991. An unfortunate side effect of Gramm-Rudman-Hollings was the tendency for Congress to side-step difficult decisions and come up with budget tricks to exempt certain programs from deficit reduction efforts.[15] In the end, even with "creative" accounting, the Gramm-Rudman-Hollings budget targets could not be met and Congress acted to extend them indefinitely. Congress completely failed to deal with the fastest growing budgetary programs in the area of entitlements. Entitlements are especially problematic because they are available to anyone meeting the eligibility criteria specified in law.[16] As the population ages into the 21st century, entitlements for elderly citizens, such as Social Security and Medicare, are expected to skyrocket. Republicans continued to push for budget reform to address spending on entitlements, but, without majorities in either the House or Senate, they were largely ignored. On the House side, Charles Stenholm (TX) has been a vigorous Democratic proponent of a balanced budget amendment. Stenholm's measures came up in 1990, 1992, and 1994 only to be defeated by narrow margins. Time and again, the proposal has fallen just short of the required two-thirds majority. With the election in 1994 of a Republican majority, most of whom had signed the Contract with its balanced budget proposal, things were about to change.

The Contract's Balanced Budget Proposal

As introduced, H.J. Res. 1 provided that the President transmit to Congress a budget in which outlays (expenditures) are not greater than receipts (revenue). Any deficit must be explicitly approved by a three-fifths (261 votes in the House; 60 in the Senate) majority of both the House and Senate. During times of war, the balanced budget requirement can be set aside provided a joint resolution is approved by a simple majority of the House and Senate. The legislation also set a debt limit at its current level that could not be increased unless approved by three-fifths of each chamber. And finally, the proposal required a three-fifths majority of the House and Senate to increase revenue. The amendment would take effect in 2002 or the second year following its ratification, whichever is later. All votes arising under this measure must be recorded, roll-call votes.

Upon introduction on January 4th, the legislation was referred to the Judiciary Committee. Protest within the Committee by Democrats was especially fierce.

Opponents charged that amendment sponsors should be required to spell out what programs would be cut in order to balance the budget. Minority Leader Richard A. Gephardt (MO) insisted that people needed to know exactly what a balanced budget would mean in their lives.[17] Republicans considered this simply a clever strategy to defeat the bill. Polls showed that support for balancing the budget dropped off drastically once specific program cuts were mentioned in such areas as Social Security and Medicare.[18] The Center for Budget and Policy Priorities, a liberal Washington think tank, issued a report claiming that a balanced budget would eliminate the safety net for the poor and redistribute money to the rich. This was the classic strategy of charging that the Republicans were engaging in class warfare. Republican leaders were confronted by these critics with the nasty problem of costs.[19] Realizing that details about costs could undermine momentum, Republicans led by Budget Committee Chair John Kasich (OH) and Majority Leader Armey (TX) admitted publicly that the enumeration of costs would bring special interests out of the woodwork in opposition. No one could estimate exactly what programs would have to be cut in a seven-year effort to balance the budget by 2002.

Perhaps the most potent argument raised against the balanced budget amendment was that it would threaten vital programs. Democrats repeatedly charged that the Contract version of the amendment would not protect the aged, sick, and poor. But there were other arguments. Chief among them was what role the Courts might wind up playing if fiscal policy were written into the Constitution. Basic taxing and spending decisions could ultimately be turned over to judges if Congress did not honor its promise to balance the budget. Several Republicans, including freshman John Hostettler (IN) and Mark Hatfield (OR), the chair of the Senate Appropriations Committee, argued that Congress should not have to have an external restraint and that it should muster sufficient will of its own to balance the budget.

Proponents also had persuasive arguments, the strongest of which was the institution's historical incapacity to make revenues match expenditures. External pressure was needed in the form of a constitutional amendment in order to force Congress to make the difficult choices it had evaded for years. Others voiced concern about the burden being passed down to future generations and damage being done to U.S. competitiveness due to the drag of the deficit. Finally, in response to arguments about the threat the amendment posed to Social Security, supporters pointed out that other provisions in the Contract supported seniors, especially the Senior Citizens Equity Act (H.R. 8), which would repeal tax increases on Social Security benefits. This measure would also raise to $30,000 (from $11,160) the amount seniors can earn before they begin losing Social Security benefits.

COMMITTEE AND FLOOR ACTION

Democrats offered amendments in committee primarily aimed at exempting certain programs such as Social Security from budget cuts and generally peppering the legislation with loopholes that would permit easy escape from a painful axe. A Clinton administration proposal sponsored by ranking Democrat John Conyers (MI), titled "truth-in-budgeting," that would require Congress to spell out what cuts would be made before the amendment was sent to the states, was also defeated. After nearly nine hours, the Chair, Henry Hyde (IL), cut off debate and passed the legislation out of committee on a party-line vote of 20–14.[20] Democrats complained about being cut off, but to no avail. The balanced budget amendment was off to the floor.

Republican leaders ran into difficulty almost immediately with the Contract version of the amendment requiring a three-fifths majority to increase revenue. The Stenholm proposal that had nearly passed the year before contained no such provision. In committee, though, the Stenholm alternative was resoundingly defeated. On the floor, it became clear that there would not be enough Democratic votes to obtain the two-thirds necessary for passage of the Contract version. The House leadership was in a double-bind. On the one side, a militant group of about forty newly elected Republicans were threatening to vote against any proposal that lacked the three-fifths revenue provision. On the other, a small bloc of moderate Republicans strenuously objected to the three-fifths provision on the grounds that it would hold a majority hostage to a minority. It soon became clear that if there were no compromise, there would be no amendment.

A few grassroots groups mobilized in favor of the stricter provision. These included the Christian Coalition, Americans for Tax Reform, Citizens for a Sound Economy, and the National Federation of Independent Businesses. But these groups found themselves preaching to the converted. Republicans were solidly behind the three-fifths provision, but as several more days passed, it became obvious that there were not enough Democrats who would go along. Moderate Republican Mike Castle (DE) summed up the reality of the situation by pointing out that the amendment required bipartisan support, plain and simple, and that the leadership was going to have to come around.[21]

On the floor, the balanced budget legislation came up under a new "winner-take-all" rule. During the first two days of debate, there would be only a single vote on the Contract version of the bill. The House would then move on to amendments, including the Stenholm version. Whichever proposal received the most votes that met or exceeded the 290 requirement would be the one passed on a final vote. Republicans were instructed by their leadership to vote against other proposals if the Contract version met the 290 goal. In total, Republicans limited the number of Democratic amendments to five, all in the nature of a substitute. Predictably, Democrats again protested that Republicans were going back on their promise to keep debate open. The minority party had prepared some 40 amendments.

By Day 22, January 26th, Gingrich and Armey could see that the Contract version of the balanced budget amendment would not pass. They abandoned it even before it was voted on and began campaigning instead for the Stenholm version which was identical in every respect save the three-fifths provision. Freshmen members initially opposed anything less than the Contract version. According to a key leadership aide, "some even discussed letting the amendment fail and blaming the failure on the Democrats!" But leadership prevailed by arguing that a failure to pass this first item in the Contract would throw the momentum to the opposition. Armey's pitch was that the "best should not be the enemy of the good." "We managed to bring them on board by convincing them of the merits of the measure itself, that elimination of the three-fifths provision is better than no balanced budget amendment at all," said Ed Gillespie, Armey's press secretary. "We emphasized that they have a collective responsibility to make the party look good."[22] The leadership's appeals worked. The freshmen began trickling back into the fold.

THE VOTES—DAY 22

On the evening of Day 22 of the first 100 days, the Contract version of the amendment came up for a vote. Republicans mustered 253 votes, 37 short of the necessary 290. Thirty-three Democrats backed the Contract version along with 220 Republicans. The Stenholm provision came up a short time later and easily passed by a vote of 300–132. Seventy-two of the 204 Democrats supported Stenholm, along with all but two of the Republicans.

Explanations for the Votes

In his recent book on the relationship between representatives and represented, William T. Bianco argues that it is more useful to study individual decisions (votes), rather than blocs of votes such as those represented in interest group ratings.[23] By looking at individual votes, one can tell whether a legislator is "choosing between personal policy concerns and constituent demands,"[24] or between party leadership and constituency. For years, scholars of Congress have argued that constituency preferences override the desires of party leadership when the two collide.[25] But in the first 100 days of the 104th, this may not be true. David Brady has pointed out that party influence on voting is vastly strengthened following major electoral shifts.[26] Republican leaders spent most of 1994 building unity behind a party program. Although it is true that the items in the Contract have widespread constituency support, few constituents knew many details about the specific proposals. Leadership had the signatures on the Contract, however, generating an unusual accountability to party leadership that might hold legislators away from taking constituency cues when those cues might point in the opposite direction.

These considerations lead us to ask what might explain the voting division on the floor. Although party is certainly relevant, it cannot be the only factor inasmuch as many Democrats backed both versions of the bill. Region is one explanation that indicates ideological orientation: the majority of Democrats behind the bill were southerners. Other explanations, however, could be rooted in more precisely measured constituency characteristics.[27] One might expect, for instance, that those with significant constituencies that are over age 65 might be hostile to a balanced budget amendment given the threat it poses to Social Security, Medicare, and other programs that benefit the elderly.[28] Similarly, those with large African-American populations that have long benefitted from government action, including the members of the Congressional Black Caucus, would probably be anxious about service cuts that would be forced upon their districts under a balanced budget amendment. We can also hypothesize that legislators from districts that are poor and urban would be opposed to the amendment. Finally, the figures in Chapter One suggested that in districts where Ross Perot ran strongest, Democrats did not do well in the 1994 elections. The "Perot factor" may influence recorded votes, too, as legislators from districts where Perot's reform message ran strongest, would be less likely to oppose the balanced budget amendment.

An analysis of the voting cleavages on the Contract and Stenholm versions of the balanced budget amendment appears in Table A1 in the Appendix. The variables included in the analysis of the two amendments were selected from among those thought to be theoretically relevant to the issue.

Constituency influences, it turns out, played a role independent of party and region in the vote on the Contract version of the legislation. Specifically, those with large elderly, African-American, and urban districts were more likely to vote against the Contract (Barton) version than they were the Stenholm measure. This is to be expected since Stenholm's proposal produced a stronger consensus across geographic and partisan lines. What is noteworthy about the Stenholm version was that it reduced partisan and regional cleavages by unifying Republicans and southern Democrats. As predicted, a rural/urban division is apparent in the vote on the Stenholm amendment with the most urban legislators about 14 percent less likely to vote for it than the most rural legislators. The proportion of Perot voters in each district made little difference to the decision to vote yea or nay on either balanced budget alternative.

The vote shows how critical the small group of southern Democrats had become to Republican success—at least on votes requiring a two-thirds majority. The conservative coalition of southern Democrats and Republicans has, of course, been influential in congressional politics for years. But with the Republicans' slim majority, the remaining southern Democrats were even more critical on supermajority votes. On the other side were the stalwart northern, urban, liberal Democrats who voted no on both proposals.

While constituency characteristics captured at the district level apparently had little direct impact on the Stenholm vote, it is important to remember that, in addition to being an indicator of member affiliation inside Congress, partisanship is also a constituency characteristic.[29] Republicans at the grassroots overwhelmingly favor the balanced budget amendment while Democrats have given it qualified support. In addition, voter stereotypes of the Democratic and Republican parties as the parties of higher and lower spending, figure into mass support for deficit reduction tending to favor Republicans.[30] Hence, the vote to balance the budget reflects the electoral connection of representatives to represented more than it would initially appear.

Conclusions

The development of the balanced budget legislation showed that, while Republicans were bent on passing the amendment, they were not in complete control. On difficult supermajority votes, conservative Democrats were a necessary part of the team. Passage of the Stenholm compromise made it clear that Republicans had taken a big step toward learning what it means to be a *narrow* majority. Rather than falling back into their minority role as the stubborn intransigents, they were shrewd enough to realize that their first step toward fulfillment of the Contract would require bipartisanship.

The need for party discipline and Democratic votes was equally important in the U.S. Senate, where the balanced budget amendment came to the floor on February 28th. With Republicans having 53 votes,* Senate Majority Leader Robert Dole (KS) would have to hold all of his own troops in line, while attracting the votes of fourteen Democrats. After delaying the vote to build pressure on one hold-out Republican (Senator Mark Hatfield (OR)) and a couple of fence-sitting Democrats, Dole finally called the vote on March 2nd. The measure fell one vote short. Freshman Senators, several of whom had just been elected from the House, were angry at Hatfield's disloyalty and launched a short-lived bid to impose party discipline. But there was little enthusiasm for punishment among more senior Republicans. Majority Leader Dole promised to bring the measure to the floor again just prior to the 1996 elections.

THE LINE-ITEM VETO

Members have long established their incumbency on the basis of spending programs that benefit constituencies back home. Whether the monies go to constituents in terms of projects, entitlements, or contracts, most members agree that constituency service includes going after a piece of the federal pie. David R. Mayhew puts the truth of the matter this way:

> *How much particularized benefits count for at the polls is extraordinarily difficult to say. But it would be hard to find a congressman who thinks he can afford to wait around until precise information is available.*[31]

The problem seems ultimately to be rooted in the strong belief, whether based in fact or not, that reelection is guaranteed by getting your colleagues to help you spend the taxpayers money in your district. Legislators catch on to this game quickly, even in an environment of fierce austerity such as the opening days of the 104th Congress. One Republican freshman reported that another freshman who was fortunate enough

*With the switch of Colorado Senator Ben Nighthorse Campbell, Republicans would eventually have 54 members in the U.S. Senate. At this point, however, Campbell had not yet switched.

to land on a pork-barrel committee had been "going around to the entire freshman class asking everyone what projects they wanted for their districts."

The practice of wrapping spending packages into inches-thick, omnibus bills has long been a vehicle for concealing particularistic benefits. These bills, in turn, have a much better chance of passing than do free-standing measures that would be vulnerable to deficit hawks or a presidential veto.[32] The Constitution has ordinarily been understood to allow the presidential veto to reject entire bills, not parts of bills. The threat of a veto is real if Congress appropriates considerably more than the president requests,[33] but Congress has found ways of minimizing the threat of a veto. Through the use of mega-bills, the president is forced to accept the entire spending package or reject it, possibly shutting down the entire government. Government shut-downs are almost always unpopular and usually blamed on the president, thereby discouraging the use of the veto.[34] Given the congressional incentive to pass massive appropriations bills in this manner, it is no surprise that reformers have repeatedly advanced the idea of giving the president line-item veto power. Proponents argue that it is the one sure way of limiting the policy effects of log rolling.[35]

BACKGROUND ON THE LINE-ITEM VETO

The line-item veto actually has its history in the Confederacy. The Confederate Constitution gave President Jefferson Davis this power, although he never exercised it.[36] Soon after the Civil War, many states began granting their governors this power. Whether it actually works to restrain spending, the idea has caught on. Currently forty-three states provide their governors with some kind of item veto power. Numerous line-item veto bills have been introduced in Congress, and all of the recent presidents have endorsed the measure, including Presidents Ford, Carter, Reagan, Bush, and Clinton.

For most proponents of a balanced budget amendment, giving the president line-item veto authority is a necessary means for obtaining serious deficit reduction in any reasonable length of time. Because of their complimentarity, the two proposals were originally packaged into the Contract as the *Fiscal Responsibility Act.* Upon introduction, the measures were split apart because the line-item veto is designed as a statutory rather than a constitutional control and did not require the supermajority vote required of a constitutional amendment.

Most discussions of presidential budget authority are placed in the context of the executive's impoundment power. Impoundment refers to any executive action to withhold or delay the spending of funds appropriated by Congress.[37] Throughout the 1950s and '60s, interbranch disputes arose over the president's impoundment authority. Conflict between the executive and legislative branches peaked during the Nixon administration. Nixon assumed substantial impoundment authority going so far as to block spending on subsidized housing programs, community development activities, and rolling-back spending on disaster assistance and farm programs.[38] In response, Congress retaliated by passing the Budget and Impoundment Control Act of 1974. This Act gutted presidential impoundment authority by requiring all "recisions" to have Congressional approval before they take effect. A recision is a cancellation of the Congressional appropriation by the president. Under the 1974 law, funds had to be made available unless both Houses of Congress took action to approve the recision request within 45 days. What this meant, in practice, was that no recisions would ever take effect.

Subject to broad but not overwhelming Congressional support in previous sessions, versions of the legislation repeatedly came up but were narrowly defeated on the floor. When they did pass, they were generally so riddled with loopholes and qualifications that they were meaningless. Such was the case in the 103rd Congress when an amended version of the legislation passed the House by a solid vote of 342–69. It was never acted on in the Senate. Clearly, a strong line-item veto would strengthen the president at the expense of Congress. Therein lies the controversy.

The Contract's Line-Item Veto Proposal

The Contract with America put forward a strong version of the line-item veto, technically called "enhanced recission." The president's basic veto authority would remain unchanged. As introduced, H.R. 2 provided the president with the power to "line-out" any portion of an appropriations bill or targeted tax provision (a provision that gives a class of taxpayers a special break) in a bill.[39] Once the president submits a "recission message" to Congress detailing the cuts he has made, Congress must act to *disapprove* the recission within twenty calendar days of a congressional session. If they do not disapprove the recission by a simple majority vote, it is automatically effective. If they disapprove the recission, the president has the power to veto the disapproval resolution. However, his veto can be overridden by a two-thirds vote of both chambers. This contrasts sharply with current law in which Congress must act to approve recissions, and, if it does not, they are void.

Upon introduction, the line-item veto proposal was referred to the Committee on Government Reform. In hearings, hostile Democrats argued that H.R. 2 would "result in a dramatic shift in responsibility and power from the legislative to the executive branch."[40] Not only would this violate the Constitutional separation-of-powers principle, but it would give the president extraordinary power to reshape national priorities in a highly partisan direction. Republican presidents will use the line-item veto more against Democratically controlled Congresses than Congresses controlled by their party, and vice versa. There is some evidence that this is, in fact, the way the line-item veto operates at the state level. Use of the line-item veto appears to depend largely on the political setting.[41] Drawing on this argument, Congressman Robert Torricelli (NJ), a Democrat, asked his colleagues to imagine how Lyndon Johnson might have used a line-item veto to punish the detractors of his policy in Vietnam, or how Richard Nixon could have used this power to intimidate those who threatened to impeach him.[42]

There was also some question as to whether a line-item veto could aid in deficit reduction given how much federal spending is not controlled through annual appropriations measures. The amount of money that could actually be reached by the president's new enhanced recission authority would constitute a small percentage of the budget. Supporters of the legislation even pointed out that it may not save very much but that the point was to provide an impetus in that direction. Ultimately, some spending reduction is better than none.

Opponents of the line-item veto legislation are right in pointing out that the measure would diminish Congressional power. But supporters of the measure see this as exactly the right prescription for the spending ills Congress cannot seem to cure by itself. The knowledge that item veto power exists would take away the congressional incentive to insert pork-barrel spending projects into more laudable bills, thereby slipping it past the president.[43] In addition, proponents constantly point out that most state governors have the line-item veto, like it,[44] and reportedly use it to reduce spending.

Those opposing the line-item veto have much of the limited research on their side. In several studies, the line-item veto was shown not to have any impact on state spending levels.[45] Where effects have been found, they are quite small.[46] Others have pointed out that governors rarely use their line-item veto powers. These studies may not find effects, however, because most legislatures are forced to submit balanced budgets. There is more fiscal restraint at the state legislative level because states are not in the position of being able to print more money.

To the extent that state legislatures are more fiscally responsible than Congress to begin with, the line-item veto is infrequently used. If a balanced budget amendment to the U.S. Constitution successfully forces Congress to restrain spending, one could see that the president may have no more use for a line-item veto than many governors. In other words, the line-item veto will function to reduce spending, only in cases where restraint is badly needed.

Proponents have made a final point in that the line-item veto can have an effect on spending even when it is not used.[47] Simply the threat of a line-item veto can induce Congress to act responsibly to restrain spending. Congressman Bob Ney, who spent several years as the Chair of the Ohio Senate's Finance Committee explained:

> *It is used sparingly. Governor Rhodes didn't use it at all because he reached into both chambers and negotiated behind the scenes. He had very thick relationships with people in the legislature.*
>
> *But the line-item veto serves as a pressure point. The threat of its exercise is enough. It makes you communicative. The governor's staff would often come into a meeting and say, "You're going to get a veto on that," and we'd go back and change it.*[48]

The example set by the states gives proponents hope that the effect of giving the president item-veto authority will be that Congress will adapt itself by turning in less costly appropriations bills.

COMMITTEE AND FLOOR ACTION

As in the case of the balanced budget amendment, many amendments were proposed in the committee markup session to weaken and otherwise undermine the Contract's item veto proposal. Paul Kanjorski (PA), a Democrat, offered an amendment to impose a sunset provision on the line-item veto by 1997. This was narrowly defeated 17–22. A proposal whereby the president would submit his proposed cuts to Congress and both the House and the Senate would be required to vote to approve them before the recission takes effect was also voted down. In a major change of the original language of the bill, the Committee accepted a Democratic amendment governing the president's power to eliminate special tax breaks. The bill emerging from committee allowed the president to reject those tax provisions affecting 100 people or companies or less. The original provision allowed the president to veto only those tax breaks that would benefit five or fewer individuals. An additional amendment offered by Christopher Shays (CT) directed that any savings from the use of the line-item veto go directly to deficit reduction.

On day 21 of the first 100 days, H.R. 2 was passed out of the Government Reform Committee on a lopsided 30–11 vote. All of the Republicans were joined by six of the Committee's Democrats. It went to the floor under an open rule permitting amendments so long as they were first available for study and allowing one amendment in the nature of a substitute and one motion to recommit (a motion to send the legislation back to the Committee with explicit instructions to revise it). Most amendments were given ample time for consideration—up to one hour of debate.

On the floor, several major amendments were considered. All of the major Democratic amendments were voted down. The one coming closest to adoption was a substitute by Charles Stenholm (TX) whose proposal for the balanced budget amendment had just passed the House. His line-item veto proposal had passed the House the year before on an overwhelming 342–69 vote. This measure had been offered in committee and would force Congress to vote to approve presidential recissions rather than vote to override them. The Stenholm measure would require only a simple majority to approve a recission whereas the Contract version would require a two-thirds majority to overrule one. Stenholm argued that his version of the legislation would better withstand a constitutional challenge that could occur given that the measure appears to hand over the power of the purse to the executive branch.[49] This time, the House rejected the Stenholm proposal by a solid margin of 266–156. After all other amendments were defeated and a vote on final passage was called for, the Contract legislation passed on a 294–134 vote, with Stenholm joining Republicans on their measure. The victory came on February 6th, in celebration of Ronald Reagan's birthday.

THE VOTES—DAY 34

An analysis of the roll-call votes on the line-item veto legislation reflects much the same pattern observable in the vote on the balanced budget amendment. Seventy-one Democrats voted with the Republicans to pass the Contract version of the legislation. Four Republicans voted against it.

Explanations of the Votes

Deficit reduction does have a constituency and it is mostly, although not entirely, with the Republicans.[50] For this reason, we should not be surprised to find a partisan division in the vote. Looking at the roll call analysis in Table A2 (see Appendix), it is clear that party is a strong influence with Republicans about 85 percent less likely than Democrats to vote with the Stenholm substitute and about 56 percent more likely to vote with the Contract bill.[51] Southerners tended to favor both versions of the line-item veto legislation but came most strongly on board the Contract version. A number of legislators from minority districts voted with the Democratic substitute but did not go along with the Republican plan, including: Kwiesi Mfume (MD), Julian Dixon (CA), Floyd Flake (NY), and Bobby Rush (IL). Finally, in the districts where Perot ran well in 1992, members were inclined to vote for the legislation.[52] This is not surprising given that the economic thrust of the Contract was specifically designed to attract independent voters.

Comparing the vote on the line-item veto legislation with that of the balanced budget amendment yields some striking comparisons. First of all, the degree of partisan polarization is about the same on the legislation that passed the chamber; that is, Stenholm's version of the balanced budget amendment and the Contract version of the line-item veto. This similarity is surprising given that the item veto required no supermajority. No pressure needed to be applied to Democrats to get them to vote in favor of the measure. But in the end, seventy-one Democrats did vote for it, mostly conservatives, suggesting strong bipartisanship when bipartisanship wasn't strictly necessary. The South provided slightly more support for the balanced budget amendment than for the line-item veto. Thirty-eight southern Democrats voted for final passage of the balanced budget amendment compared with only 27 on the line-item veto bill. Finally, those in minority districts were far more hostile to final passage of the line-item veto legislation than to the balanced budget amendment.

CONCLUSIONS

As the balanced budget amendment came up for a vote, it was crucial for the Republicans to win this first victory. A loss would have almost certainly slowed their momentum. Mustering the 290 votes necessary to pass the Contract version of the legislation was impossible. In the face of this, Republican leaders decided to compromise by accepting the Stenholm substitute. In Majority Leader Armey's office, the climate was tense. Freshmen Republicans were threatening to vote against any compromise of the original Contract bill. If a significant number of them bolted the party, the first item in the Contract would fail. But the freshmen respected Armey and Gingrich. As one leadership aide put it, Gingrich and Armey have "moral authority and credibility with the freshmen. The freshmen realize that Newt and Armey had something to do with getting them here." The Majority Leader's argument that it would be a bitter disappointment to see the first item in the Contract fail eventually won them over.

By contrast, the line-item veto was much less work. Without having to obtain 290 votes and not having to worry about renegade Republicans, the leadership could relax. Only four Republicans eventually voted against the legislation, and only one of those was a freshman. The Republicans had remained united behind the first two steps in their plan to get the deficit under control. Ten percent of the Contract now stood fulfilled.

The Senate went on to approve a slightly different version of the line-item veto in late March. President Clinton even promised to sign the bill once the conference version of the legislation had passed both chambers. Republican enthusiasm for passing the proposal into law cooled, however, as congressional leaders realized how President Clinton might use this authority to rearrange House and Senate priorities. By late summer, the conference committee had not even convened.[53] Most Republicans remained committed to passing the legislation, but they wanted to win their first budget and appropriations battles outright. The Republicans were just beginning to feel the immense institutional power of the purse that comes with being a congressional majority. Giving up that power so soon after taking control would be to compromise with the devil they had just defeated at the polls. Democrats would be sure to remind them, though, of their promise to pass the line-item veto. And undoubtedly some Republican appropriators would regret that they had made that promise. The lesson from this: What you promise to enact as a minority hoping to gain the majority is not what you would promise to enact as a majority hoping to maintain your position as a majority.

5

Rewriting the 1994 Crime Bill

Crime is one of those "can't-miss" issues in American politics. People fear crime and eagerly cast votes for politicians who promise to keep their streets safe. While other programs are on the deficit reduction chopping block, crime control seems almost immune to budgetary pressures.[1] Unsurprisingly, Republicans and Democrats compete for the upper hand on this popular campaign theme.

While concern for crime is evenly distributed throughout the population, incidences of crime are not. The most serious crime problems are in poor, big-city neighborhoods.[2] African Americans are far more likely to suffer from violent crimes than are whites, and the perpetrators are usually other blacks.[3] Since the locus of crime is in low-income minority neighborhoods, criminal justice policy inevitably takes on a redistributive tone: taxes for crime control are collected from wealthier neighborhoods to be spent on law enforcement and prevention programs in poorer, mostly African-American and Hispanic neighborhoods. In this respect, anti-crime policy is similar to anti-poverty policy. All communities divert some resources to combatting crime, but for those areas with high crime rates and weak tax bases, redistribution of resources by the state and federal governments is necessary.

Politicians of all ideological hues agree that crime control is a government function, but there is no consensus on how resources should be mobilized to that end. This is partly because social scientists have been unable to pinpoint what causes crime. Economic inequality, substance abuse, family disintegration, racial oppression, school performance, lenient punishment, neighborhood decay, moral character—everything seems correlated with crime, but there is less certainty about its origin.[4] In the absence of other leads, researchers have even been at work investigating whether there is a genetic predisposition toward violence. With no conclusive evidence for any particular cause, politicians are left to make up their minds based on the only thing they have to go on: their own beliefs and the fears and prejudices of their constituents.

Because Democrats and Republicans often represent very different constituencies, their approaches to crime control differ. At the extremes, one focuses primarily on preventing and deterring crime through the punishment and incapacitation of criminals, while the other focuses on providing an assortment of intervention and diversion programs to those at high risk for developing a criminal lifestyle.[5] Accordingly, the two policies send resources in very different directions. The get-tough-on-crime approach favors police protection and corrections. Most of the money is spent on (or in support of) state and local police and corrections efforts. While citizens in poor neighborhoods benefit by having fewer criminals on the streets,[6] few of the resources from traditional law and order policies actually fall directly into the hands of the poor. By contrast, the liberal approach directs a much larger share of the resources at the poor communities themselves in the form of literacy, job training, youth diversion programs (such as midnight basketball leagues) drug rehabilitation programs, and spending on community housing, education, and infrastructure. It is little wonder, then, that politicians from such areas insist on including these programs in crime legislation.

An added political dimension is that those representing poor and minority areas are convinced that the criminal justice system is discriminatory. The recent beating of black motorist Rodney King by Los Angeles police officers reinforced this impression. The subsequent acquittal by a mostly white jury of several of the officers involved added more anecdotal evidence of racism. African Americans greatly fear criminal victimization, but they also have far less confidence in the police than whites have. Given our history, it is not hard to believe that this discrimination has occurred. One study by the Rand Corporation suggested that race affects the likelihood of post-arrest release, as well as the length and type of sentence imposed,[7] although more recent studies have been less conclusive on this point.[8] Evidence that the death penalty is racially discriminatory has been mixed with at least one study suggesting that it is the race of the victim that matters most. In other words, defendants charged with killing white victims are more likely to receive a death sentence than are those charged with killing blacks.[9] The belief that the system is unfair turns many politicians in the minority community away from the enforcement-oriented approach to crime control.

Crime as a Republican Issue

A majority of Americans have recently developed strong sympathies toward stricter law enforcement. Hence, Republicans have been in a better position to take electoral advantage of this issue. Because of their reputation for championing equality, fighting for civil rights and the rights of the accused, Democrats have been typecast by Republican opponents as "soft on crime."[10] Even today Democrats appear more willing than Republicans to entertain challenges to the fundamental values of the majority.[11] Naturally, in our competitive political system, Democratic tolerance for deviance has been exaggerated, but Democrats have been unsuccessful in shaking this image. Even in mid-August of 1994, as President Clinton and the Democrats were about to pass their crime bill, the public saw the Republicans as the party best able to deal with the problem.[12]

Background: President Clinton's 1994 Crime Bill

In an effort to shake the Democrats' soft-on-crime stereotype, the Clinton Administration launched its major anti-crime initiative in early 1994. The Democrats had generated momentum with the passage of the Brady Bill in November 1993. The Brady legislation requires a five-day waiting period before anyone can buy a handgun. The Clinton crime plan was introduced by then-Chair of the Judiciary Committee's Subcommittee on Crime, Charles Schumer (NY). As introduced, it included a mix of enforcement and social programs, including a large grant program for the hiring of about 50,000 new police officers;[13] a $13.5 billion grant program for prison construction; an expansion of the list of federal crimes that warrant the death penalty; $7 billion for prevention programs; new sentencing guidelines; a schedule for providing drug treatment for federal prisoners; among other provisions.[14] A controversial ban on certain assault weapons was also added. The total cost of the package at the time it passed the House was about $28 billion. In House floor debate on the measure, Democrats won passage by a slim 216–214 majority.[15] Thirty-eight Republicans supported the measure while many conservative Democrats bolted on account of the weapons ban.

The legislation went to the House-Senate conference committee in the summer and was reported in early August. Democrats moved to bring it up for final passage on the House floor but as always had to first vote on the rule that would govern its consideration. In a rare defeat, the rule went down 225–210 with many conservative Democrats joining the Republicans, mostly on the basis of opposition to the gun ban. This temporarily stalled the legislation. Republicans also complained that the legislation was laden with social spending that was more objectionable than the assault weapons ban.[16] Republican conferees insisted on major cuts in social programs and a consolidation of other funds into a block grant.[17] Under a block grant, funds are distributed to state governments with minimal federal management.

In response, Democrats took the bill back to the conference committee and reformulated it to meet several objections. The cost of prevention and treatment programs was cut by about $3 billion and funding for prison construction was cut by slightly more than $1 billion. Republicans also managed to cut a $10 million grant for a criminal justice research center at a university located in the district of House Judiciary Committee Chair Jack Brooks. The assault weapons ban remained.[18] Republicans insisted on other changes, but Democrats needed to sway only about a dozen votes. They had made just enough changes to bring some of their own members and a few moderate Republicans on board. In a late August vote, the legislation passed the House by a 235–195 vote. The bipartisan coalition included 46 Republicans who voted in favor. Sixty-four Democrats voted no.[19] This would prove to be a fatal vote for several Democrats. The Judiciary Committee Chair, Jack Brooks (TX), went on to lose his seat in November based partly on his vote in favor of gun control.

The Contract's Crime Proposal

Although a number of Republicans voted for the Clinton crime legislation, most of the conservatives remained hostile to both the gun ban and the social spending. Polls in late summer indicated that people overwhelmingly favored the death penalty but were opposed to repealing the assault weapons ban.[20] Out of respect for the party's moderates and for public opinion the Republican leadership decided against placing the repeal of the assault weapons ban in the *Taking Back Our Streets Act,* the Contract's crime bill. Gingrich and Armey figured that a repeal of the assault weapons ban would be controversial and that they might not win. Even if the repeal of the ban did pass, the President would veto it. In addition, Newt Gingrich's leadership planning team anticipated that a fight over the weapons ban would overshadow the rest of the Contract. "We didn't want this package of provisions to be drowned out by a furor over assault weapons. We wanted to focus the public's attention on the other issues in the legislation."[21]

What were those issues? The Contract bill contained eight major provisions. Title I dealt specifically with limiting death penalty appeals or "habeas corpus reform."[22] There are over 2,300 convicts on death row around the country. Because of the lengthy appeals process, however, few are executed: in 1992, only 31 death sentences were carried out. Sponsors of the legislation argued that the abuse of the habeas corpus system keeps states from implementing credible death penalties.[23] With appeals that can take up to 14 years, the list of death row inmates expands monthly.[24] Unsurprisingly, then, the appeals process is damned as a miscarriage of justice.[25]

The Contract's legislation proposed new limitations on filing appeals. Juries are also to be instructed to recommend the death penalty if "aggravating factors" (circumstances of the crime that increase the level of guilt) outweigh "mitigating factors" (circumstances that diminish guilt). This represented a significant change from the 1994 legislation, which stated that juries are never required to impose a death sentence.

Title II of the Contract's *Taking Back Our Streets Act,* strengthened mandatory minimum sentences for drug crimes. Title III of the legislation provides for the payment by the convict of restitution to the victim(s) for damages caused as a result of the crime. The Court is directed to determine the amount of restitution based on the victims' circumstances and not according to the economic resources of the offender.[26] The Court is to set up the payment schedule and has discretion to determine the method of payment.

Title IV repealed major segments of President Clinton's legislation dealing with social spending for crime prevention as well as the authorization of $8.1 billion for the hiring of new police officers. Instead of specifically targeting spending for certain purposes, it authorizes $10 billion (over five years) in block grants to state and local governments. The changes effectively deleted programs such as midnight basketball leagues, job training, drug counseling, and the creation of Boys and Girls Clubs in public housing projects.

Title V authorized an additional sum of $10.5 billion to states for the construction and operation of prisons. States would have to enact tougher sentencing requirements to be eligible for the money. Currently, many states attempt to reduce prison populations with so-called "back door" policies, that give inmates credit for "good time," effectively shortening sentences for serious crimes by as much as eighty percent.[27] The Contract legislation would force states to end such practices as a condition for receiving grants. No such conditions were in the 1994 legislation.

Title VI expanded the "good faith" exception that allows for the consideration of evidence that was obtained in a warrantless search. If federal authorities were acting in "good faith," on the basis of an "objectively reasonable belief" that they were acting properly in conducting a search, the evidence obtained could be considered in court.

Title VII directed federal courts to dismiss frivolous or malicious lawsuits brought against prison officials by inmates. This provision was designed to cut down on the number of frivolous law suits clogging the criminal justice system. Finally, Title VIII provides for the expedited deportation of illegal aliens convicted of felonies.

COMMITTEE AND FLOOR ACTION

Investigative hearings were held on the 19th and 20th of January in the House Subcommittee on Crime. The legislation was marked-up in the full committee on January 27th. Following the initial hearings, Judiciary Republicans quickly recognized that germaneness rules would expose the legislation to many controversial amendments. House rules forbid amendments that are not related (germane) to the main topic of the legislation. There were nine titles in the Act, eight of which were substantive. Given that the legislation had such a wide scope, Alan Coffey, the Judiciary Committee's chief counsel, suggested breaking it up into several separate bills, which would restrict the number of amendments that could be offered. For example, the repeal of the assault weapons provision in the 1994 legislation could easily be brought up as a germane amendment if the legislation were introduced as a whole. By breaking up the legislation, Republicans could avoid a full-scale fight on the ban, which they wanted to put off. In addition, the Judiciary Committee Chair, Henry Hyde (IL), opposed repeal of the ban. Political scientist Keith Krehbiel has noted that the scope of legislation may be a primary determinant of the restrictiveness of rules used in governing its consideration.[28] In dividing the legislation, the scope of each bill was much narrower. House Republicans could therefore avoid the practical necessity of considering the legislation under closed rules. A final rationale for this strategy was that it would be less easy to veto if it went to the president in separate vehicles. Breaking up the bill would force the White House to deal with ideas that stand on their own.

Judiciary Committee Republicans, in consultation with the Rules Committee, decided on six vehicles. The two titles dealing with prisons, V and VII, went together. The title dealing with enhanced penalties for crimes committed with firearms was put off for fear that it would trigger the assault weapons debate. The criminal alien deportation title formed a separate bill, as did habeas corpus reform, the victim restitution title, the block grants for law enforcement, and the title that would allow for the admissibility of evidence obtained in good faith.

In committee markups of the individual bills, Democrats had three basic reactions. One group, led by the ranking Democrat on the crime subcommittee Charles Schumer (NY) and joined by Barney Frank (MA), Pat Schroeder (CO), and John Bryant (TX) argued that revisiting the crime legislation was a waste of time. They emphasized that the Republican effort was just a political ploy to recapture the crime issue. The original legislation was not broke; the Republicans were only trying to fix it because it wasn't theirs. These Democrats also charged that Republicans were attempting to take back one of President Clinton's few victories of 1994:

> *We were too successful. This was one of their traditional issues. The Republicans were resentful of how well we handled the crime bill. These were clear successes for Chuck Schumer and Bill Clinton.*
>
> *. . . If last year we [had] done what they did this year, they would have come along this year and changed it by doing the opposite. This was change for change's sake.*[29]

A second bloc of Democrats was ideologically offended by the bills, especially the streamlining of death penalty appeals, the elimination of social spending on crime prevention, and the criminal alien deportation. These were the African Americans on the committee: Mel Watt (NC), John Conyers (MI), and Sheila Jackson-Lee (TX). They were joined by liberal Democrat Jerrold Nadler (NY) and Hispanic member Xavier Beccera (CA). Their approach was to launch a vigorous debate on the merits of various approaches to crime. Watt (NC) surprised members and staff on both sides with his intense and well-prepared statements. These members considered the enforcement-dominated approach, and the death penalty in particular, to be flawed and racially discriminatory. The acrimony in the committee was mostly a result of this group's angry protests.

Several Democrats took the crime legislation more seriously and attempted to negotiate to advance individual policy goals.[30] One of these was Zoe Lofgren (CA), a newly elected Democrat. She raised objections from time to time but these objections were less partisan. As a former county official, she was very concerned about practicality. Lofgren (CA) focused on issues of implementation and contributed to at least one amendment. She impressed staff on the Republican side as both able and willing to work with the new majority.[31] Jack Reed, a Democrat from Rhode Island, also took a less ideological approach, raising substantive issues in a more conciliatory tone. A third was Howard Berman (CA) who, realizing that the Republicans had the votes, decided to do what he could to improve the bill.

Several amendments came up, and a few were adopted. One of the most politically interesting was the amendment by Berman (CA) to H. R. 668, the criminal alien deportation bill. His amendment would require the federal government to pay the cost of incarcerating criminal aliens in state prisons, something about which California has long complained. In current law, there is a similar provision but it is capped at a certain amount. The Berman amendment would have removed the cap.[32] This proposal split the Republicans and produced a geographical cleavage between sunbelt and rustbelt states. Republicans from Florida, California, and Texas, supported it, arguing that states should not be forced to bear the costs of weaknesses in federal border control. Republicans from nonborder states opposed the amendment, arguing that the federal government simply did not have the money to pay for a problem that was isolated to the borders. The amendment passed the committee on a 20–14 vote and later passed the House with Speaker Gingrich's blessing.[33]

Throughout the markup, Republicans were more relaxed and far more cohesive than the Democrats. Their position was that federal agencies should not dictate justice policy to cities and states and that the Democratic legislation of 1994 had not been tough enough on hardened criminals. The six bills easily passed onto the floor, often with bipartisan support. The closest vote, 19–14, came on the legislation to allow prosecutors to use evidence obtained by faulty searches that were conducted in good faith, the so-called "exclusionary rule" provision.

The legislation came to the floor on February 8th, Day 35 of the Contract countdown. Republican solidarity was never much in question, although certain noncommittee Republicans quietly complained about the cost of new prison construction. Moderates raised objections about streamlining death penalty appeals and permitting searches without a warrant. Leading Judiciary Democrats such as Schumer (NY) and Frank (MA) were quick to point out inconsistencies in the six bills. The Contract legislation placed strict conditions on the prison grants, for example, but did not condition the law enforcement block grants. They also pointed out that few of the states could meet the sentencing conditions on the prison grants and that therefore the legislation was soft on prisons.[34]

While restricting the time for debate on each bill, Republicans allowed amendments on the floor and several were adopted. Harold Volkmer (MO), a Democrat and gun rights advocate, offered an amendment to exempt the Bureau of Alcohol, Tobacco and Firearms (ATF) from the bill permitting warrantless searches (H.R. 666). He derided the ATF for overzealousness, saying, "I did it because I don't like the ATF and the abuses it heaps on people. They're like a 'Rambo' operation and people here are realizing that."[35] His amendment prevailed over objections by the Judiciary Chair, Henry Hyde (IL), and won 73 Republicans along with many

Democrats. Another Democrat, James Traficant (OH) sponsored a similar measure restricting IRS agents from using the provision as an excuse to conduct warrantless searches. The Traficant amendment passed on a voice vote.

THE VOTES—DAYS 38–42

The first five bills to be considered won easy bipartisan passage: victim restitution (431–0); the use of evidence from warrantless searches (289–142); streamlining death penalty appeals (297–132); prison construction grants (265–156); and the deportation of criminal aliens (380–20). The sixth bill ran into opposition not only from leading Democrats but also from President Clinton. This was the legislation (H.R. 728) to convert the funding for police and prevention programs to a block grant program. Democrats attacked the measure as a giveaway because it required no matching funds from states and localities. Opponents charged that it was the same kind of pork-barrel politicking that Republicans had attacked the previous year in the debate over the Democratic version. Republicans replied that it was arrogant to tell local officials how to spend the money. Nevertheless, in response to the Democratic criticism, Republicans changed the legislation to require a 10 percent match, compared with the 25 percent match written into the 1994 law.

Meanwhile, the president promised to veto any proposal that threatened his plan to place 100,000 police officers on the streets over five years. The block grant approach allowed states and cities a measure of discretion in how the money was spent. The veto threat was unusual given the president's reluctance to exercise this power. In his first two years and two months in office, he had still not vetoed a single piece of legislation.

As the time for debate wound down, Democrats remained unconvinced that the money in block grant form would be wisely spent. Voting for block grants meant that federal authorities could not aim the expenditure of funds toward social programs that would directly benefit Democratic constituencies. Not surprisingly, all but 18 of the Democrats voted against the measure. Republicans were more cohesive, however, with only nine no votes.

An analysis of the floor votes is useful as a means of evaluating the wisdom of the Republican strategy to break the bill into six separate vehicles. Not only did this strategy help to limit amendments, thereby avoiding a fight on the gun ban, it also helped draw crucial Democratic support.

Explanations of the Votes

As with other items in the Contract, we might expect a split between northern and southern Democrats. Southern conservatives would be more likely than the northern liberals to vote with the Republicans. In addition, the issues of crime are likely to split members representing substantial black populations from the rest of the chamber. Throughout the debate, members of the Congressional Black Caucus criticized the GOP for its one-sided emphasis on enforcement. Similarly, urban legislators and those from lower income districts would be far more likely to support President Clinton's bill last year than the Republican rewrite this year. Much of the grant money from the 1994 legislation was directed toward inner-city social programs. Since the victim restitution and criminal alien deportation bills were overwhelmingly approved, they are not included in the vote analysis.

The results presented in Table A3 (see Appendix) for the four most controversial crime bills indicate that the sharpest partisan division occurred on H.R. 728, the crime block grants that stripped the social spending from President Clinton's crime package. Southerners were most united on the prison construction grants, although they were more likely than northern members to vote in favor of all the bills. Aside from partisanship and region, district characteristics such as the percentage of black constituents and the rural/urban character of the district played a role in shaping preferences. Members of the Black Caucus, nearly all of whom have large African-American constituencies, were particularly hostile to the streamlining of death penalty appeals. They also voted overwhelmingly against relaxing the rules on warrantless searches. Notably, two black members, William Jefferson (LA) and Mel Reynolds (IL), joined Republicans in voting for the prison construction grants. Finally, urban legislators voted against the crime block grants and both the exclusionary rule and death penalty appeals measures. There was no significant difference between urban and rural legislators on the voting for prison construction grants.

Traditionally, students of Congress have thought that the way to make tough votes easy was to bundle them into omnibus packages. Here, Republicans did the opposite. Given the difference in the number of Democrats who voted with Republicans on the four measures and the strength of the Democratic opposition to the crime block grants, it probably made good sense to divide the legislation into six separate bills. Democrats could vote for popular measures such as victim restitution, the expedited death penalty, prison construction and the good faith exception to illegal searches, while still voting with the president against the block grants. With this strategy, Republicans were able to muster substantial bipartisan support bringing on conservative southern Democrats while losing just a few of their own members.

CONCLUSIONS

Observers in both parties agreed that Republicans hoped to reap political gains by including crime legislation in their Contract with America. Republicans acknowledged that the public probably did not follow the specifics that closely, but "this allows Newt and the leadership to say 'crime'," said Paul McNulty, the chief counsel for the crime subcommittee. "Republicans now look tougher on crime than Democrats."[36] The difference is that Democrats saw the Contract legislation as an attempt to steal the issue from the Clinton administration: "They saw that crime was one of

Bill Clinton's only victories last year and they wanted to deny him that," said conservative Virginia Democrat Owen Pickett.[37] Republicans admitted that they had to get the issue back but also saw their new majority as a means of enacting policy that they had talked about for years. Still, this example of the Republican attempt to rewrite the president's crime legislation is the most baldfaced attempt to translate a new majority into policy change.

Democrats complained about the climate of the Committee and the attenuation of debate. "The Judiciary Committee is a shambles," said Barney Frank (MA). "The quality of the work coming out of the committee is shabby. It has to be rewritten on the floor."[38]

"Shambles!" snapped a Republican leadership aide, "The fact is that the Committee has never been run better! If it was a shambles we wouldn't have the bills out. It should have been such a shambles under the Democrats!"

During the long hours of debating such polarizing issues, and under constant pressure from the leadership, there was bound to be some hostility in the give-and-take. With no proxy votes, all of the members had to be present to vote all the time. With only a 20–15 ratio of Republicans to Democrats, only a few Republicans could be absent and a given proposal would fail. Under these conditions, it was a wonder the Judiciary Committee was able to move at all.

The crime legislation shows that Republicans have adapted to majority status in the House. There are two tasks the majority must master if it is to succeed. The first task is the ability to translate the popular will into public policy when that will is clearly expressed. Undoubtedly what contributed to the rewriting of the 1994 crime bill was the widespread popularity of several of the measures Republicans were pushing. This is particularly true of expedited executions and victim restitution, where public sentiment is so supportive. Under the Democratic leadership, however, such reforms were kept off the agenda by a band of powerful liberal committee members who successfully bottled-up popular measures.

Second, a majority must exploit to its advantage the areas in which public opinion is silent. Republicans seized on the popularity of several of these measures but then went on to use the opportunity to make changes in other areas where the public had no clear opinion, i.e., on the funding of state and local crime and prison programs. There is potential risk in this as inattentive publics can sometimes be awakened. Inattentiveness today does not always mean indifference tomorrow.[39] But the calculation Republican leaders made in changing the block grants was that those constituencies likely to be alienated by the changes, namely urban populations that stood to benefit from the social programming, would not be Republican anyway. Therefore the risk was not only negligible today, but would be minimal tomorrow.

The Contract's crime legislation provided an opportunity to revisit an old debate about the proper approach to crime control. The size of the majority vote on the four most divisive measures shows that the tone of the debate was more partisan than the floor division itself. An average of forty-four Democrats joined with the Republicans on the four most controversial bills—with 60–70 Democrats joining Republicans on the expedited executions and search and seizure measures. By late summer, the Senate Judiciary Committee was moving forward with similar crime legislation and the Senate passed habeas corpus reform as part of an anti-terrorism bill in June on a vote of 91–8. It would be difficult for President Clinton to ignore the sizable majorities on these bills once the legislation reached the other end of Pennsylvania Avenue.

▶ 6

Revitalizing National Defense

In the hearings on H.R. 7, the Contract With America's *National Defense Revitalization Act,* Defense Secretary William Perry charged that the Republican legislation, "usurps the responsibilities of the secretary of defense."[1] He then proposed that if the committee found him incapable of meeting those responsibilities they should ask him to resign. He denounced the legislation as "deeply disturbing," and its authorization of new funds for a ballistic missile defense system wasteful and unnecessary. "We were surprised by the rhetoric and vitriol of the Secretary of Defense, given what we had heard from Pentagon staff," said one Republican committee aide. For weeks, Republicans had been reassured by Pentagon contacts that the military had no objections to the bill. To then have the Secretary of Defense make the legislation a matter of personal prerogative was more than a little surprising.

Article II of the U.S. Constitution gives the president considerable responsibility for setting defense and foreign policy priorities. To the extent that the president must deal with crisis situations requiring prompt action, this arrangement is in the national interest. The framers, however, did not excuse Congress from responsibility in this area.[2] The Constitution gives Congress an impressive set of national security powers, including the power to declare war, establish an army and navy, and regulate foreign commerce.[3] The effect of the delegation of these tasks to both branches has been frequent institutional struggle. Congress regularly tries to reorder executive branch priorities in the authorization and appropriations process.[4] What was different about national security policy at the opening of the 104th Congress was that a Republican Congress was challenging a Democratically controlled defense establishment. The Republican minority had challenged President Carter's defense program, and Democrats had frequently challenged the arms buildup of the Reagan years, but for the first time a Republican majority was challenging a Democratic administration's defense posture. Add to this the rapidly changing international political context of the last five years, and there were bound to be new twists to the debate.

Background: Defense and Foreign Policy in the 1990s

The end of the Cold War era brought about a sea change in American defense and foreign policy. Only a short ten years ago, defense policy was based on the reality of a bipolar world: the United States and the Soviet Union, with the presence of a third power, China, nested in the background. The communist threat towered over Western Europe and the near and far reaches of Asia. At home, an anticommunist consensus prevailed to determine foreign and defense policy. The practical implication was that American defense spending and policy were driven by Soviet defense spending and policy.[5] In the wake of the Soviet invasion of Afghanistan in December, 1979, and the Iranian hostage crisis, public opinion was unambiguously supportive of the Reagan defense buildup of the early 1980s.[6]

The collapse of the Soviet Union and the Warsaw Pact alliance undercut the strategic necessity for high defense expenditures. The threat of war on a global scale faded from peoples' minds. The Persian Gulf War and the numerous local conflicts that have broken out from Bosnia and Somalia, to Haiti and Panama, provided a new argument. In the bipolar world, one superpower's attention was always focused on the other. In a world of many actors, the task of monitoring is much more complicated.[7] The United States had to prepare itself to intervene in smaller scale, regional conflicts to act as a force for stability in a multipolar world. This mission of thwarting numerous simultaneous threats could easily be more costly and complicated than defending against a single global threat. The upshot is that much of the consensus that once governed foreign and defense policy has evaporated.

The future of Ballistic Missile Defense (BMD), formerly called SDI (Strategic Defense Initiative), has also been put in doubt by the decreasing tension between East and West. The original idea behind SDI was to create a space-based anti-missile system that would permanently protect the United States from Soviet missile attack. Critics argue that our ballistic missile defense priority should be on the maintenance of short-range missile defenses. Some have also argued that a space-based missile defense system would never work against anything but the most rudimentary missile delivery system. These critics have been gaining ground. In the wake of the break up of the Soviet empire, President Bush did not have the commitment to the deployment of SDI that President Reagan had. This left the program open to budget cuts in both the Bush and Clinton administrations.[8]

Just a few years ago, the necessity of the NATO alliance was unquestioned. Now the necessity of NATO, and whether it should be expanded to encompass the nations of the former eastern bloc, is very much in dispute. The young democracies of eastern Europe are understandably concerned about the "security vacuum" of their region.[9] They are clearly uncomfortable being merely a buffer zone between the West and the former Soviet republics. But absorbing them into the NATO alliance will be cumbersome and costly if it is accomplished at all.

The need for multilateral approaches to international problems has fueled a debate about the role of the United States in United Nations peacekeeping operations. The United States currently contributes up to 31.7 percent of the United Nations' budget for peacekeeping operations—more than twice the contribution of any other country.[10] In the face of the U.N.'s ineffectiveness in resolving the conflict in Bosnia and Somalia, there are questions about the extent to which the United States should participate in such efforts at all.

The problem is complicated because the U.S. military simply does not have the resources to respond unilaterally to every conflict and coup around the world. In hearings on H.R. 7 before the International Relations Committee, President Clinton's U.N. representative Madeline Albright, argued that "the United States is not the world's policeman" and that U.N. peacekeeping is a bargain that "enables us to influence events without assuming the full burden of costs and risks."[11] To the extent that the U.S. military assumes the role of resolving every small conflict, the capacity to respond to major conflicts, say, in Korea or the Persian Gulf, is correspondingly lessened. By their very nature, short-term operations such as those of Haiti, Rwanda, and Somalia are unplanned. Because they are unplanned, the funds and equipment to carry them out come out of existing readiness resources. The unpredictable strategic situation of the 1990s may require some multilateral division of labor, especially given current fiscal constraints.[12]

Members of the national security community are quick to point out that spending on defense even in the absence of an imminent threat is important just to maintain industrial capability. It would be unwise to rely upon foreign manufacturers for critical defense supplies. "What do you do if you only have one submarine builder in the nation? If you are not building subs, there are no sub builders," explained Joel Hefley, a Colorado Republican. "We don't need six manufacturers, but we need to keep up the capability."[13]

Of course, allocation of defense resources is not merely a matter of strategic necessity, capability maintenance, or popular opinion. Members of Congress have another concern: how cuts in defense spending would affect jobs back home.[14] Force reduction has returned nearly 500,000 people from active duty to the civilian workforce. This has caused corresponding job losses in defense related industries.[15] After emphasizing the new threats to national security, the Chair of the National Security Committee explicitly made this point:

> *When we cut back the funding for know-how and technology, we are basically undermining our industrial base. It is government's responsibility to ensure that our industrial base remains strong. This has to come first.*[16]

The defense committees consist of members who have a disproportionate share of Pentagon-dependent payrolls within their districts.[17] Members keep defense programs alive not just for the sake of national security but as government-subsidized employment programs. For many members, the interest of employment drives policy and program decisions as much if not more than the interest in security. In this respect, defense policy resembles traditional pork-barreling—or the awarding of federal largess to a limited number of districts by members of Congress who desire to stay in office.[18]

The Contract's National Security Bill

Against the backdrop of this amalgam of issues, the Republican Conference's national security task force, led by Congressman Robert Livingston (LA), framed the Contract's *National Security Revitalization Act.* While Livingston was not a member of the Armed Services or Foreign Affairs Committees, he was on the Defense Appropriations Subcommittee responsible for military spending. He was also chosen to lead the task force because of his close relationship to Majority Leader Armey (TX) and Speaker Gingrich (GA).

The underlying motif of the Act was to erect a barrier against the cuts in defense spending that had occurred under the Democratic leadership on the committee and in the White House. "Under the Democratic chairman, this committee should have properly been called the House *Un*armed Services Committee," said Floyd Spence (SC), the Republican Chair. "Having them running the committee was like having a fox in the chicken house."[19]

As originally drafted and introduced on January 4, H.R. 7 contained several major provisions. A title on missile defense directed the Secretary of Defense to deploy at the earliest possible date an anti-ballistic missile system that can defend the United States against ballistic missile attacks.[20] In addition, the Secretary was directed to develop short-range anti-missile systems, so-called "theater missile defense."

An additional aim of the legislation was the creation of a commission to undertake a "comprehensive review of the long-term national security needs of the United States." The appointment of members to this commission was heavily weighted in favor of Republican selections by the Speaker of the House and the president *pro tempore* of the Senate, each having the choice of four members. The president would also choose four members, for a total of 12. This is a kind of procedural legislation that Congress has often used to create institutions inside the executive branch that will be sympathetic to congressional preferences.[21] The goal of these commissions and oversight boards is to ensure the executive branch's accountability.[22]

A third major title dealt with "command and control" issues. This section prohibits the use of Department of Defense funds by the United Nations for peacekeeping operations. The Clinton Administration had moved some U.N. peacekeeping expenditures from the State Department to the Defense Department in order to fund peacekeeping operations without full Congressional authorization. This title further specified that, to the extent that Department of Defense funds are utilized for U.N.

peacekeeping efforts, these funds must be counted toward the United States' overall annual contribution to U.N. peacekeeping operations.

Republicans were most concerned about ceding control of U.S. forces to U.N. officials. They pointed out that placing the U.N. in control of multinational (including American) troops in Somalia only led to disaster due to the varying languages, cultures, and overall lack of joint training for such missions. Troops have been put under foreign command under NATO arrangements, but, under NATO, sophisticated working relationships have been developed and problems posed by language differences have been resolved. The Contract legislation places explicit limits on the president's capacity to put U.S. troops under the command of foreign nationals.

Title VI, the last major provision, expressed the sense of the Congress that NATO membership should be expanded to encompass nations in eastern and central Europe, specifically Hungary, Poland, the Czech Republic, and Slovakia. Other European countries emerging from communist domination would be eligible for NATO membership providing they have made "significant progress toward establishing shared values and interests, democratic governments, free market economies, civilian control of the military, police and intelligence services" along with certain other conditions, including the willingness to bear the responsibilities and costs of NATO membership.

COMMITTEE AND FLOOR ACTION

The National Security Committee

The National Security Committee is generally characterized by consensus. Many of the Democratic members on the committee believe in a robust defense program so they found it easy to go along with most of H.R. 7. Early objections were raised on the timing and schedule of the legislation. Democrats complained that given the bill's significance, it should not be pushed through so quickly. They demanded extensive hearings on SDI but Republican staff only scheduled one followed by a generic hearing on the remainder of the bill.

During the markup on January 31, Day 27 of the 100-day countdown, the Democrats came prepared with a series of amendments to radically overhaul the bill. The Democratic strategy was to assign a title of the bill to a member or set of members for the purpose of offering title-by-title amendments. They chose to have their most conservative members take the lead knowing that outspoken liberals such as ranking Democrat Ron Dellums (CA) and Pat Schroeder (CO) had very little influence on the rest of the committee.

Congressman Ike Skelton (MO) was assigned to offer an amendment substituting for Title I of the legislation addressing general concerns about military preparedness and defense cuts. He negotiated with Republican staff behind the scenes to make a few changes to which the Republican leadership agreed. When ranking

Democrat Dellums (CA) called on him to offer his substitute at the markup, he reported to the minority leader's dismay that he had no substitute because he had worked out his differences already.

Democrats John Spratt (SC) and Chet Edwards (TX) were assigned the responsibility of offering a substitute for the title on Ballistic Missile Defense. Their argument was that the proper path to missile defense was to move toward theater (short-range) missile defense systems, as opposed to a major national defense system. This approach was consistent with the Clinton Administration's decision to allocate a far greater share of resources to theater missile defense programs. Spratt complained about the language in H.R. 7 being too loose and vague. His intention was to place architectural limits on missile defense. On a vote, however, his amendment was defeated 18–33 with four liberal Democrats opposing any kind of national defense system voting with the Republicans against the amendment.[23]

"The most smoke and fire came on the commission," reported a Republican committee staffer. "This was surprising given that Dellums himself is the father of several of them." And indeed, it was the commission that the Secretary of Defense had so strenuously objected to at the January 27th hearings. In response, Democrat Sonny Montgomery (AL) moved to replace the commission in Title III with the Secretary of Defense and the Joint Chiefs-of-Staff. Jane Harman (CA) went even further to offer an amendment to strike the commission altogether. Neither amendment passed but Republicans did agree to allow the President and Congress to divide the appointments equally, thereby allowing the president to name two additional appointees, while stripping legislative leaders of two.

Norman Sisisky (VA), an influential conservative Democrat, offered an amendment to the title that limited the operation of U.S. troops under U.N. command. His amendment would have erased the language that limits the president's ability to place troops under U.N. command, reaffirming the president's constitutional power as commander-in-chief. He received almost no support for this amendment, even from members on the Democratic side. Following a short discussion, he allowed it to be defeated on a voice vote.[24]

With virtually all of the substantive amendments failing, Chair Spence called for a final vote. In spite of the Democratic attempts to overhaul the bill, and their frustration at failing, eleven joined the Republicans in reporting the bill on a 41–13 vote. Consensus had been maintained on the National Security Committee.

The International Relations Committee

The International Relations Committee also held hearings on H.R. 7, but the climate there was far more contentious. This committee has historically lacked the consensus of the National Security panel.[25] The focus was on the foreign policy aspects of the legislation, specifically the measures on reducing U.S. funding to the United Nations and the placement of limits on the president's authority to place U.S. troops under U.N. command. The Democrats focused on these two issues and tried to muster support for far more amendments than the six dealt with in the National Security markup. Republican committee member Ileana Ros-Lehtinen (FL) explained the reason for the hostile climate of the hearing room:

> *It may appear to some on the outside that the National Security bill wasn't handled right. But we could never appease the Democrats on that committee. They were obstreperous and had no desire to improve the bill. The appearance was that we weren't good negotiators with the other side, but in reality [Chairman] Ben [Gilman (NY)] did the best job he could given the membership of that committee. They just weren't interested in compromise.*[26]

A review of the hearing transcript verifies Ros-Lehtinen's account. Democrats spent the first hour of the January 27th markup quarreling with the Republicans about minor points in the preamble of the legislation and raising countless points of order to stall the proceedings. Eventually, substantive issues were discussed, but the climate of the committee was hostile to the end. Conservative Republican Dana Rohrabacher (CA) observed that the Democrats had a common message but no organized effort:

> *The Democrats were coming up with every scenario possible that would lead people to believe that we were headed for war and pestilence. On restricting U.N. command of our troops, this drove the liberals crazy! This would disrupt the world order! American cowboys would be riding roughshod all over the world instead of being part of a U.N. cavalry unit!*
>
> *. . . But they [the Democrats] were pretty much in disarray, much like the Union Army after the battle of Bull Run. They were spouting random expressions of outrage and frustration. Their theme was obstruction but they had no coordination.*[27]

Democratic committee member Albert Wynn (MD) naturally had a different point of view, but confirmed the basic point about the ideological distance between Republicans and Democrats on the panel:

> *The Republicans are very hostile to the U.N. and isolationist in their thinking. There is a big ideological split on the committee. The Democrats are very pro U.N.*
>
> *There was some bad blood between the groups [Republicans and Democrats] particularly because of the cutting off of debate. Ben Gilman is a fair-minded, evenhanded guy and tends to be accommodating. But he was being pressured from his side to get the legislation out.*[28]

In spite of stout Republican resistance, Democrats did manage to eliminate language in the bill stating that Poland, Hungary, the Czech Republic, and Slovakia should be invited to join NATO no later than early 1999. Following the bitterly partisan three-day markup in which nearly every Democratic amendment was defeated, the International Relations committee reported the bill out on a sharply divided 23–18 vote.

H.R. 7 came up for debate on the floor on Day 43, February 15th, of the 100-day countdown. The Rules committee assigned a modified open rule that permitted eleven hours of debate; one hour of general debate, with ten hours of debate on amendments. The time for debate was further diminished by the stipulation that voting time (17 minutes for each amendment) would be subtracted from the total time allotted for debate. This infuriated Democrats who charged that Republicans were unfairly demanding consideration of important legislation under unreasonable rules. During debate on the rule, leading Democrats rose one after another to complain about the time limit for debate. "In about the same time it would take to watch the movie 'Dumb and Dumber' five times, the Republicans are asking us to totally redefine America's national security interests!" exclaimed David Bonior, the Democratic Whip.[29]

Indeed, throughout the first 100 days, Democrats charged that the majority had reneged on their campaign promise to keep the rules open. Barney Frank (MA) led the Democratic criticism of Republican floor procedures. He acknowledged that the Republican rules were about as open as Democratic rules had been, but he blasted them for their lack of openness given their campaign promises:

> *Given their campaign, they shouldn't be running things the way we did. Much of their Contract is procedural. They made promises about openness and fairness. They talked about how the Democrats were unfair and corrupt, how we always put our self-interest ahead of governing. But they're totally failing to live up to their promises because the pressure is to produce.*[30]

Even Democratic freshmen with no experience of previous Republican-Democratic wars bitterly complained:

> *On these "open rules," it is an issue of language. What they are calling "open" isn't really open at all. They may allow a few amendments, but that's not open. My expectation is that when someone promises open rules, they meet that obligation they've made. Look at the first day. They didn't allow any amendments. They called it open but it wasn't.*[31]

Republicans stood their ground insisting that they were still far more fair than the Democrats had ever been:

> *The Democratic charge that the rules haven't been open is absolutely preposterous. First of all, we never promised totally open rules. We said we would consider these items under open and fair debate. We are using modified open rules with time limits . . . It is ironic to have the same people who used to jam closed rules down our throats now claim we are not open.*[32]

This kind of exchange on the rules, whether on the floor or in the Rules Committee, would continue throughout the remainder of the first 100 days.

Following passage of the rule on H.R. 7 by a party line vote of 227–197, debate on the bill opened up with Chair Gilman (NY) controlling the time on the foreign policy sections of the legislation. Republican arguments underlined their suspicion of the United Nations and the costs associated with participation in U.N. peacekeeping efforts. Democrats emphasized the importance of U.N. peacekeeping missions to our foreign policy and national security. To them, the Republican proposal to cut back NATO contributions signaled the coming of a dangerous isolationism.[33] They pointed out that this legislation would have hampered President Bush's ability to conduct the Persian Gulf War had it been enacted then. Democrats also attacked the Republican plans to expand NATO membership claiming that they would arbitrarily include some countries, but exclude others.

On the defense-related portions of the bill, Democrats focused attention on the Republican plans to revive a national ballistic missile defense system (BMD). Republicans advanced the idea as a protection against rogue commanders, terrorists, and accidental launches that would threaten the U.S. mainland with nuclear attack. Democrats replied that the cost of the "star wars" program would come out of funds to promote military readiness.[34] They pointed out that the Pentagon had spent nearly $35 billion on missile defense since 1985 but there was still nothing deployed. Opponents of H.R. 7's statement on missile defense also included moderate Republicans such as Jim Leach (IA).

The unexpected climax of the debate came when John Spratt (SC) offered the same amendment that had been defeated in committee redirecting the Pentagon's policy emphasis from national, space-based anti-missile systems to theater, that is, short-range, ground-based weapons systems.[35] This amendment was expected to fail, but to everyone's surprise it passed by a slim 218–212 vote. The Republican leadership had suffered its first defeat. The leaders had wrongly assumed that because Spratt's measure had failed in committee, it would fail on the floor. Several prominent Republicans abandoned their party's position, including Budget Committee Chair John Kasich (OH), Leach (IA), and Massachusetts Republican Peter Torkildsen, along with twenty-two others. The chamber only narrowly rejected (206–223) a later amendment by Democratic committee member Chet Edwards (TX) that would have prohibited the deployment of space-based anti-missile systems altogether. Stunned but not routed, Republicans came back to defeat subsequent amendments to strike the national security commission title and two attempts to reassert presidential control over U.S. troops in U.N. operations and policy toward NATO.

THE VOTES—DAYS 43–44

As time for debate expired, H.R. 7 came to a vote on Day 44 of the 100-day calendar and passed on a vote of 241–181 with a small bloc of conservative Democrats joining all but four Republicans. An analysis of the floor division on two central motions appears in Table A4 (see Appendix). The first vote was the Spratt amendment that effectively knocked out the Contract with America's ballistic missile defense plank. The second vote was on passage of H.R. 7, as amended.

Explanations of the Vote

The explanatory variables have been selected on the basis of their relevance to defense and foreign policy voting. Constituency characteristics have some relevance to defense and foreign policy inasmuch as public opinion tells members what not to do.[36] Constituencies also benefit from certain defense policies. Based on their policy preferences, my expectation is that Republicans and southerners are likely to support passage of H.R. 7 in the form in which it came out of committee. Legislators from urban areas, because of their likely liberal and internationalist tendencies, would not be as inclined to favor H.R. 7 as those from rural areas. I have also added a variable for the number of citizens employed in defense industries within each congressional district.[37] Legislators from defense-dependent districts would be more likely to support this generally pro-defense legislation, especially the original title on Ballistic Missile Defense.

Not surprisingly, Table A4 shows that both votes were highly partisan and somewhat regional. Republicans were 91 percent more likely to vote in favor of the final passage of H.R. 7 than Democrats were. The only Republican defectors were moderates Connie Morella (MD), Jim Leach (IA), John Porter (IL), and conservative Frank Wolf (VA). Wolf expressed reservations about the hasty admission of Eastern European countries to NATO for fear that their current governments still contain communists.

Southerners were 19 percent more likely to vote for H.R. 7's final passage than non-southerners were. Reflecting the lead they took against the legislation, many southern Democrats on the National Security Committee voted against the bill, but they were not entirely unified. John Tanner (TN), Gene Taylor (MS), and Pete Geren (TX) voted with the Republicans.

Differences in the voting are also traceable to districts with defense-related industries. Those from the most highly defense-dependent districts were about 8 percent more likely than those with no defense jobs to vote with the majority on final passage and substantially more likely to vote against John Spratt's amendment to modify the ballistic missile defense title.

CONCLUSIONS

The consensus that held Republicans and conservative Democrats together in the committee evaporated on the floor. Conservative Democrats who had led the charge to change the bill, only to be beaten back by the committee leadership, found themselves joined by liberal and moderate members of both parties. This time, it appeared that the Republicans had lost their discipline while the Democrats had maintained it. How did this happen?

For the first time, the Democratic leadership allowed their most conservative members to take the lead in opposition to the bill. Ordinarily, the conservative Democrats are not on good terms with the liberal leadership. As Owen Pickett (VA) explained, "I haven't communicated with the leadership in quite some time. I don't have a hostile relationship with them, they just don't talk to me."[38] When asked about his relationship with the Democratic leadership, Mississippi Democrat Mike Parker explained, "Let's just say that [Minority Leader] Dick Gephardt's (MO) family won't ask me to be a pall bearer at his funeral."[39] The defense legislation was different, however. For once, Democratic leaders allowed their conservative, pro-defense members to offer proposals that were reasonable alternatives to the Contract. The Spratt amendment, in particular, successfully attracted a large number of Republican moderates and deficit hawks concerned about costly defense programs. As freshman Republican Bob Ney (OH) put it in defending his no vote:

> *I had a mandate to vote on the Contract, yes. But that doesn't give me discretion to vote on anything that comes out of committee under the name of the Contract. I voted against the star wars legislation. I am a good strong defense person, but I am against spending $37 billion on something that doesn't yet exist, then sinking another $60 billion into it without knowing when it will be built.*
>
> *Another member came up to me and asked, "How can you vote against star wars?! That's the Contract with America! People sent you out here to pass that!" But I look at my copy of the Contract and I don't see anything about star wars.*[40]

The lesson learned from the floor vote on H.R. 7 was that Republicans could not take their majority for granted on every issue related to the Contract. Every measure would have to be checked and rechecked by the whip system to ensure sufficient votes. The Republicans are fortunate that their defeat on ballistic missile defense came early in the voting on Contract legislation. They would be more vigilant from then on. On the Democratic side, the leadership appeared clueless as to what had contributed to Spratt's remarkable victory. Their tendency was to return to their majority strategy of allowing their liberal members to take the lead. Now in the minority, this strategy would force the liberals only deeper into the minority as their conservative wing defected to the Republicans.

As for policy, Republicans once again found that they had changed sides with the Democrats. Republicans were now second-guessing a president's foreign and defense policy. This would continue in the Senate when the Armed Services Committee conducted its authorization hearings and markup in late July. The Senate bill incorporated many of the Contract's themes and ideas, including the emphasis on the development of high technology weaponry.[41] The Senate Foreign Relations Committee, headed by conservative Republican Jesse Helms also moved forward on legislation to restrict American participation in U.N. operations. The most serious defeat for President Clinton's foreign policy came in the passage of Majority Leader Dole's resolution to lift the arms embargo against the Bosnian Muslims.[42] Always the predictable critics of presidential prerogative in foreign policy, the Democratic leadership in Congress now found itself opposed to measures designed to limit the executive's discretion over foreign policy. Testimony to the persistence of institutional rivalry that goes far beyond partisanship and personality, it is almost as if Defense Secretary Perry had dusted off the old notes of his Republican predecessors.

7 Reforming Welfare

"Ten years ago, we didn't have a handful of goddamned Republicans who could spell AFDC," said a veteran Republican leadership aide who contributed to the Contract's effort to overhaul the government's largest welfare program. "Democrats knew the programs, it was their constituency, but we didn't." Since the Great Society, welfare legislation had been almost exclusively the product and province of liberal Democrats in Congress.[1] Republican administrations would frequently speak of reform but could make little headway on Capitol Hill. Even Ronald Reagan's attack on welfare in the 1980s did little to alter entrenched practices.[2] With the election of 1994, Republicans were finally in a position to push for serious reform.

Republicans had been well equipped by some unlikely allies in their drive to enact sweeping changes in the welfare system. These allies were academic social scientists, some conservative but most liberal. Mounting academic studies indicated that after twenty years of Great Society programming and the considerable economic growth of the early 1980s, there was still no antidote to long-term poverty and dependence.[3] For a substantial group of welfare recipients, nothing seemed to work. A few studies suggest that the AFDC program offered incentives for women to have illegitimate children since mothers receive the assistance on behalf of their kids.[4] Much stronger evidence suggests that impoverished single parents pass poverty and welfare dependency down to their offspring.[5] Researchers also found that AFDC contained incentives for family dissolution because it provided benefits primarily to female-headed families with a heavy penalty on those who do marry.[6] Once fathers abandoned their children, single-women would stay on welfare rather than work. This is primarily because most jobs available to such women do not pay as well as welfare.[7] Few single mothers have spent any time in college and about one-third haven't finished high school.[8] For many reasons, then, a program originally designed to be a temporary bridge to better times became a permanent way of life.

The upshot of this research was that long-term welfare dependency was a problem after all.[9]

Republican arguments that welfare was due for major reworking were also amplified on Capitol Hill through public opinion. Welfare is bewildering to outsiders but, one thing is clear, the American people do not like handouts, especially to the able-bodied. The public structures its attitudes toward welfare policy according to some notion of merit.[10] The deserving poor consist of the disabled, elderly, sick, mentally ill, and/or those who have personal crises of some kind. The undeserving are those who are not disabled but would rather remain on welfare than work for low wages. These notions of who does and does not deserve welfare lead other Americans to view welfare recipients as pathetic at best, and as lazy, irresponsible, and menacing at worst.[11] Citizens resent that recipients who are not disabled are generally not required to work for their benefits. There is also a widespread perception of fraud in the system. Many members of Congress hear these complaints about fraud and non-work in every town meeting:

> *From what I hear back home, welfare fraud is widespread. People are running welfare scams all over the place. Even if there is no fraud, the system still needs to be reformed. We have created a class of people completely dependent on welfare. It's their living! They have no thought of working!*[12]

By the time the 104th Congress convened, even Democrats had come around to the conviction that something needed to be done. "There's no dispute. The welfare system isn't working, neither for the people paying the taxes nor [for] the recipients," said Rosa DeLauro from progressive New Haven, CT.[13]

With the two sides agreeing that the existing welfare experiments have failed, the question then became: What kind of reform and how much? The answer lies in where the two parties place blame for the problems of poverty. Liberal Democrats trace welfare dependency to the absence of employment opportunity for recipients. Either there are no jobs that pay sufficiently, or the recipients are not properly trained for the jobs that do pay. Hence, Democratic reforms, including the 1988 Family Support Act, have emphasized the maintenance of benefit levels in areas of high unemployment while encouraging job training for the able-bodied.

Conservative critics charged that the 1988 Act was little more than an attempt to reintroduce previous welfare-to-work programs that had failed during the early 1970s. They emphasize that poverty among the able-bodied is the direct result of pathological behavior. Their response: to remove the reinforcement for that behavior. As one Republican committee aide explained:

> *It's a basic principle of economics: if you want more of something, subsidize it. Or in psychology: if you want a positive outcome, reward it. We believe it is morally wrong to reward illicit, stupid, rotten behavior.*

Background on the Contract's Personal Responsibility Act

The development of the Contract's welfare reform bill is traceable to 1991 when former Representative Vin Weber (MN) introduced the first legislation to place a time limit on welfare benefits.[14] Republicans had always been suspicious that welfare programs were not working, but had never taken much interest in the operation of the programs, the delivery of services to clients, or the needs of welfare recipients. Weber's interest stemmed from his position on the Appropriations subcommittee dealing with welfare spending and his interest in developing conservative social policy. He had been an active member of the House Wednesday Group (one of the legislative service organizations that was abolished during the transition—see Chapter 3) where ideas for reforming the welfare system had first been advanced. The Wednesday Group consisted of moderate-to-liberal Republicans, the most prominent of whom was Nancy Johnson (CT), a member of the Ways and Means Subcommittee on Human Resources, the panel in charge of AFDC. Following Weber's retirement in 1992, she played a major role in the formation of *The Personal Responsibility Act.*

Johnson was joined in her developing interest in welfare by Republican E. Clay Shaw (FL), who transferred to Ways and Means from Judiciary in 1988 to assume the ranking position on the Human Resources Subcommittee. Conservative Republicans in the leadership were initially nervous about Shaw and Johnson taking the lead on welfare reform. Johnson is a strong supporter of abortion rights. Ultimately, however, permitting moderates to frame the legislation would ensure that the Republican Conference would not divide when it came to a vote.[15] Johnson and Shaw had credibility with the moderate wing of the party that more conservative members lacked.

Together, Shaw and Johnson introduced Vin Weber's time-limited welfare proposal following Weber's retirement in 1992. By late 1993, however, a working group in the House made up primarily of Ways and Means Committee members had added several new titles. The bill placed a 2 percent cap on the growth of poverty entitlement programs. New provisions threatened to cut benefits to recipients who did not establish paternity for their children, denied AFDC and other benefits to most resident aliens, and cut costs by transferring several nutrition programs into a block grant to states. While, to some, the idea of cutting aid to resident aliens was an extreme step, there had been a precedent set earlier that year. The Democratically controlled Ways and Means committee had voted to delay the eligibility of legal immigrants for disability (SSI) benefits in order to redirect $331 million to pay for emergency unemployment benefits.[16]

The momentum in the direction of reform was greatly aided by President Clinton's promise to "end welfare as we know it." He did not send a proposal to Congress in 1993 but had a twenty-seven-member working group designing a bill for introduction in early 1994. The charter for this group was consistent with the president's campaign emphasis on transforming welfare into a temporary safety net rather than a permanent resting place.[17] His proposal would include the two-year time limit on welfare benefits that had been a part of the Republican bill.

Framing the Contract's Personal Responsibility Act

In the summer of 1994, Newt Gingrich directed an already formed Welfare Reform Task Force to pull together what would become the Contract's bill. In addition to Nancy Johnson (CT) and Clay Shaw (FL), two young conservative members on Ways and Means were active in this effort: Dave Camp (MI) and Rick Santorum (PA).[18] Another brainy conservative, Jim Talent (MO), was not on Ways and Means but was very aggressive in insisting on more sweeping reform than that contained in previous legislation. Talent had introduced a bill with fellow freshman Republican Tim Hutchinson (AR) in the 103rd Congress (H.R. 4566) that would bar unmarried mothers under age 21 from receiving AFDC, food stamps, or public housing. This controversial proposal was an attempt to address the rising tide of illegitimate births, estimated to be 30 percent of all births in 1992. Johnson, Santorum, and Shaw were satisfied simply to use the bill they had introduced in the 103rd Congress (H.R. 3500) as the Contract's welfare proposal. Talent and Hutchinson, encouraged by Armey and the Republican leadership, pushed to cut cash benefits altogether, as their bill suggested. As newly elected members at the time, the views of Talent and Hutchinson were not welcomed by the more established Ways and Means members. "We weren't well received," Hutchinson recalled.[19] "Ways and Means greatly resented a couple of freshmen coming along and putting a bill in and getting involved in the welfare debate." But Gingrich and Armey favored the tougher approach of the Talent-Hutchinson proposal. "Their support increased our leverage," Hutchinson said.[20] Many of the conservative pro-family interest groups also favored the cutoff of AFDC as a means for curbing illegitimacy. Like the cutoff of benefits to noncitizens, the Talent-Hutchinson approach was not entirely unprecedented. Some states had enacted laws to deny additional AFDC benefits to welfare recipients if they had more children.

Within the task force, the move to discourage young unmarried women from becoming pregnant by cutting off AFDC was a source of controversy. "When Nancy Johnson first heard about cutting off aid to unwed mothers, she had a goddamned conniption fit," said one leadership aide. "She has now become one of its strongest supporters." What brought the more moderate members on board was the realization that nothing else has worked to reduce illegitimacy. "Nothing works to keep young mothers from having babies," reported a committee researcher. "We try to reach the important outcomes and nothing works. It's like a scarlet letter. Once you have an out-of-wedlock birth, none of our puny interventions help." Several academics had issued reports suggesting that the cutoff of AFDC may have no impact on the birth of illegitimate children either. But the trends in illegitimacy, Republicans reasoned, were clearly heading in the wrong direction under current programs.

Compromises were made on the way to the final draft of the legislation, and, by September 27th, the Contract's *Personal Responsibility Act* contained all of the provisions mentioned above except that the denial of benefits to teenagers was restricted to those under 18, rather than under 21. Following the election, Gingrich captured nationwide attention by proposing that states be permitted to use federal funds to establish orphanages. Under current law, full-scale orphanages are prohibited from receiving federal funding by a cap of 25 on the number of children allowed to be served in a "congregate setting" (group home). "A change in the cap was never seriously considered by the Ways and Means Committee," a staffer there reported. "This was just Gingrich letting everyone know that he was in charge. He deliberately provoked a fight to call attention to the fact that some kids get smashed-up by their families and would be better off in orphanages. He was setting the terms of the debate."

The suggestion to bring back orphanages ignited a firestorm of controversy that ensured it would not be a serious legislative proposal.[21] The orphanage issue was ultimately preempted by the overall goal of decentralizing welfare policy. States were given added flexibility to terminate AFDC benefits after two years if at least one year had been spent in a job training program. States were allowed the flexibility to cut benefits to those under age 21 who had not completed high school or its equivalent. State control also meant the freedom to reduce cash assistance for those who refused to work or to participate in job training. The bill would impose a spending cap on the growth of its funding consistent with the Talent proposal mentioned above.[22]

During the transition, the staff of the Ways and Means Committee held several meetings with Republican governors John Engler (MI), Christine Whitman (NJ), William Weld (MA), and Tommy Thompson (WI), who pressed for the conversion of several poverty and nutrition programs into block grants. With gubernatorial input, the bill was rewritten to favor the block grant approach. Among the converted programs were AFDC; 23 child welfare, foster care, and adoption assistance programs; programs for child care; school lunches; and several family nutrition programs.[23] By converting AFDC to a block grant, the legislation would effectively end it as a federal entitlement program. The block grant proposals were added to H.R. 4 upon its introduction in the 104th Congress on March 13th.

Also folded into the legislation was the Agriculture Committee's proposed changes to the food stamp program. The food stamp reforms stopped short of giving the program to the states. As Bill Emerson (MO), the chairman of Agriculture's Nutrition Subcommittee, put it:

> *Now I basically agree with the block grant approach. My big reservation, though, is with the food stamp program. I want to reform it before we give it to the states. The governors and the legislatures will have a very full plate with all the stuff we're going to give them.*
>
> *Food stamps needs a full-scale reform. It is rife with abuse and illegal trafficking. What I want is to hasten the use of technology in the administration of welfare. My goal is to straighten some of this out first and save the governors some problems they don't need.*[24]

Emerson pointed to Maryland's use of EBT (Electronic Benefit Transfer) systems to prevent food stamp fraud as the type of technological innovation he wanted all states to adopt. Under an EBT system, recipients do not receive stamps that they can then trade for cash at seventy-five cents (or less) on the dollar. Instead, recipients receive a card, much like a bank teller card, that only they can use to buy food. The food stamp title transfers the entire food stamp program into a block grant as soon as states implement such a system.

Within the party, the Contract's welfare reform plank was the most divisive of the items outside of term limits and tax cuts. On the right, several members expressed concern that the cutoff of AFDC benefits to teens would lead to more abortions. At least one member, Jim Bunn (OR), refused to sign the Contract on this ground. There was also opposition from the two Cuban-American members of Congress, who also refused to sign the Contract because of the proposed elimination of benefits to legal residents (see Chapter 2). Other Republicans supported the general thrust of the bill but had reservations about specific provisions. With strenuous and vocal Democratic opposition, this bold set of proposals would generate the most intense committee and floor debate of the first 100 days.

COMMITTEE AND FLOOR ACTION

Three committees possessed jurisdiction over separate titles of the *Personal Responsibility Act.* The Agriculture Committee produced the food stamp reform title. The Education and Economic Opportunity Committee held hearings on Title III, which included the nutrition block grants (especially school lunches); the child care block grants; and the block grants for family nutrition programs (including the Supplemental Nutrition Program for Women, Infants and Children, or WIC). The bulk of the legislation was marked-up in Ways and Means.

"It was unbelievably hostile," chuckled Congressman Phil Crane (IL), the second ranking Republican on the Ways and Means Committee, when he recalled the climate of the committee hearings on welfare reform.[25] "It surely was hostile. I had to gavel a few down," recalled Bill Goodling (PA), the Chair of the Education and Economic Opportunities Committee.[26] "It was the most unenjoyable markup I have ever sat through." "It was typical," said Bill Emerson (MO), rolling his eyes with a tone of disgust in his voice, when asked about the Agriculture Committee's hearings. "All they [the Democrats] did was make rhetorical statements about how mean-spirited Republicans are taking food out of the mouths of poor people,"[27]—three different committees, nearly identical combat taking place in each.

Ways and Means

The Ways and Means Subcommittee on Human Resources held hearings for seven days in late January. Among those testifying was Governor John Engler (MI) who argued for the conversion of all welfare entitlements into block grants. Engler had sought permission from the federal government to experiment with Michigan's welfare system upon assuming office in 1990 in the middle of a recession.[28] These experiments appeared to generate considerable savings without cutting aid to the truly needy.

At the subcommittee markup on Day 41 (February 15th), Democrats remained resolutely hostile to the block grant approach. "It very quickly turned into an us-versus-them affair," Clay Shaw (FL) recalled.[29] "The Ways and Means Democrats have stacked my subcommittee with its first string." Subcommittee Democrats, including Sander Levin (MI), Barbara Kennelly (CT), Pete Stark (CA), and Harold Ford (TN), argued that the states could not be trusted to run their own welfare programs. At least some governors and legislators would throw people out onto the streets. The reason why federal government stepped in to begin with is that states were not responsibly caring for the needy. The Democrats offered a series of amendments to soften the bill, but they were all defeated except two minor provisions accepted on a voice vote. Republicans responded that the current system clearly wasn't working and that some of the state experiments were. "The ultimate cruelty is to continue the present system, which is corrupting the poor," said Subcommittee Chair Shaw.[30] Democrats charged that Republicans were involved in allowing America's children to be "crash test dummies."[31]

At the Ways and Means full committee markup of the legislation on February 28th and March 1st, 2nd, and 3rd, fatigue had set in. Majority Leader Armey's (TX) relentless schedule was taking its toll on the civility of the members. "The tone was so rancorous, the substance of the legislation didn't matter," recalled committee Republican Dave Camp (MI).[32] The opposition to the bill was led by Democrats Jim McDermott (WA), Harold Ford (TN), Charles Rangel (NY), and Pete Stark (CA). McDermott is respected on both sides as one who is well studied on welfare programs and can easily win a debate. Rangel generally used an effective mix of sarcasm and humor to attack the Republicans. Ford and Stark were more emotional in their approach. Together, they repeated the arguments that were voiced in the subcommittee hearings about maintaining AFDC's status as an individual entitlement.

Republicans agreed to alter the provision of the legislation that would deny benefits to single mothers under 18. Instead, states would be given cash bonuses if they could reduce their "illegitimacy ratio," defined as "a percentage equal to the sum of the total number of out-of-wedlock births in the state and the total number of abortions, divided by the total number of births in the state in the applicable year." Democrats attacked the revision as an inducement for states to shut down abortion clinics.

The climax of the hearing came at the very end when Jim McDermott (WA) raised a procedural objection that the bill could not be voted out of a committee since it was not in final form. This protest violated a longstanding rule of comity on the committee. For years, Ways and Means had conducted "conceptual markups." Members would discuss what was to go into the bill in nontechnical language. The bill would then be voted on and the staff would draft the legislation in its final form. McDermott (WA) invoked a rarely used House rule stating that "proposals must be reduced to writing at the demand of any member..." before they can be voted on. Not knowing of the obscure rule, Chair Bill Archer (TX) declared that the motion was out of order and proceeded to call for the vote. Pete Stark (CA) loudly protested that Archer (TX) was not permitting the minority to review the actual text of the legislation before the vote was called. Phil Crane (IL) described the scene:

> *Stark was screaming and yelling that we couldn't report this out. Archer broke his gavel trying to restore order. Finally, Archer yielded to the objection, and we wound up with a two-day delay on the vote. In all the years on the committee, no one had ever done that.*[33]

Congressman Bill Thomas (CA), the third-ranking Republican, moved to call for the sergeant-at-arms to restore order, and Stark (CA) then accused the Republicans of using Nazi-style tactics to ram the legislation through the committee. Andy Jacobs (IN), who sits next to Stark on the Democratic side, moved in to calm him down, "I'm used to that from when I did police work," Jacobs explained.[34] "The Democrats are smarting and irascible. Some of the Democrats are embarrassed to be in the minority. I'm not bothered by it, 'to the victor belong the toils,' to quote Adlai Stevenson, but some of my colleagues' egos have really been hurt."[35]

"McDermott may regret he ever made this move," said a top Republican aide in a tit-for-tat tone of voice. "From now on, we will always have statutory language present before we vote on a bill. Never again will we move forward without legislative language." "The demand to have statutory language is far harder on the minority than it is on the majority," said Clay Shaw (FL).[36] "The majority can now demand that any amendments the minority offers must be in final, legal form before we accept them."

Democrats were hampered in their opposition to the legislation because they could not agree on what to include in a substitute bill. While certain members were more vocal than others, there was no leadership to pull together a substitute bill until the last minute. "If they had a strategy," it sure wasn't obvious said one Republican leadership aide. Andy Jacobs (IN) pointed out that he never attended the caucus meetings on the welfare bill because they never went anywhere. "There's lots of discussion but never any resolution," he reported.[37] Although the Democrats managed to stick together in voting against the Republican proposals, they could do little to advance their own ideas. Virtually all of their amendments were defeated in committee. This put them in a position of having little to do but complain. At the end of the hearing, they were able to pull together a substitute that was defeated on a 13–21 partisan vote, with Democrat Gerald Kleczka (WI) refusing to vote. Kleczka then joined the Republicans in support of their plan after they accepted several of his amendments on a voice vote.[38] "Kleczka's done a lot to revise the SSI [Supplemental Security Income] program," one Republican aide pointed out. "He wanted to be able to take credit for it."

Education and Economic Opportunity

On Bill Goodling's (PA) committee, the Republicans won the battle on school lunches but lost the war. With no southern Democrats on the committee, Education and Economic Opportunities is perhaps the most ideologically divided panel in Congress. The Democrats maintained a cohesive front railing against the Republican plan to turn over several large food and nutrition programs to the states. Democrats leading the charge included the ranking minority member, Bill Clay (MO), along with Dale Kildee (MI), George Miller (CA), and Patsy Mink (HI).

Much of the point of the Republican plan was to reduce the cost of these programs by cutting out the federal bureaucracy. In fact, Republicans were not reducing expenditures under the program, they were simply cutting back the rate of increase. Under the Republican plan, the authorization for the school lunch program would increase funding from 1996 to 1997 by 4.47 percent, from $6.7 billion to $7 billion. The Democrats said this was tantamount to a cut, since, under existing law, the increase would have been 5.3 percent. "Only in Washington, D.C., can you call a 4.5 percent increase a cut," said Goodling.[39] "The program must need fixing since only 50 percent of the eligible children even participate. School lunch professionals have repeatedly complained that they are being strangled by the paperwork from Washington."

But the Democrats were relentless in seizing upon the school lunch revisions as a sign of the Republicans' cruelty to children. Under the block grant approach, some $7.3 billion would be saved through 2002. Democrats refused to go along with the Republican contention that the savings would be from cuts in administration rather than in the number of clients served. Bill Clay (MO), the would-be chairman, called the block grants a "giant money-laundering scheme . . . a blank check to governors while imposing no standards of accountability. It violates all sense of human decency."[40] Even Republicans agreed that Democrats won the public relations battle. "We got our asses kicked on school lunch," admitted one Republican aide. "We could have done a better job getting the governors to defend us on this."

In spite of the deluge of negative press, Goodling kept Republicans together to vote against most Democratic amendments. As on Ways and Means, the Democrats had no discernible strategy but offered nearly two dozen amendments aimed at softening the legislation. The bill was finally voted out on strict party lines, 23–17, on February 23rd. Goodling reflected on his conduct of the markup:

> *I tried to give them every opportunity to offer amendments and work things out, but eventually we had to move. I hope I was more patient than I had to be. Certainly people on my side thought I was.*
>
> *One day, near the end of last year, someone on the other side asked me how I would run the show if I were chairman, in the majority. I told them that I would be kinder and more benevolent than they had been. Just then,*

the chairman, William Ford (MI-retired in 1994) walked in and said, "You won't live long enough to be in the majority." And now, here I am.

Agriculture

The Agriculture Committee, with its jurisdiction over the food stamp title of the bill, was the last to act on welfare reform. The legislation was referred first to the Food and Nutrition Subcommittee for a series of hearings in late February. On the agenda were two items: how to reduce the costs of the program by cutting waste and fraud and whether the entire program should be converted into a block grant in the same manner in which the school lunch and nutrition programs were. The same governors who had negotiated block grant proposals with the Ways and Means and Education Committees were back to press for state control. Unlike the other committees, however, Agriculture's members seemed reluctant to give up their turf. Almost all of the Agriculture Committee's members come from farm districts that benefit from the $27 billion spent on food stamps. While Republicans elsewhere were willing to take programs that were failing and give the governors a chance to make them work, Emerson (MO) and Committee Chair Pat Roberts (KS) insisted that the food stamp program needed to be reformed first.[41]

By abandoning the Contract and deciding to keep the food stamp program at the federal level, Roberts, Emerson, and other committee Republicans agreed to maintain one national safety net. The Republican governors, led by John Engler (MI) and William Weld (MA), continued to lobby for more discretion, insisting that control over food stamps, Medicaid, and AFDC were all necessary to effectively run a welfare system.[42] Committee members bowed to this pressure and agreed to exempt states from federal standards governing the program as long as the states adopted electronic monitoring systems to reduce food stamp fraud. With electronic monitoring, transactions are recorded and maintained by computer, allowing state officials to trace misuse of food stamp funds. The governors also insisted on the ability to provide cash to food stamp recipients who are working in private sector jobs.[43] Finally, strict new work requirements were written into the legislation. People between 18 and 50 would be denied food stamps after 90 days unless they were working at least twenty hours per week.[44] Republicans also moved to cap the growth of benefits to 2 percent per year, rather than at the rate of food-price inflation. Republicans insisted that all of these measures were necessary to control the costs of the program.[45]

Because the Republicans tempered their demand for reform, the atmosphere of the full committee markup was not as vitriolic as on the other panels. Democrats were not entirely shut out of the policy formation process. Several Democratic amendments were accepted on voice votes. Republicans and Democrats also joined together to cosponsor several amendments that won voice-vote approval. But the Democrats did not forgo the opportunity to make forceful points. Their charge was led by Earl Pomeroy (ND), Tim Johnson (SD), and Harold Volkmer (MO). The criticisms paralleled the "children as casualties" theme heard on other panels. Volkmer complained that the legislation was hard on children, hurting "the neediest of the needy." He even sponsored an amendment to retitle the legislation, "The Food Stamp and Commodity Reduction to Make Americans Hungry Act."[46] Tim Johnson (SD) called the bill "radical right-wing extremism" designed to hurt children. Pomeroy (ND) labeled it "God-awful."

Even so, there were several committee Republicans who wanted to go further with food stamp reform more along the lines of the Contract's original proposal. Freshman committee member John Hostettler (IN) suggested dismantling the program altogether in favor of state-operated food assistance programs. This proposal didn't get far with only five Republicans voting in favor. "He's a fine fellow, definitely up and coming," said Emerson of Hostettler, "but he wants to get there faster than is prudent."[47]

The Committee voted the food stamp reform title out on a strongly party line (26–18) vote on March 8, roughly a month before the 100-day deadline. Republicans won the support of one southern Democrat, Scotty Baesler (KY). "I voted for it because nobody put up an alternative proposal," Baesler explained.[48] "It was sure better than what we had. There was no reason to vote against it simply because it was presented by the Republicans. I didn't think it was strong enough. It struck me as rather milk-toasty." A leadership working group then combined the food stamp provision with the work of the other two committees and the legislation was sent to the floor on March 21st.

Once on the floor, several major controversies threatened to delay consideration of the bill. Rules governing floor debate are seldom defeated, but this one came dangerously close to losing. The modified closed rule worked out with Republican leadership allowed 31 amendments, twenty-six by Republicans and five by Democrats, including two major Democratic substitutes. Each amendment was to receive twenty minutes of debate. Only two of the four amendments sought by anti-abortion critics of the legislation were ruled in order. Several Republican members voted against the rule on the grounds that the reduction in AFDC benefits to young women would prompt more abortions. Republicans narrowly won approval of the rule by a scant six votes (217–211).[49]

In the opening minutes of the debate, Democrat John Lewis (GA), a member of Ways and Means, set the tone by suggesting the Republican welfare plan was similar to the Nazi Holocaust.[50] Clay Shaw (FL) responded angrily:

> *There is no one in this House that I have had more respect for than you. But for you to come on this floor and compare the Republicans to the reign of the Nazis is an absolute outrage, and I'm surprised that anybody with your distinguished background would dare to do such a horrible thing.*[51]

Shortly thereafter, Jim McDermott (WA) who had so fiercely opposed the legislation in Ways and Means, referred to a New Testament passage contrasting how much

Jesus cared for little children with how Republicans would treat them under H.R. 4.[52] Republicans responded that it was the current welfare system that was cruel to children, "encouraging self-destructive behavior, dependency and out-of-wedlock births."[53] One by one, members from Ways and Means from both sides took to the floor to defend or attack the legislation. They were followed by members of the Education committee and finally those on the Agriculture committee. Their general arguments echoed the tenor of the debate in the committees.

The second day of debate brought up the consideration of several key changes. The first two were brought by the Ways and Means Chair, Bill Archer (TX), who bundled several alterations into two amendments. The first of these ensured that any savings resulting from the cuts in entitlement programs would pay for subsequent tax reductions (see Chapter 9). This drew howls of protest from Democrats who argued that any savings from welfare reform should be put toward deficit reduction. This move also called the Republican motivation for welfare reform into question. During the first day of debate, Republicans had credibly argued that the system needed to be reformed because it was bad for the clients. Now, Democrats could call attention to the possibility that the true motive for welfare reform was to pay for tax cuts for middle- and upper-income Americans. Dave Camp (MI) refuted this accusation:

> *We are first trying to fix a badly broken system. We want to help people who are truly in need.*
>
> *. . . We had 170 witnesses at our [Human Resources] subcommittee hearings and not one of them spoke in defense of the status quo. Whether they were advocates, recipients, or experts, there was a consensus that something needed to be done.*[54]

Republicans insisted that with 340 welfare programs and billions of dollars spent, welfare reform would be both better for clients and better for taxpayers. When the vote was called, the amendment passed on a party line (228–203) vote.

The second amendment was offered "en bloc," meaning that it combined several amendments, in this case eleven, into one. Bundling amendments together is a common practice to save valuable debate and voting time for more controversial issues. In consolidating eleven amendments into one, it meant that the new mega-amendment would receive only twenty minutes of debate under the rule. Democrats protested that the changes contained in the en bloc amendment required more time for discussion. They had a legitimate point. One of the amendments would prohibit states from using any block grant funds to pay for abortions, not exactly a trivial matter. The sponsor, Henry J. Hyde (IL), feared that in their attempt to reduce out-of-wedlock births, states would turn to abortion counseling as an option. Sam Gibbons (FL), the Democratic leader of the Ways and Means Committee repeatedly called the en bloc procedure "outrageous" complaining that no one on the Democratic side knew which amendments were contained in the proposal.[55] After demanding that everyone "sit down and shut-up," Gibbons was met with boos and hisses from the

Republicans who were on the floor, to which he replied, "Boo if you want to. Boo if you want to. Make asses out of yourselves for the American people . . ."[56] The debate proceeded and the en bloc amendment passed with a solid majority of 249–177.

Several other amendments were offered during the second and third days of debate. One of these, offered by Jim Talent (MO) (the conservative Republican who had pushed the original welfare reform task force to toughen-up the legislation) sought to require specific and strict work requirements for parents with children over the age of five. Talent demanded that work mean work, "It [work] should not mean carte blanche job searching, it should not mean carte blanche education and training. Those are not work."[57] In requiring 30 hours of work per week rather than 20 hours for those with children over age five, Talent's proposal went well beyond the Contract's original legislation. The most persuasive Democratic objection was that there was no endless supply of unfilled jobs for unskilled workers and that the jobs that were available didn't pay a living wage.[58] Leading Republicans also opposed the amendment, including Johnson (CT) and Shaw (FL). When the roll was called, it mustered a mere 96 votes in its favor.

The third and fourth days of debate were typified by consensus votes on several proposals to toughen child support enforcement provisions. A Republican amendment to authorize states to withhold or suspend the drivers' licenses of individuals who owe back child support had been defeated in the Ways and Means Committee when offered by Democrat Barbara Kennelly (CT). Sensing that the idea had strong support, Republicans then gave the amendment to one of their own, Marge Roukema (NJ). Democrats considered this boldfaced thievery, but the amendment passed on the floor by an overwhelming 426–5 vote.

The last amendments considered were Democratic substitutes. The most viable one was offered by Nathan Deal (GA), a moderate southerner who would later switch parties. His substitute proposal was close to the welfare reform legislation President Clinton had proposed. It included a time limit on AFDC participation of two years and was strong on both work requirements and child support enforcement. The principal difference between it and the Republican plan was that the Deal proposal lacked the spending authorization cuts. Even Republicans recognized that it was a highly credible alternative, although some suggested that, had the Republicans brought it to the floor, Democrats would have still charged them with child abuse. The Deal alternative won over every Democrat and was narrowly rejected on a party line vote of 205–228. Liberal Republican Connie Morella (MD) was the only Republican voting in favor. A more liberal substitute that would expand existing programs and guarantee a minimum wage was rejected the next day on a lopsided 96–336 vote.

THE VOTES—DAYS 78–80

After the substitutions and the motion to recommit the bill failed, the final vote on passage of the *Personal Responsibility Act* was called for. It passed 234–199 on

March 24th. Republicans had completed action on the most comprehensive policy proposal of the first 100 days, with a little more than two weeks to go.

With the charges of cruelty to children and class warfare, it is worthwhile to examine the floor division on several of the key votes for traces of class, race, and urban/rural cleavage. An analysis of several of the key roll calls appears in Table A5 (see Appendix). The first vote in Table A5 is on the Archer en bloc amendments. The second vote is on the Talent amendment to toughen the work requirements. The third vote is on the Democratic substitute offered by Patsy Mink (HI) and the last vote is for final passage of H.R. 4, as amended. Since the Deal substitute amendment was almost a perfectly party-line vote, with only one Republican voting with the entire Democratic caucus, it will not be included in the analysis.

Explanations of the Votes

The explanatory variables reflect characteristics of constituencies thought to be relevant to redistributive policy making. While partisanship played the decisive role in the debate, my expectation is that it is not the only relevant factor. The vote may also divide along class and racial lines, with members in minority and low-income districts voting against final passage. Members from rural areas and from southern districts, where socially conservative populations prevail, would also tend to favor stricter welfare reform measures.

The results are mostly consistent with these expectations. Using income as the indicator for the socioeconomic status of districts, there is no decisive polarization by class except on the vote for Archer's (TX) en bloc amendments. Even here, though, the sign of the coefficient shows that wealthier districts tended to vote against the Republican position, not for it. Is this a sign that there is no class warfare in the 104th Congress as the Democrats so frequently charged? Certainly there isn't much sign of class cleavage once partisanship is included in the model. Since partisanship is associated with wealth, however, ($r = .23$; $p < .01$), the presence of significant partisan cleavages on each measure stands in for whatever income differences exist.[59]

The remaining variables show that majority-minority districts were most hostile to the Archer amendments and most favorable toward the Mink substitute. Every black Democrat except one (Bill Jefferson (LA)) voted with Mink. Rural districts, home to the most conservative constituencies, were highly supportive of Congressman Talent's (MO) conservative work initiatives but hostile to Congresswoman Mink's (HI) proposed liberal reforms. Finally, southern members were also attracted to the Talent amendment and were unable to go along with the liberal substitute. Nearly half of the Talent amendment's votes came from the South.

Final passage boiled down to a partisanship that overshadowed income differences among districts coupled with the conservatism of a few rural members. Of the nine Democrats voting for the legislation, seven were from nonurban districts. Southerners, however, were not necessarily drawn to the Republican legislation since they had sponsored its principal substitute (the one offered by Democrat-turned-Republican Nathan Deal (GA)).

CONCLUSIONS

The welfare debate showed little of the bipartisan consensus that formed around earlier Contract items such as crime, the line-item veto, and the balanced budget amendment. In these areas, many southern Democrats joined the Republicans generating a margin of victory well above the majority's 230 votes. On welfare reform, however, Democrats allowed one of their southern, conservative members to offer a challenging, credible substitute. It came very close to winning, whereas the more liberal measure preferred by many in the Democratic leadership was a dismal failure. Clay Shaw (FL) even told Democratic leader Richard Gephardt (MO) on the floor after the vote that had Deal's amendment been offered last year, it would not only have passed, it would have allowed the Democrats to maintain the majority.

> *That would have saved them. The American people are begging for welfare reform. This was the most important piece of legislation to come out of Congress this century except for declarations of war. It will affect the lives of millions of people for years to come.*[60]

What a shock it was to Democratic leaders when Nathan Deal (GA) switched parties less than a month later. Gephardt (MO) figured he had gone out of his way to allow him to offer a principal substitute on a major piece of legislation. Although Deal had earlier discussed the possibility of switching parties, this did not appear to be the time.

The close, party-line vote both on the Deal substitute and on the Republican welfare reform plan is the exception that points to—but perhaps doesn't yet prove—an important rule. When Democratic leaders made room for their shrinking southern bloc by allowing them to take the lead, the party could offer a serious alternative. The same was true of the winning amendment offered by John Spratt (SC) on the national defense measure (see Chapter 6). By contrast, when the liberal Democrats left their southern members out of the legislative process, they watched those members comfortably vote with the Republicans. Mike Parker (MS), one of the most conservative southern Democrats, emphasized a related point:

> *Liberals are important to society. They bring issues to the forefront. The problem with liberals is that the solutions they come up with have no basis in common sense. In the past, the solutions were always engineered by conservative Democrats. Where the Democratic party lost its way was when they decided they didn't need the conservative Democrats anymore.*[61]

The proposals offered by the liberals, such as the welfare substitute by Patsy Mink (HI), may be appropriate for the safe, progressive constituencies of northern, urban districts. But such proposals are not viable for the maintenance of a Democratic majority in Congress. The liberal, northern members may not be comfortable allowing their southern bloc to lead, but they cannot be a national majority without them. Republicans will continue to woo southern Democrats by treating them better than their own leadership has. This is why Gingrich appointed Gary Condit (CA), a conservative Democrat from California, to a conference committee when Gephardt (MO) would not. Unless the Democrats recover an appreciation of the importance of these conservative members, there will be more southern Republicans in Congresses to come.

In early June, the U.S. Senate Finance Committee voted on a much narrower welfare-reform proposal than that of the House. This proposal was amended to incorporate many of the House's provisions during senate floor debate in September. The Senate legislation passed on an overwhelming 87–12 vote on September 19th. By late September, the legislation was awaiting a conference committee to work out major differences between House and Senate versions. "Remember, conference committees are structured the way the leadership wants,"[62] Representative Talent pointed out. "[Senate Majority Leader] Dole and [Senate Majority Whip] Lott are a lot closer to Gingrich and Armey than most people think. Even if it were to die in the Senate, we will have accomplished an enormous amount," Talent continued. "It is ideas that are important in the long run." The British Parliament took years to finally abolish the slave trade following repeated defeats. Full-scale welfare reform of the kind promoted by the House may require several attempts.

8

Limiting Congressional Terms

"It's foolish to bring legislation to the floor that you know won't pass," said Democrat Paul Kanjorski (PA) in reference to the Republican effort to pass term limits. "This is just a p.r. exercise. These people are good vote counters, they know the votes aren't there. This entire week has been a waste."[1] Kanjorski was right about one thing. Republicans knew that they could not muster the 290 votes necessary to send the proposed Constitutional amendment to the Senate and then on to the states for ratification. He was expressing a long-standing philosophy of congressional government, namely, that the goal of legislating should be to write a bill that will pass.[2] Republicans disagreed, though, about whether it was wise to bring a sure loser to a vote:

> *We brought it to a vote for two reasons. One, sometimes it's important to rush the wall to see if you just might be able to get over it. Second, we wanted accountability. We wanted people on the record. Now there are those who voted yes and those who voted no. The record is very clear. There will be people who will lose in '96 because of that vote.*[3]

Others pointed out that Constitutional amendments rarely pass on the first vote. Some momentum is required and that means taking the initial step of bringing the measure to a vote even if it falls short.

ARGUMENTS FOR TERM LIMITS

While the idea of limiting congressional terms is as old as the Articles of Confederation, the popular movement for constitutionally limiting congressional terms is a

20th century development. In the 19th century, seat turnover through electoral defeat and voluntary retirement was far more common.[4] Term-limits supporters now question whether elections are adequate instruments of accountability given high reelection rates. Incumbents are heavily advantaged in their pursuit of reelection. They benefit from subsidized travel, the franking privilege, professional television and radio studios, tremendous fund-raising advantages and staff that serve as a reelection machine.[5]

The 1994 election saw substantial seat turnover, but such elections are rare. Between 1974 and 1992, an average of 93.9 percent of incumbents were returned to office.[6] According to proponents of term limits, this low turnover rate makes voter choice an illusion. Yet it is choice that is essential for democratic rule. The framers of the Constitution never imagined a system in which turnover would be so low. Term-limits supporters also claim that, in their constant pursuit of reelection, members become captive to special interests. PACs (political action committees) give 90 percent of their contributions to incumbents. Seeking perpetual incumbency, members put Congress up for sale.

The desire for reelection also undermines the capacity to focus on policy.[7] Members of Congress know that they must look good. Much of an incumbent's activity, then, is symbolic rather than effectual.[8] The desire for reelection is a powerful force. "We can be certain that over the years lies have been told, crimes have been committed, and responsibilities have been neglected all because of the desire to be elected or reelected."[9] Limiting congressional terms, so it is argued, would permit members to focus on legislating rather than engage in a flurry of activities that has no cumulative effect except to aid reelection. Those who are good at getting reelected are often the best actors and self-promoters rather than the best at policy formation. Some have even found an inverse relationship between attendance in committee and the amount of time members spend drawing media attention to themselves.[10]

Proponents point out that the president is limited by the 22nd Amendment to two terms and that 36 states have limited terms for governors. Since 1990, about twenty states have limited the terms of state legislators.[11] Until state laws limiting congressional terms were struck down by the Supreme Court in May, 1995, legislation had been introduced in virtually all other state legislatures. Extending term limits to members of Congress is an expression of popular will. Between 1990 and the Supreme Court ruling, twenty-one of the twenty-four states that have the ballot initiative process passed ballot measures limiting congressional terms.[12]

A final argument for term limits, then, is their very popularity. Support over the last thirty years has never fallen below 47 percent and has been recently as high as 80 percent.[13] Voter hostility focuses more on Congress as an institution than on individual members. Republican Bill Emerson (MO) said that when he talked to supporters of term limits in his district they demanded limits for everyone else, but not for him. "They were adamant about me staying on! So I asked them, 'Oh, so term limits should apply to everyone but me?' You see, they were just frustrated with the Democratic leadership and wanted the playing field to change."[14] And this points out the very source of long-term incumbency: people are satisfied with their own representatives, it's everyone else's that they wish would go away.

ARGUMENTS AGAINST TERM LIMITS

Politicians opposed to term limits commonly indicate that the popular movement to impose them is misguided. Although members opposed to term limits seldom question public opinion in the areas where it is with them, they readily challenge popular wisdom on this issue. "I don't believe the public understands the problems with term limits," said Emerson (MO).[15] "We have a very good process in place to limit terms. It's called elections and it just worked in 1994."

Opponents of term limits reason that experience should count. When choosing a surgeon, a patient prefers one with experience. A legislature made up of citizens who are here today, gone tomorrow, would allow for control by bureaucrats, special interests and congressional staff members. With term limits, even greater power would flow to Washington's permanent insiders.

Perhaps the most potent argument against term limits is that they are a denial of citizens' fundamental right to choose who should represent them. As one Republican reasoned,

> *Now I'm a Presbyterian. I even thought about going into the ministry. For me, public service is a calling. I believe my abilities to serve are best placed in this public arena. I don't feel that I own the seat. But I believe that as long as I'm working hard for my constituents, and they think I'm doing a good job, they should not be denied the right to elect me.*

Members opposed to term limits rationalize their desire to remain in office with solid constitutional arguments backed by a narrow 5–4 Supreme Court ruling in May 1995 in *U.S. Term Limits* v. *Thornton.* "We are . . . firmly convinced that allowing the several states to adopt term limits for congressional service would effect a fundamental change in the constitutional framework," wrote Justice Stevens in the *Thornton* case.[16] Term limits were considered at the 1787 Constitutional Convention in Philadelphia but rejected.[17] The Constitution specifies the qualifications for office in Article I, Sections 2 and 3. These qualifications require only that members be of a certain age, be citizens of the United States, and residents of the state from which they are elected. The Court ruled that these qualifications are exclusive. Any measure that adds to the list of qualifications explicitly listed must be adopted through the amendment process.[18]

Since the Court has now ruled that state-imposed limits are unconstitutional, a constitutional amendment will be necessary. Had the Court ruled in favor of the states' power to impose term limits, then a constitutional amendment would not have been required.

BACKGROUND ON THE CONTRACT'S TERM-LIMITS PROPOSAL

In spite of its overwhelming popularity with the public, the Republican leadership's commitment to term limits was questionable from the beginning. Even in the 103rd Congress one could find a substantial plurality of Republicans who were opposed, including a majority of the older members. Only a few members of the other party favor term limits. Democrats held symbolic hearings on the matter in 1993 when Democrat Don Edwards (CA—now retired) chaired the Civil and Constitutional Rights Subcommittee but never intended to bring the issue to the floor.

While Newt Gingrich (GA) publicly supported the entire Contract, he had never been enthusiastic about term limits and the new Majority Leader, Richard Armey (TX), had suggested in interviews that he had little ardor for them. "Term limits was put into the Contract because they couldn't credibly run on a reform platform without it,"[19] said David Mason, a congressional reform specialist at the Heritage Foundation. Given the popularity of term limits, it was just too difficult to ignore the issue. GOP leaders could assure opponents within the party that the Contract's promise was to bring term limits to a vote, not to pass them.

Still, term limits were a divisive issue within the Republican Conference. "To show you how little influence I had last year, I thought term limits shouldn't be included in the Contract," said Colorado Republican Joel Hefley.[20] "I didn't think term limits brought the party together." Several members, including the influential Henry J. Hyde (IL), had such strong reservations that they nearly refused to sign the Contract.

The task force on term limits was led by several junior members: John Linder (GA), Tillie Fowler (FL), and Bob Inglis (SC). Inglis has placed a six-year, self-imposed term limit on his service in the House. All of the House proposals recommended a limit of twelve years (two terms) for U.S. Senators. Tillie Fowler's (FL) bill recommended an eight-year maximum term of service for House members. Consistent with his own pledge, Inglis (SC) recommended a three-term or six-year limit for House members. Fowler pushed the four-term limit primarily because Florida had just adopted such a measure for federal legislators. A more senior Republican, Bill McCollum (FL) offered a third proposal for a six-term, twelve-year limit on service in the House. McCollum later added a provision that would preempt state laws to ensure national uniformity in congressional terms. This would effectively strike down any state laws that imposed less than the twelve-year limit. So there were three original proposals that came to be known as "8–12" (Fowler), "6–12" (Inglis) and "12–12" (McCollum).

Although capturing the full 290 votes necessary for a constitutional amendment would be difficult for any of the proposals, McCollum's legislation had the best chance. Inglis's proposal for a three-term limitation was widely popular with Washington-based grassroots groups that were influential in pushing the state-level initiatives. The most important of these groups was U.S. Term Limits (USTL), an organization with an energetic following of 70,000 people. Based on this support, the leadership decided to bring both the 12–12 and 6–12 proposals to a vote as part of the Contract.

COMMITTEE AND FLOOR ACTION

The effort to pass term limits was the most disorganized and halfhearted operation of the first 100 days. The failure was predictable well ahead of time. Even the usually optimistic freshmen interviewed in late January and early February were predicting the loss two months prior to the vote.[21]

During the transition and through the month of January, momentum was steadily building in favor of McCollum's twelve-year proposal. Even Inglis (SC), the sponsor of the 6–12 proposal, agreed that the McCollum proposal was acceptable if it could muster the 290 votes. On January 31st, however, U.S. Term Limits came out opposing any compromise with the forces behind the McCollum proposal. The group's executive director, Paul Jacob, even announced that USTL would run advertising against Republicans who supported term limits but were joining the push for the twelve-year proposal.[22] Jacob said that he would prefer no amendment to one that second-guessed the states by imposing a twelve-year nationwide limit. This stubborn and self-defeating move by USTL did little more than marginalize the group. Republicans were incredulous that longtime term-limits supporters would be targeted by USTL's negative advertising. One of these was Dave Camp (MI), a longtime supporter of the 12–12 proposal. USTL spent about $1,200 on advertising against him on two television stations in his central Michigan district. "They ought to go after people who oppose term limits," Camp said. "They left alone all the people who voted against the twelve-year limit. This was dumping on their own side. It didn't make any sense."[23]

The legislation was marked-up in the House Judiciary committee on February 28th. "This was the Democrats' finest hour," said Barney Frank (MA) as he puffed in Churchill-esque fashion on his cigar.[24] "We totally bogged them down. Their strategy was a joke. We stuck together pretty well and the Republicans kept peeling off on things." "He's right," said Bob Inglis (SC) responding to my account of Frank's comments. "They had the votes to tip the boat over on any given issue."[25]

The lack of consensus on term limits was amplified in the close quarters of the Judiciary Committee hearing room. Senior Republicans Carlos Moorhead (CA) and James Sensenbrenner (WI) were resolutely opposed to term limits. An even bigger obstacle was Chair Henry J. Hyde (IL). He spoke out against them during the hearing and refused to state the majority position after each vote. Democrats joined with several of the senior Republicans to amend the legislation to permit members to serve twelve years, sit out for one term, and run for an additional twelve years. McCollum further amended the legislation to provide for federal preemption of state laws.

The legislation was then voted out on a 21–14 vote looking nothing like the Contract's original proposal. Gone were both the 6–12 proposal, defeated on a 20–13 vote; and the original 12–12 proposal (by McCollum). "It was awful,"[26] recalled Inglis of the markup session. "We made no effort to caucus ahead of time to straighten out what our goal was. I made a mistake. I assumed that everyone knew what the goal was. The result was that Republicans split in all directions." Critics complained that the bill no longer constituted a serious limitation on terms. A member could serve for twelve years, run a spouse for the seventh term, and then return for another twelve years. "That's not term limits," said Inglis.

The Leadership Intervenes

When Gingrich and Armey realized that the Judiciary Committee had abandoned the original Contract's term-limits proposals, they knew they would have to act. "So many changes have been made, now no one likes the bill,"[27] reported one committee staffer. Gingrich and Armey made the decision to scrap the committee's version of the legislation and bring the original Contract items to the floor.

Postponing the floor action, the leaders scheduled a meeting to decide which alternatives would be considered. Present at the meeting were Armey, Gingrich, and several other Republican leaders, the sponsors of the term-limits measures, along with representatives from the interest group community—including the Christian Coalition, H. Ross Perot's United We Stand, the National Taxpayers Union, and the Heritage Foundation. U.S. Term Limits was not invited. A majority of the Republican freshmen had closed ranks behind a new twelve-year proposal of Congressman Van Hilleary (TN) that prohibited federal preemption of state law. McCollum and Hilleary argued about their bills with Hilleary insisting upon states' rights and McCollum insisting upon federal preemption. Gingrich spoke in favor of McCollum, complaining that Hilleary's proposal had surfaced late in the process while McCollum had worked for months to build support. Gingrich launched into a tirade against U.S. Term Limits and then left the room.

With Armey still searching for a rule to govern debate, the interest group representatives spoke almost unanimously in favor of the Hilleary proposal. "The grassroots efforts were more like Hilleary," explained David Mason of the Heritage Foundation who was present at the meeting.[28] "Many of the groups represented term-limits efforts at the grassroots." While Gingrich had argued against Hilleary's proposal, Armey was more willing to accommodate the groups and seek consensus with the members present. Armey then asked if anyone could outline a rule for floor debate. The emergent rule allowed three Republican alternatives: the two Contract proposals 6–12 and 12–12, along with Hilleary's proposal preserving lower state limits, and a Democratic substitute.

The Democratic substitute would apply the twelve-year limit retroactively, forcing many sitting members out of office. This proposal, which few members took seriously, had been roundly defeated in committee when it had been offered by term-limits opponent Barney Frank (MA). Frank's name was subsequently dropped from the legislation to make it more palatable to term-limits supporters.[29] The rule governing consideration was the same winner-take-all provision used in the debate over a balanced budget amendment (see Chapter 4). Each substitute would get a vote, with the one garnering the most support presented for final passage.[30]

Just prior to the debate, the term limits cause received a boost when Republican Conference Chair John Boehner (OH) announced that he was changing his mind on the issue. He had always opposed term limits but decided to vote in favor. As he explained in an interview a few days after the vote,

> *I've always been against term limits. I believe that you can always get rid of people you don't want at the ballot box. [The elections of] 1992 and 1994 proved this. I believe that limiting terms would only drive power to the staff and the bureaucracy.*
>
> *Then Ohio voted overwhelmingly for term limits in 1992. And I got to thinking, who am I to say I know better than you do what's good for you? This got me to reconsider my role in our system as a representative.*
>
> *Then I was watching the debate on the balanced budget amendment in the Senate. This was the crowning blow. I watched six Democratic Senators who had voted for the identical language a year ago thumb their noses at the American people by voting against the amendment. This helped me to understand why people are so frustrated with Washington. I also believe that states should be the center of power in our system. The states ultimately have to approve term limits if it's a Constitutional Amendment. So who am I to stand in the way of states considering a constitutional amendment to limit congressional terms?*[31]

Term limits came to the floor on March 29th, just two weeks prior to the 100-day deadline. McCollum's twelve-year proposal with the added provision for preemption of state laws (H.J. Res 73) served as the base text. Time for debate was limited to three hours for the general resolution and one hour for each of the three substitute amendments.

Debate opened with general arguments. Members active on each side filed to the floor to wait their turn. In an electrifying speech, Judiciary Chair Hyde (IL) called the term-limits movement "angry, pessimistic populism" and hailed the tradition, history and institutional memory that come with seniority.[32]

The debate then moved toward consideration of the Democratic substitute that would apply retroactive term limits. Republican Martin Hoke (OH) accused the sponsor of the Democratic substitute, John Dingell (MI) of being "hypocritical" and "cynical" for introducing a measure he had no intention of voting for. Dingell and other leading Democrats had long opposed term limits of any kind and had pushed this substitute simply to goad Republicans. Dingell objected to Hoke's characterization of his [Dingell's] motives and Hoke eventually had to apologize.[33] Republicans continued to insist that the Democratic substitute was a "killer amendment" designed to derail any serious term-limits initiative.[34] When the vote was called, the Dingell version was defeated 135–297.

The Inglis substitute came up following the disposal of the Democratic measure. Inglis (SC) argued that a majority of states adopting term limits had adopted a six-year limit for House members.[35] Inglis garnered the vocal support of a large bloc of freshmen, including Fred Heineman (NC), Tom Coburn (OK), Jack Metcalf (WA), Jon Fox (PA), John Shadegg (AZ), and George Nethercutt (WA). Although no Republicans spoke against the substitute, there was ample opposition from a cadre of senior Democrats led by John Conyers (MI). When the roll was called the Inglis version went down 114–316.

Van Hilleary's (TN) twelve-year limit without state preemption was next. Once again, Republican freshmen were at the forefront of the debate with senior Democrats in opposition. This time, however, several of the African-American and Hispanic Democrats made forceful points. Jose Serrano (NY) argued that term limits was a form of minority power dilution. Serrano (NY) suggested that just as minority representatives were gaining power and seniority in Congress, the movement to curtail terms had gained momentum.[36] In a rare moment, John Conyers (MI) the Democratic floor leader on the bill, gave Bill McCollum (FL) time to speak against the Hilleary alternative on the ground that it did not demand uniform limits on terms. McCollum's insistence on preempting state term-limits laws was considered incongruous by many Republicans given their penchant for federalism. On the other side, Bob Inglis (SC), whose amendment had just been defeated, spoke in favor of Hilleary's substitute. The Hilleary proposal also won the support of Rules Committee Chairman Gerald Solomon (NY). Nevertheless, when the vote was called, the measure was defeated 164–265. Momentum was building far too slowly for the next vote to yield the necessary 290.

With the substitutes out of the way, McCollum's 12–12 proposal was brought up for consideration and final passage. At the close of the debate, Speaker Gingrich took the floor to make a final pitch in favor of the proposal. He compared the debate on term limits to the debate that brought about the adoption of the 17th Amendment on the direct election of U.S. Senators. The idea took some 20 years to take hold, but it finally passed. Gingrich predicted that the same might be true of term limits. He closed by promising to bring the term-limits proposal to a vote as the first item in the 105th Congress of 1997.[37] The vote on McCollum's measure was called and in the most successful attempt of the night to "rush the wall," it gained 227 votes in its favor, falling 63 votes short of the necessary two-thirds.

THE VOTES—DAY 85

The halfhearted effort to pass term limits stands as an exception to the overall success of the Contract. The disunity among committee Republicans and the ambivalence of the leadership were partly to blame. The question is whether the leadership could have mustered the 290 votes had they been fully mobilized behind it given that so many senior Republicans were in opposition. The answer is, probably not. Very few Democrats joined the cause. Perhaps more votes could have been swayed had the largest grassroots group, U.S. Term Limits, ran ads against term-limits opponents rather than supporters. But they would have had to target enough members to bring over sixty-three votes—a tall order even for such a large group.

Explanations of the Votes

An analysis of the votes reveals just how critical various kinds of opposition were to the term-limits effort. Table A6 (see Appendix) reveals the influence of partisanship and seniority on the vote for the four versions of the legislation brought to the floor. Other variables suggest the way in which constituency influences may have played a role. Key among these is H. Ross Perot's support in the 1992 election. Perot supporters are overwhelming term-limits backers. Perot's grassroots organization, United We Stand, helped put term-limits ballot initiatives together in 1992 and 1994. The influence of region on the vote is included with a control for the conservative influence of southern congressional districts. The percentage of the population in rural areas is included to evaluate the extent of urban/rural cleavage in the vote. Because big-city, urban districts are generally less competitive than rural and suburban districts, I hypothesize that urban members will have more to lose from term limits than will those from less-urban areas.

The data show that there is a strong measure of partisanship in the term-limits dispute. The vast majority of Democrats are opposed while most of the Republicans are in favor. Republicans had incorporated term limits into their presidential platform in both 1988 and 1992. Accordingly, Republicans were about 60 percent more likely to vote for passage of the McCollum 12–12 version than Democrats were. Table A6 (see Appendix) also shows that seniority and Perot support played a role almost equal to party in several of the votes. Those in districts where Perot received his strongest support were about 64 percent more likely to vote for final passage than members in districts where Perot had very little support. Similarly, the youngest members were 75 percent more likely to vote for McCollum's measure than the oldest members. The generational split was also evident on the alternative measures. Even some of the younger Democrats from non-Southern states, such as Bill Luther (MN), Karen McCarthy (MO), Jane Harman (CA), and Jim Barcia (MI) voted for McCollum's proposal, suggesting that the generational split was not on the Republican side only. Why do younger members tend to follow public opinion on this issue while older members do not? Surely not all of those who voted for term limits really believe in them. The younger generation's deference to the popular movement probably reflects their inexperience in taking politically difficult stands. Older members are more confident casting occasional votes against their constituency.[38] Finally, southern members were more attracted by term limits than northern members, and urban legislators apparently felt more threatened by term limits than rural members did.

This analysis suggests that the votes on term limits may have had roots in factors other than party efforts or the personal beliefs of the members about the propriety of limiting congressional terms. Junior members in Republican districts where Perot ran strongest, as well as those from the South, were most favorably disposed to vote for both the Hilleary substitute and the McCollum proposal. What this suggests is that Republicans will get closer to passing a constitutional amendment on term limits as older members retire and the GOP increases its share of southern seats.

CONCLUSION

Recalling the Contract's original promise, to bring these measures up for discussion and a vote, one can reasonably ask whether the debate on term limits really was a waste of time. Did it accomplish anything? While the loss of the term-limits vote was obvious as early as 1994, there was much to be gained in bringing the measure to the floor. These votes served as a baseline to put the members on record. It takes time to build momentum behind controversial proposals. The Balanced Budget Amendment required several votes and a full thirteen years of support building before it finally passed the House. There had never been a committee markup on term limits. For supporters of the measures it was an important start. Arguably, those who were against term limits also benefitted from the debate. Democrats had bottled up the issue, stifling discussion and preventing the opponents of term limits from airing their arguments. For many, this was the first time the other side had been heard.

While there was a strong partisan tone to the debate, the term-limits issue shows that Republican factionalism was not cured simply by collecting the Contract signatures on September 27th. In this case, the split emerged between the zealous junior —mostly freshmen and sophomore—members against many of the more senior and experienced members. A similar division exists in the U.S. Senate, where term limits is opposed by a large proportion of senior Republicans. Majority Leader Robert Dole (KS) has pledged to bring term limits to the floor of the Senate anyway.

In reform movements, the typical division is between the young and their new ideas against the experienced pols—trying to maintain the power and privilege of old age. The young usually win these battles in the long run, especially if they are as popular at the grassroots as term limits is. But as in other efforts to pass constitutional amendments by daunting supermajority margins, substantial consensus must be in place first. The hope of term-limits supporters is that the no votes will be used against the reelection bids of anti-term-limits members in 1996. If this hope becomes a reality, Republicans will have taken their first step toward forging a supermajority consensus by keeping their promise to bring term limits to a vote.

9

Cutting Taxes

"The tax cut promise is a false promise," said freshman Republican Ray LaHood (IL) who replaced retired Republican leader Robert Michel in Illinois' 18th District.[1] "Our party has tilted too far toward tax cuts. How can we promise a check when there's no money in the checkbook? Any savings we get from program cuts we should apply to the deficit." LaHood even refused to sign the Contract on the ground that he opposed its tax cut provisions (see Chapter 2).

For most other Republicans, tax cuts were a popular element of the 1994 campaign. A majority of the Republican freshmen made some promise of tax reduction as part of their broader theme of cutting government. President Clinton made middle-class tax relief a major campaign theme in his 1992 election. He later abandoned that pledge in favor of deficit reduction and higher marginal tax rates for the wealthy.[2] Given the president's turnabout, it was inevitable that tax cuts would find their way into the Contract with America.

For most Democrats and a few Republicans such as LaHood, tax cuts and deficit reduction did not mix. The Congressional Budget Office (CBO) estimated that the tax bill could increase the deficit by $41.6 billion by the year 2000 without offsetting spending cuts.[3] Most Republicans, however, reasoned that deficit reduction and tax cuts were complementary. A review of the economic arguments on each side illuminates this fundamental dispute.

Proponents argue that tax cuts serve as an economic stimulus. High taxes and government spending are a drag on the economy. Corporate and personal income taxes, in particular, are costs imposed on the work, saving, and investing central to a productive economy.[4] People try to avoid costs by not being as productive. In this sense, higher taxes reduce productivity. Tax cuts, therefore, reduce the costs imposed on these productive activities.[5] In the absence of other disincentives, then, tax cuts yield economic growth. The argument is strengthened if one looks at comparative data on industrial economies. Countries with the fastest growing economies have the lowest average tax rates. The countries with the slowest growing economies have the highest tax rates.[6]

Supply-side Republicans take the argument one-step further. If tax cuts result in a burst of productivity of sufficient strength, the increase in income can offset the losses in revenue. Their assumption is that the tax cuts will provide businesses with more to invest, and their investments will pay off. The additional taxable income will ensure no substantial rise in the deficit. In fact, the deficit may actually shrink.[7]

Such was the rationale for the adoption of 1981 Economic Recovery Tax Act (ERTA) early in the Reagan Administration.[8] Pushed by the increasing proportion of members from business-oriented sunbelt states,[9] Congress slashed taxes. By a vote of 323–107, individual income tax rates fell by 25 percent and numerous forms of corporate tax relief were enacted, including increased depreciation deductions, investment tax credits, and a 25 percent tax credit for research and development.[10] The 1981 law allowed certain corporations to pay no taxes, which paved the way for political and economic problems in subsequent years.[11] Faced with the fact that the 1981 tax reform would not significantly reduce the deficit, the Reagan Administration supported subsequent efforts to close loopholes, culminating in the 1986 Tax Reform Act that repealed the investment tax credit and raised corporate income taxes.[12] Much of what was done for the sake of corporate investment in 1981 had been undone by 1987.

Democrats frequently point out that the deficit soared through the 1980s. Furthermore, much of the spending was defended both by people within the Reagan and Bush administrations and by Republicans in Congress.[13] Federal spending outstripped economic growth and the gains from tax reduction largely went unrealized. The conclusion Democrats draw from this is that tax reduction and deficit reduction cannot go hand-in-hand. The attempt to do both failed in the 1980s, so it must always fail. Deficit reduction will require a tax increase or (at the very least) a reduction in the growth of federal spending at current tax rates.

THE CONTRACT'S TAX REDUCTION PLAN

Tax policy is governed by far more than just the size of the deficit, objective economic conditions, and complicated arguments by economists. Two other factors are determinative: (1) public opinion and (2) political ideology. First, tax cuts are usually popular.[14] Regardless of the unsettled quarrels among economists about the tradeoffs of tax cuts, deficit reduction, and government spending, the popularity of tax cuts ensures that politicians will usually favor them.

Second, the Republican leadership believes in tax cuts as a matter of principle, or ideology. Republicans have traditionally been opposed to government spending. Tax cuts coupled with spending cuts are considered a sure means of reducing the growth in government programs.[15] Republicans in the 104th Congress did not lament the tax reductions of the early 1980s, they lament the absence of serious spending cuts. They are convinced that George Bush's breach of his no-new-taxes pledge played the key role in his 1992 loss. In spite of the skepticism about the wisdom of cutting spending and cutting taxes, Gingrich and Armey pushed for both as a means of breaking free of what they considered the failed fiscal politics of the Bush administration. The centerpieces of the tax cut proposal were a 50 percent reduction in capital gains taxation and a $500 per child tax credit for those earning incomes up to $200,000 (also called "family tax relief").

The capital gains legislation was originally introduced in 1991 by Senator Malcolm Wallop (WY) and Congressman Tom Delay (TX) (now the Majority Whip). The point of reducing the tax on capital gains is to stimulate economic growth by encouraging maximally profitable investment activity.[16] High taxes on capital gains discourage investors from acquiring assets with the highest available yield. Fearing the high taxation resulting from the sale of an asset, investors simply keep it to avoid the tax when they would otherwise be better off by selling. These so-called "lock-in effects" are so powerful that economists have suggested that capital gains tax cuts would boost the economy.[17] Politically, however, the capital gains tax reduction has always been controversial. Democrats perpetually charge Republicans with pandering to the rich since wealthy investors are most likely to reap the immediate benefits.

The family tax relief measure originated in the 103rd Congress with Representatives Rod Grams (MN) (now Senator) and Tim Hutchinson (AR). Republican leaders realized that the tax credit was not likely to stimulate much economic growth. But the point of this reform was to further reduce the tax burden on American families. The ability to pay taxes varies directly with family size. Given two families, each earning $65,000 per year, the one with one child is better able to pay taxes than the one with three children (all other things equal). Granting an additional tax credit to the larger family reduces that family's tax liability. Freshman Republican Enid Waldholtz (UT) said that this subsidy for larger families became a significant issue in her campaign against Democratic incumbent Karen Sheppard and a third-party candidate:

> *Before the Contract went public, I was supporting the $500 per child tax credit. My opponents accused me of pandering to Mormon families in the district. They said 'large Utah families' but what they really meant was Mormon families.*[18]

With a large proportion of Mormons in her district, Waldholtz managed to turn back these attacks by pointing out their anti-Mormon and anti-family bias. The family tax relief proposal originated in the 1994 Republican budget plan but was capped at $200,000 at the insistence of several moderate Republicans, including Christopher Shays (CT) and Olympia Snowe (ME) (now Senator). It was incorporated into the Contract with the $200,000 cap.

These tax cuts were a step toward Majority Leader Armey's (TX) more ambitious goals for the tax system. Armey had long championed full-scale tax reform in the form of a flat 17 percent tax on income with the elimination of all deductions. He declined to add this provision to the Contract on the ground that it would be too difficult to muster support within the 100-day time frame (see Chapter 2).

The Contract's tax provisions were scattered among three bills: H.R. 6, titled the *American Dream Restoration Act,* H.R. 9, the *Job Creation and Wage Enhancement Act* and H.R. 11, the *Family Reinforcement Act.* In addition to the capital gains tax cut and the family tax relief measure, the bills included a reduction in the tax liability of married couples and an enhanced IRA that is tax free if withdrawn for use for retirement, a first home, a college education, or medical expenses. H.R. 11 contained tax credits for adoptions and elderly care and H.R. 9 contained new tax breaks for businesses. The Ways and Means Committee had jurisdiction over all of these provisions[19] and combined them into a single bill (H.R. 1215) before the markup in mid-March.

COMMITTEE AND FLOOR ACTION

The Ways and Means Committee held hearings on the combined tax proposals in mid-January. The Clinton Administration opposed every element of the plan, saying that reductions in the capital gains tax would crowd out government spending for child care, education, and worker training.[20] Congressional Democrats immediately inflated the specter of class warfare. Although they were reluctant to attack the $500 per child tax credit, they criticized the high cap, saying that wealthy families did not need this tax break.

President Clinton countered the Republican tax initiative with a proposal to raise the minimum wage. In early February, Senate Majority Leader Dole (KS) suggested the possibility of trading a minimum wage increase for the capital gains tax reduction. House Democratic leader Richard Gephardt (MO) then blasted the Republicans for trying to get something for their wealthy backers in exchange for a reasonable proposal to assist the lower and middle classes.

By late February, the prospect of passing the tax cut package looked bleak. The total tax cost of the cuts was estimated at $189 billion to be paid for through offsetting budget cuts. Senate Republican Budget Chair Pete Domenici (NM) said that tax cuts would probably not be a part of his plan for reducing the deficit. Senate Finance Committee Chair Bob Packwood (OR) also came out against tax cuts. Democrats pointed out that the public's enthusiasm for tax cuts had waned. "They are pushing too hard for something the people don't want," said Paul Kanjorski (PA).[21] "They will find an inconsistency when they go back home and see that the people aren't interested in a tax cut." Kanjorski had noted that polls suggested the public's willingness to postpone a tax cut for the sake of deficit reduction.[22] Even Newt Gingrich (GA) announced that he wasn't sure a majority could be found for what he later described as the Contract's "crown jewel."[23]

Coming in the home stretch of the 100 days, the tax reduction measure met little opposition in the Ways and Means markup from beleaguered Democrats exhausted from the battle over welfare reform. They predictably focused on the capital gains provision and the $200,000 cap on the child credit. Committee Republicans expressed surprise that the Democrats offered only one amendment on the legislation:

> *Last week on the tax bill, we were prepared to go very late on Tuesday and Wednesday, anticipating opposition. They had been ranting and raving all morning. We broke for lunch, we came back in, they introduced one amendment and then dropped everything. They didn't offer any amendments.*[24]

Apparently, the Democrats could not organize an amendment strategy. They offered a single amendment to sunset the Republican tax provisions after five years. It was defeated on a party-line vote. "We were really surprised," said a top committee aide. "They had prepared 99 amendments and didn't offer but one. I don't know who came up with their strategy, but we sure liked it." Many of the amendments were controversial and would have put Republicans in a difficult position. In the days leading up to the markup, Democrats suggested changing the per-child credit by limiting it to families with incomes under $95,000. Many Republicans favored this change and Republican committee member E. Clay Shaw (FL) admitted that the committee would have reduced the cap had Armey (TX) not intervened to maintain it:

> *The high limit on the tax credit was a serious political mistake. This was an obvious lightning rod. This gave the Democrats something to shoot at. They should have either gone with no cap at all, or reduced it. Leadership was so insistent that it be kept. [Majority Leader] Armey [TX] came in and talked to us and pushed it.*[25]

Committee Republican Dave Camp (MI) echoed these remarks while explaining the leadership's rationale:

> *I think we should have lowered it. But the leaders felt that it was something we had promised in the Contract. It had been a compromise between those who wanted no limit and those who thought the limit should be even lower. So since it was already the product of compromise, they decided to leave it as it was.*[26]

Democrats had also drafted several amendments to ensure that savings from tax cuts would go to deficit reduction. This would have also won Republican support. But the Democrats themselves were divided on these issues. Senior committee Democrat Andy Jacobs (IN) explained the Democrats' dilemma:

> *We just decided not to bother with amendments since they [the Republicans] wouldn't accept them. They should be thankful that we saved them an entire day of committee work when we could have caused trouble. But on this tax legislation, there isn't anything we could have done anyway. We only have 20 or so members and we don't usually agree.*
>
> *... Compared to welfare, tax cuts were a waltz. Now there isn't a single Republican on that committee that I don't like, but they are paying for a tax cut for the rich by cutting poor children. That was the thrust of our argument.*[27]

So the Democrats contented themselves with voting no. Republicans speculated that they feared being televised on C-SPAN attempting to eliminate cuts in a popular tax-reduction package. But the decision to let the package go to the floor unamended also served the Democratic rhetorical emphasis on class warfare. Now they could not be charged with compromising with the Republican favoritism of the rich.[28] On the other hand, tax bills customarily go to the floor under a closed rule—no amendments are permitted. In choosing not to amend the legislation in committee, House Democrats gave up their last chance for changes.

As the bill moved to the floor, opposition within Republican ranks spread. Some of the opposition came within the usually loyal freshman class. Freshman Bill Martini (NJ), a moderate, joined with more senior Republicans Mike Castle (DE) and Fred Upton (MI) and about twenty-seven other members to build support for a change that would not allow the per-child credit until deficit reduction targets were met.[29] The rule could have been defeated had the leadership not yielded to the pressure to include a modified version of this proposal. Another freshman, Greg Ganske (IA), again complained that the $200,000 limit on the child tax credit was too high and mustered 102 signatures on a letter to the leadership insisting on the chance to offer an amendment to lower the cap to $95,000. Here, however, the leadership refused to yield, arguing that abandonment of the $200,000 limit would alienate the more conservative wing of the party. Ganske (IA) and his cosigners were persuaded to withdraw their proposal for the sake of party unity.

Consistent with tradition on tax legislation, the rule allowed no amendments. The Democrats were permitted one substitute, offered by Minority Leader Gephardt (MO), and were allowed a motion to recommit the bill to committee. Conservative Democrat Glen Browder (AL) had drafted a far more credible substitute emphasizing deficit reduction, but Gephardt refused it in favor of his own. The rule passed on a 228–204 vote, with eleven Republicans voting against and nine Democrats voting in favor.

The debate opened on April 5th, on Day 92 of the 100-day countdown with members from the Ways and Means, Budget, and Commerce Committees taking the lead. The rule provided for two hours of opening debate, with one hour of debate devoted to the Democratic substitute. Democrats immediately charged that Republicans were playing games with the deficit. Just as Ronald Reagan promised deficit reduction on the heels of a tax cut, with a resultant increase in the deficit, Republicans were making the same empty promises again.[30] The legislation is only making the rich richer while not giving poor and middle income voters any breaks. Democrat John Lewis (GA) underlined the class warfare theme:

> *I have heard Speaker Gingrich refer to this tax proposal as the crown jewel of the Republican Contract. I could not agree more. Like the crown jewels, this bill is for royalty, it is for the truly wealthy among us. If you are middle class, if you are poor, you can look but you better not touch...*[31]

Republicans responded that most of the tax savings would go to middle-income families. The capital gains cut would encourage entrepreneurship, strengthen businesses in difficult international markets, and create jobs.[32] Liberal Democrats refused to buy the idea that business incentives create jobs for anyone other than the privileged few. Charles Rangel (NY) spoke of the capital gains tax reduction and the other pro-business measures as merely another form of corporate welfare.[33]

Following the debate among members of the Ways and Means Committee, members of the Budget Committee streamed to the floor. Democrats charged that the tax cuts had not been offset with spending cuts. Budget Committee Chair John Kasich (OH) had released a proposal illustrating how it could be paid for, but none of those cuts had been enacted. Other Democrats attacked Kasich's proposed cuts as harsh on children, infants, seniors, and students.[34] After each individual Democratic criticism, Republicans quoted figures about the amount of tax relief that would accrue to the complaining Democrat's congressional district by enactment of their plan.

Finally, members of the Commerce Committee were given their turn. One Democrat, James Traficant (OH), spoke in favor of the legislation, calling on his fellow Democrats to stop the talk of class warfare.[35] On the other side, Republican Scott Klug (WI) spoke in opposition to the legislation, saying, "I am not Santa Claus... it is my job tonight to remind everybody in this chamber that we are flat-out broke."[36]

With the expiration of the first two hours, action moved to consideration of the Democratic substitute. This legislation narrowly focused tax cuts on those earning less than $65,000 without cutting the range of government programs as recommended in the Republican legislation and with neither the capital gains tax reduction nor any of the other breaks for businesses. Additional provisions allowed certain families to deduct educational expenses and the interest paid on student loans.

Republicans assailed various inadequacies of the Democratic proposal and attacked the Democrats for not supporting stronger measures. As time expired, the Gephardt substitute mustered a mere 119 votes. The motion to recommit the Republican proposal to committee was rejected 168–265, and the vote on final passage was called. The last item in the Republican Contract with America passed on a vote of 246–188, with twenty-seven Democrats voting in favor and eleven Republicans in opposition.

THE VOTES—DAY 92

The debate was rife with the talk of class warfare. The rich were not only cutting entitlements to the poor, they were doing so to further enrich themselves. This argument failed to persuade a large number of Democrats. Nor did the more narrowly focused tax cuts of the Gephardt substitute attract much support. The 119 votes in favor of the Democratic substitute was similar to the support for the liberal Democratic alternative on the welfare legislation (Mink substitute, see Chapter 7).

Remarkably, Republicans managed to keep all but a handful of their members on board. Ultimately, the desire to prove they could govern overruled other impulses, as moderate Republican Christopher Shays (CT) pointed out in my interview the day of the vote:

> *I'm a bit uncomfortable with the tax cuts. But I think they should move forward. I am more concerned, though, with deficit reduction. I will vote yes on final passage of the tax cuts...*
>
> *The press says this is the beginning of the end and that after the first 100 days our unity will dissolve. But it is the height of absurdity to suggest that we are going to break apart. We want to show the people that this Congress can work, that we can govern. That desire will hold us together. It matters to me that we work out our disagreements. But we can do that ahead of time before the floor.*[37]

As a postscript, Shays was right about Republican unity after the 100 days. The House GOP would maintain its cohesion even without the Contract.[38] The Republican leadership's most persuasive argument throughout the 104th Congress was that unity was required for maintenance of their majority status. At the end of their forty years of control, Democrats had forgotten about the importance of unity.

Explanations of the Votes

An analysis of the principal votes on the tax cut legislation appears in Table A7 (see Appendix). As on the other votes on the Contract, I expect party membership to be highly influential. Certain constituency characteristics may also be relevant, though. Members from districts with large proportions of urban and minority residents are expected to be hostile to final passage of the tax cuts. Southerners are hypothesized to support the cuts. Because H. Ross Perot's campaign placed a strong emphasis on deficit reduction, members from districts where Perot ran well in 1992 are expected to vote against the tax-cut legislation.

The results show that partisanship was not highly relevant to the Gephardt substitute with so many Democrats voting against their leadership. Republicans were far more likely than Democrats to support final passage. Members from districts where Ross Perot did well were slightly less likely than members from anti-Perot districts to vote in favor of the Gephardt substitute, although, contrary to my hypothesis, members from strong Perot districts were not especially hostile to final passage of the tax cuts. Southerners were 27 percent more likely to vote for final passage of the bill than non-southerners were, regardless of party. Mississippi Democrat Mike Parker defended his yes vote:

> *Personally, I believe we pay too much in taxes and the federal government does too much. I want to force the issue of cutting government by forcing the tax cuts. I'm hard line compared to most people. I want it all and I want it all today.*[39]

Like many conservative Democrats who voted for the legislation,[40] Parker represents middle-class voters (especially by Mississippi standards). The dominant theme of the party liberals, that the rich were picking on the poor, would not resonate well with people who believe they benefit more from tax cuts than from government services. Indeed, there is little evidence of class warfare in the vote as measured by variation in the median incomes of congressional districts. Once partisanship is taken into account, members from high-income areas appear to be about as likely to vote no as members from low-income areas. Of course, as on the welfare votes, partisanship slightly overshadows class cleavages since the variables are related ($r = .23$, $p < .01$).

CONCLUSIONS

Next to term limits, the tax-cut legislation was the most internally divisive bill for Republicans. Unlike term limits, however, tax cuts were a far higher priority for the leadership. Gingrich and Armey were insistent that the party emerge from the dark days of the Bush administration and refocus the party on the tax-cutting agenda of the 1980s. The passage of the Republican budget proposal on May 18th proved that Republicans did not need the Contract to hold them to their tax-cut and deficit-reduction pledges.

More important, the tax-cut legislation provided a diversion from the months-long controversy about programs that would be cut under Republican rule. Tax cuts gave the new majority something to favor. It prevented interest groups and the public from focusing entirely upon the pain associated with deficit reduction. Certain groups would suffer more than others, but with the tax reduction, Republicans could now argue that at least someone would benefit. Conservative pro-business and pro-family groups lobbied for this legislation when they otherwise might have either campaigned against cuts in favored programs or remained on the sidelines.

Democrats focused attention on two major provisions of the legislation: the $200,000 cap on the per child tax credit and the capital gains tax reduction. These two measures best served their arguments that Republicans were out to help the rich at the expense of the poor. "There are seven or eight tax provisions that are designed to help Mr. and Mrs. Average Joe," countered Bill Goodling (PA), the Chair of the Education and Economic Opportunities Committee on the day of the vote.[41] "The [Republican] leadership didn't get that message out." "The problem is that we are stepping on ourselves," said freshman Republican Dan Frisa (NY).[42] "We've been doing one of these issues after another, one week this, next week that. It's too much to digest. Last year, they worked on the crime bill for a solid month." The Republicans and Democrats were in the middle of a full-scale communications war that was difficult for Republicans to fight at the pace they were legislating.

Democrats lost the tax cut vote but their rhetoric was sufficiently familiar and contained enough truth that it could not be dismissed by either the Republicans or the American people. After initial resistance, the U.S. Senate followed the House in providing $245 billion in tax relief as part of a seven-year deficit reduction plan in June of 1995.[43] Given the popularity of tax cuts it would be difficult for President Clinton to ignore this politically tempting proposal. If he rejected the legislation, he would have to account for the veto in the 1996 presidential campaign. The Republicans have yet to prove that tax cuts and deficit reduction are compatible means to balancing the budget. If President Clinton can be persuaded to go along with the Republican scheme, Republicans will have the opportunity to rerun their 1980s experiment.

▶ 10

Conclusion: The Contract Sets a New Agenda

Promises made, promises kept. This was the jubilant but weary chant of the Republicans at the completion of the most intense legislative period in decades. "This is a much harder working Congress than I've ever seen. People are tired," said Republican Carlos Moorhead (CA), a House veteran of twenty-three years. The new majority succeeded in bringing every Contract item to a vote within 92 days. In doing so, the Republicans had managed a sweeping change in the political agenda that would shape law and policy into the new century. Every measure passed the House except the constitutional amendment to limit congressional terms (see Chapter 8, and Appendix Table A8). Although House leaders recognized that the Republican Senate had less commitment to the Contract, several of the bills had passed even that chamber or were well on their way to passing in the second (1996) session of the 104th Congress. President Clinton quickly signed into law the Congressional Accountability Act and the unfunded mandates legislation. He nevertheless threatened to veto some of the Contract's more ambitious initiatives and, by midyear, it was doubtful whether the President and the Republicans could work together.

THE RULES CONTROVERSY

Democrats charged that the Republicans had used closed rules to push the Contract through, but the rules were reasonably open. Republicans allowed Democrats to offer both substitutes and motions to recommit on nearly every element of the Contract. A comparison of the rules in the 104th Congress with those of the 103rd is instructive (Table 10-1). At the end of the 100 days, Republicans had brought 72 percent of the bills to the floor under open or modified open rules. An open rule is one under which any member may offer a germane amendment. A modified open rule is one under which any member may offer a germane amendment subject to a time limit on the amendment process or to a requirement that the amendment be printed ahead of time in the *Congressional Record.* Democrats complained that "modified open" rules were really very restrictive and should hardly be combined with the open rules in Table 10-1. Republicans had also complained about such modified open rules when they were in the minority. But now the roles were reversed and the Rules Chair Gerald Solomon (NY) could determine how the various rules were to be classified.

A modified closed rule specifies the amendments that may be offered. Only 28 percent of the legislation during the first 100 days came to the floor under such a rule. A closed rule is one under which no amendments may be offered. Republicans did not legislate under any totally closed rules during the first few months of 1995.

While the process was not totally open, it was surely more open than the Democrats had been in the previous Congress when they rarely offered Republicans both a motion to recommit *and* a substitute on major legislation. As one leadership aide indicated, "We haven't assumed the same dictatorial posture in the majority that they [the Democrats] did in terms of limiting debate. We have cut back on time and occasionally limited amendments, but generally we feel that limiting debate time is more fair than limiting amendments." Apparently, Republican leaders considered the time

Table 10-1 The Amendment Process under Special Rules Reported by the Rules Committee, 103rd Congress vs. 104th Congress (As of April 7, 1995)*

Rule Type	103rd Congress	104th Congress
Modified open/Open	44% (46)	72% (21)
Modified closed	47% (49)	28% (8)
Closed	9% (9)	0% (0)
Totals	100% (104)	100% (29)

Source: House Rules Committee.
*The measures included in this table apply only to rules that provide for the original consideration of bills, joint resolutions or budget resolutions and which provide for an amendment process. It does not include special rules that waive points of order against appropriations bills which are already privileged and are considered under an open amendment process under House rules.

limits of the modified open rule to be an effective instrument of control. In reality, the practical effect of restrictive time limits is to limit the number of amendments. The difference is that time limits affect both sides. Many Republicans who wished to offer amendments were prevented from doing so because time for debate had ended. However, just like the Democrats before them, the Republicans figured that it was worth the sacrifice to avoid casting votes on difficult Democratic amendments.[1]

Some have suggested that the more urgent a bill is, the more likely it is to receive a closed rule.[2] During the first 100 days of this Congress, every bill was on an urgent timetable. Some Republicans interviewed early admitted that closed rules might be necessary as the deadline approached, "We're going to make the deadline," freshman Mark Souder (IN) predicted in early February.[3] "The freshmen are pushing to close the rules in order to pass it [the Contract]. If worse comes to worse, we'll close the rules at the last minute and ram everything through." Republicans were ready to abandon the pledge of more open debate if meeting the deadline required it. But closed rules proved to be unnecessary given Majority Leader Armey's (TX) strategic use of rules that allowed amendments under rigid time constraints.

COMMITTEE ACTIVITY: TO AMEND OR NOT TO AMEND

One of the most enigmatic patterns of the first 100 days was the tendency for the Republican leadership to permit major amendments to some pieces of legislation, while other bills passed virtually unchanged. Why did the leadership seek to exercise more control over some pieces of legislation and less on others? My suggestion is that the extent to which a Contract measure confronted amendments depended upon four factors:

1. *The complexity of the legislation*—more complex measures (with multiple sections and titles) were more likely to be amended than simpler measures.
2. *The ideological heterogeneity of the committee*—the more ideologically divided the committee, the more likely legislation moving through that committee would face pressure for change.
3. *The public visibility or salience of issues*—highly salient provisions in legislation drew heavy amendment activity.[4]
4. *Leadership's commitment*—bills to which the Speaker and Majority Leader were strongly committed were not as subject to amendment as legislation where there was less commitment.

Simple Measures

Given their simplicity, measures such as the balanced budget amendment and the line-item veto were not subject to much change (Chapter 4). There was very little to amend. For issues that are cut and dried, the likelihood of expeditious consideration through a straight up-or-down vote in committee and on the floor is quite high. Leadership rarely has to expend resources to prevent threatening counter-proposals.

Controversial Committees

Not all committees are alike. Consensus committees, such as National Security (Chapter 6) and Agriculture (Chapter 7), have a far more cohesive membership than ideologically polarized committees such as Education and Economic Opportunities, Judiciary or International Relations.[5] Generally, more amendments were offered on the provisions flowing through the ideologically divisive committees. The volume of amendment activity did not always guarantee that the amendments would be accepted. Most Democratic amendments were defeated on party-line votes regardless of the committee. But the demand for change and the level of acrimony on the ideologically divided committees was higher. Similarly, the demand for change from members who were not on the committee was stronger than the pressure for change on more homogeneous committees.

Interestingly, the consensus committees may be in a better position to resist leadership pressures than the divisive committees. Agriculture, for instance, stood against the leadership in refusing to convert food stamps into a block grant. Because Bill Emerson (MO), Pat Roberts (KS), and other leading Republicans were in agreement on the food stamps issue, leadership was in no position to contest the committee's decision. Leadership has more leverage in the committees where consensus is more elusive. In these settings, leadership can pick sides and more effectively tip the balance in one direction or step-in and broker a compromise between the contending members.

High-Visibility Issues

Some issues generate more heat than others. Issues that generate strong public reaction are more difficult for the leadership to control. They may be so controversial that they imperil the rule for debate itself. Such was the case with the welfare reform provision denying welfare benefits to teenage mothers (Chapter 7) and the tax cut measure prior to the agreement on deficit reduction reached with the moderate Republicans (Chapter 9).

Leadership Commitment

A final, and for this Congress, most important determinant of the extent to which a bill was altered is the strength of the leadership's commitment to the originally drafted measure. As I stated in Chapter 1, the Contract was an unusually successful attempt to forge party unity and commitment to a specific program. While the new Speaker and the Majority Leader never forbade the committees from amending that program, there was also a limit on how far revisions could go. On term limits, they rejected the Judiciary Committee's work in favor of the original Contract's proposal (Chapter 8). The leadership's commitment to the tax-cut legislation was so strong that Democrats sensed no point in trying to amend it. Even after being confronted by nearly half of their own members, Armey and Gingrich refused to lower the $200,000 cap on the child tax credit (Chapter 9). Maintaining the Contract's original provision in the face of this internal pressure was probably the most remarkable exhibition of leadership power during the first 100 days.

These four explanations for the changes made during the legislative process are consistent with the legislative behavior of previous congresses. Given the Republicans' forty years of wandering in the wilderness of minority status, Republican leadership commitment was probably a stronger influence on amendment activity in the 104th Congress than in the Democratically controlled Houses of recent years.

PARTY DIVISIONS: CLASS WARFARE OR CONSENSUS

The election results suggested that the new Congress would be ideologically divided and highly partisan since both parties were rendered more homogeneous. Democrats also charged that the Contract divided the American people along class lines, pitting the rich against the poor. The consensus votes on many of the Contract's measures show that if the Congress were split, it was divided in a lopsided fashion—Republicans and conservative Democrats, against the liberal Democrats. Taking the measures reported in Appendix Table A8, I averaged the size of the bloc that voted with the majority of Republicans on final passage of each bill. None of the measures in Table A8 were double counted and the average majority was 334 votes. If the overwhelmingly popular opening day reforms are excluded from the count, it leaves the average majority at 312 votes. The Republicans only had 230 members to start the 104th Congress. That left an average of 82 Democrats voting on the final passage of the provisions in the Contract with America with Republicans losing less than ten of their own.

Members' Contract Ratings

Did the floor division reflect cleavages between wealthy and poor areas? To the extent that the parties reflect *class* differences the answer is yes. An analysis of the roll call votes on final passage of the Contract's provisions is quite revealing. By constructing a Contract "rating" or "score" for each member, one can see who was most loyal to the Contract and who voted consistently against it. The score simply tallies the number of yes votes each member cast and divides that tally by the total number of votes. I have excluded the largely consensual opening day reforms from the tally, although consensus votes on later measures have been included. A member voting for final passage of every measure in the Contract would receive a rating of 100%. Those who voted for only half of the Contract's measures would receive a score of 50% and so on.[6] Using standard, ordinary least-squares regression, one can then use many of the same variables included in the voting analyses of each chapter to explain members' ratings.

The percentage of members voting for every element of the Contract and therefore receiving a perfect 100% rating is quite high—29 percent, 124 members. Only two of these members were Democrats: southerners Ralph Hall (TX) and Billy Tauzin (LA), and Tauzin switched parties three months later. Democrat-turned-Republican Nathan Deal was almost perfect at 95 percent. At the other extreme, the three members most hostile to the Contract were Democrats Xavier Becerra (CA), Bobby Rush (IL), and Mel Watt (NC), who voted yes only 12 percent of the time. Most of the members found much of the Contract agreeable. The average member voted in favor of the Contract 70 percent of the time!

The results of an analysis predicting member ratings are presented below in Table 10-2. Included as explanatory variables are many of the same predictors used in the voting analyses in Chapters 4–9: district characteristics such as the black percentage of the population, median income, percent rural, and the percent voting for Perot in 1992 as well as the party of the member, when that member was elected and whether they were from a southern district. An interaction variable for southern Democrats is also included. The results show that, on average, Republicans ranked 49 percent higher on the rating scale than Democrats did. Southerners were generally more conservative than non-southerners, but southern Democrats were 13.5 percent closer to a 100 percent rating than all other members. The racial and urban character of congressional districts had the predicted effects. A 10 percent increase in the black population of a district led to a 2.8 point decline in the score. Similarly, the more urban the district, the less favorable the member was toward the Contract. Perot support also had a strong impact. A 10 percent increase from one district to the next made a contribution of 2.5 points toward a 100 percent rating. Finally, younger members had slightly higher ratings than more experienced members, suggesting a generational component to the Contract's support. Newly elected members had ratings about a point higher than did those who had been in office two terms (two points higher than those who had been in office four terms). Income differences across districts were not significant influences on members' propensity to vote with the Contract—apparently class differences are overshadowed by the partisanship and ideology of the members and the racial and urban composition of their districts.

To summarize, the plurality of legislators who found themselves on the losing side of these votes were from northern and western urban districts with significant minority and low-income populations. In this sense, the Contract with America was a legislative program supported most consistently by members from predominantly white, middle- and upper-income suburban and rural districts. Does this mean that the policy consequences of the Contract would not benefit lower income, minority citizens? On this the jury will be out for some time. Liberal Democrats are convinced that their constituents will only be hurt. Republicans are sure that a rising economic

Table 10-2 Explaining Support for the Contract with America

Variable	Coefficient (Standard Error)	Mean	Standard Deviation
Party (0 = D, 1 = R)	49.1*** (1.7)	.53	.50
South	3.5* (1.9)	.32	.47
South x Democrat	13.5*** (2.7)	.15	.36
% African American	–.28*** (.06)	11.9	16.2
Income	.00002 (.0001)	30,709	8,382
% Rural	.16*** (.04)	24.9	22.0
% Perot	.26* (.14)	18.4	6.1
Year elected	.26** (.08)	86.2	8.0
Constant	–34.5		
N	434		
Adj. R^2	.82		

***$p < .01$
**$p < .05$
*$p < .10$
Multiple Linear Regression, OLS Estimation (Standard Errors)

tide will lift all boats. One lesson Republicans have learned from the experience of the 1980s is that deficit reduction is a policy priority equal to cutting taxes.

Tone of Debate as a Measure of Partisanship

In spite of the consensual nature of many of the Contract's votes, the tone of this Congress was nastier and more partisan than in previous years. While cooperation between the parties' leadership cadres has been lacking for some time, it seemed totally absent in this Congress. This was predictable given the difficulty Democrats had adjusting to minority status. One freshman Democrat watched her senior colleagues with a mixture of sympathy and frustration:

> *It's like a messy nasty divorce. You go from a comfortable situation in marriage to a very uncomfortable one. There's no money, no autonomy, and*

people are bitter. John Dingell [MI] just doesn't know how to deal with it. People are bitter, and everyone is chafing.[7]

Others called attention to the so-called "caucus of 89 former chairs and subcommittee chairs." These were the especially miserable Democrats, such as former Commerce Committee Chair John Dingell (MI), who had lost considerable power in the Republican takeover. The Commerce Committee Democrats "are heavily sedated and deep in therapy," joked freshman Republican Dan Frisa (NY) referring specifically to the attitudes of Dingell (MI) and the formerly powerful Commerce subcommittee chairs Henry Waxman (CA) and Edward Markey (MA).[8] A senior Appropriations Democrat expressed frustration at minority status in straightforward terms:

It's awful! I hate it! I want to get out of being in the minority as quickly as possible. As a minority, you can have no impact on policy. You can get involved. You can make a difference, but only to the extent that the majority allows you the room.[9]

Given that the Democrats are the party that favors government, believing that government spending and intervention can solve pressing social and economic problems, their policy impotence during the first 100 days was especially painful. "Overall, there is a sense of frustration for those who came here to try to do good things."[10] In this sense, Republicans who believe in government restraint are better able to cope with minority status than their activist Democratic counterparts.

Republicans relished the Democratic fulminations. "Exhausting as the schedule has been, the thrill of being in charge keeps you going," said Phil Crane (IL).[11] "The agony of the Democrats is worth watching." For forty years, Republicans had struggled with their "permanent minority" status. Many of them couldn't resist playing payback for their years of mistreatment. For first-term Democrats, anxious to work with the new majority, the vengeful attitudes of the majority leaders were an obstacle to cooperation. As one freshman Democrat observed about the chair of his principal committee:

Chairman ____ is somewhat rigid and embittered about the past. I've been working hard to work with him. I want to work with everyone. Some of them are so embittered, though, they can't get past that.[12]

Some Republicans were trying to live up to a higher standard than their predecessors but most admitted that treating the Democrats fairly was not their primary goal:

When the Democrats had the committee they were obnoxious. So we don't exactly have a lot of sympathy on our side of the aisle for saying, "Oh we treated them badly yesterday."

... But I'm not really into paybacks either. They say I run my subcommittee like a professor. We have been more fair to them, but that isn't our top priority.[13]

Still, a few Democrats appeared to accept, if not enjoy, the role reversal of minority status. Ron Coleman (TX) wryly pointed out that the Republicans taught them minority tactics, "Gingrich called [former Speaker] Jim Wright (TX) a liar and a cheat and now he's getting the same from us."[14] Black Caucus member Albert Wynn (MD) also took a more realpolitik view, "I don't expect them [the Republicans] to be fair. That would spoil the war."[15]

THE PERSISTENTLY INFLUENTIAL SOUTH

Not all Democrats were treated with equal contempt by the leadership. Southern Democrats were generally encouraged to bring their amendments to the floor by the Rules Committee. "This has been a conscious decision," said a leadership staffer. "Their views are like ours." Democrats who pledged to work with the majority were treated better by the Republicans than by their own leadership. Mississippi Democrat Mike Parker, who, several months later, was on the verge of becoming the fourth House Democrat to switch parties, forcefully made this point when asked about his adjustment to minority status:

I've always been in the minority. I was in the minority last year. Now that the Republicans are in charge, I'm still in the minority.

... I haven't been marginally better treated by the Republicans. I've been treated much much better by the Republicans. I have learned that under the Republicans I can be treated with respect. I've been treated far better by the Republicans than by my own leadership. I will always be beholden to the Republicans for the way they've treated me.[16]

The success of the new majority in winning the support of conservative, southern Democrats is a product of the electoral forces that have reshaped the region. The southern members who formed The Coalition admitted that the point of the group was survival. Tennessee Democrat John Tanner lamented the extremism in both parties:

It can all be traced back to the 1962 Baker v. Carr *decision: one man, one vote. Now there's a bias in redistricting. Every ten years the state legislature gets a recommendation from Congress. The result is that Democratic districts get more Democratic, Republican districts more Republican. There are fewer and fewer districts in the middle. We are the roadkill. We are the yellow line in the middle of the road that gets hit on both sides. Because the districts in Congress are more and more one-party dominated, the American Congress is more extreme.*

> *What you have in Congress after 30 years of this redistricting is more and more polarization by party. The more extreme elements of the Republican leadership have risen to the leadership. They'll go over the edge. It's just a matter of time.*
>
> *I have a left-over district after everyone else got through cutting into it. Fewer and fewer districts are competitive. There are fewer moderates. We are the roadkill inside and outside of Congress.*[17]

By refusing to pursue a policy of inclusion, the liberal Democratic leadership lost the Tanners and the Parkers in their party to the other side on key votes. As alternatives, minority leaders Richard Gephardt (MO) and David Bonior (MI) generally offered amendments to Republican bills that could generate only half the support necessary to be taken seriously. In the few cases in which the liberal Democrats made room for their southern bloc, they won (Chapter 6) or came close to winning (Chapter 7).

While the number of southern Democrats is dwindling, this does not mean the region has lost influence in Congress. The Contract's prime movers were largely from southern states: Gingrich (GA), Armey (TX), Delay (TX), Livingston (LA), Spence (SC), to name only a few. Given its southern inspiration, it is fitting and predictable that the Contract with America won the widespread support of the region's white members and constituents.

THE SENATE: THE CONTRACT'S GRAVEYARD?

While the focus of this book has been on the new politics of the U.S. House, the Congress is, of course, a bicameral institution. The framers of the Constitution designed the two chambers to be different in many important respects. The Senate, for example, was intended to be a highly deliberative institution that would consider legislation more slowly than the House. Rules within each chamber have ensured that this design has been carried out. First, the Senate operates with far fewer rules and it has no rules committee to structure floor debate and limit amendments. Senate action can be held hostage to a single senator or group of senators through the use of the filibuster—a permissible procedure in which senators seize control of the senate floor with the intention of talking a bill off the legislative schedule, thereby postponing its consideration indefinitely. Ending a filibuster requires a cloture motion that must receive sixty votes to quiet the protesting member(s).[18] Through the use of the filibuster, Senator Robert Byrd (WV) had stalled action on the unfunded mandates legislation for several days—one of the least controversial pieces of the Contract. Second, the House has many more members and can therefore distribute the legislative workload in a more efficient manner, permitting members to be highly specialized. Senators must cover a broader range of issues and themes not only because they number only 100, but because they represent entire states. Finally, the Speaker is a much more powerful leader than the Senate Majority Leader. Bringing strong party government to the House has been no easy task, but enforcing party discipline in the Senate on crucial votes has been next to impossible. Hence, the Republicans' intense frustration with Senator Mark O. Hatfield's (OR) vote against the balanced budget amendment (Chapter 4).

As the Republicans in the House raced through their 100-day agenda, it was little wonder that Democrats were relieved that the Senate operated at a slower pace. When they had been in charge, these same Democrats had frequently complained about the Senate's relative incapacity to act. Now, however, the House liberals recognized that Democratically inclined interest groups opposed to the Contract would have more time to mobilize against its passage. If unable to stop the legislation, these groups would have time to force the House Republicans to compromise once the bills reached the House-Senate conference committee. There the Senate and House versions of the legislation would be reconciled and Democrats could hope that the Senate version would prevail.

Democrats were also counting upon the Senate Republicans' weaker commitment to the Contract. By fall, though, the Senate was catching up to the House. With several Republican Senators (Dole, Lugar, Specter, Gramm) running for president, the competition for leadership on issues helped win support for welfare reform. The welfare legislation even passed with strong Democratic support on an 87–12 vote.

CONGRESS AND RESPONSIBLE PARTY GOVERNMENT

The Contract can be understood as an effort to introduce responsible party government into a legislature that has heretofore been described as an inchoate collection of atomized interests. Many of the opening day reforms (see Chapter 3) were intended to strengthen the role of political parties by strengthening House leadership. While the Senate did not fully follow the House precedent, by midsummer even the exceedingly independent Republican senators adopted measures to strengthen party and leadership control. These measures included limits on seniority, secret ballots on the votes for committee chairs, and an agreement to adopt an agenda at the beginning of each Congress.[19] Impressed by the accomplishments of the new House majority and influenced by younger members newly elected from the "other body," senators now see there are advantages to the Gingrich-Armey model of leadership. House Republicans, after all, had maintained their unity well beyond the first 100 days to pass a budget plan and the major appropriations bills with little dissent within their own ranks.

The Contract also furthered party government because the Contract's framers invited the public to hold GOP representatives accountable for their reform program. This was a risky move given the independence of the Senate in the American legislative system. What if the Contract bills did not pass into law? Would the public understand that the pledge was to bring the measures to a vote, not necessarily to pass them (right away)? House leaders worried about the Senate's slow action on the Contract. "You don't get credit for enacting measures that don't pass,"[20] admitted Speaker Gingrich's Chief-of-Staff Dan Meyer. But Republicans hoped that they would get partial credit: "People are realistic. Voters are more sophisticated than you give them credit for. If it fails to pass, we can still go back and tell them that this is good stuff and that the people who voted for it should be rewarded. Let's get it next time."[21] Much depends on how patient the public is willing to be. If the Republicans failed to pass their program and the people expected it to pass, the party responsibility model would predict a thorough trouncing for the GOP in the coming election.

THE PUBLIC'S VIEW OF THE 104TH CONGRESS

The Contract with America promised that the Republicans would restore the bond of trust between citizens and representatives. Did their aggressive work of the first 100 days accomplish this worthy goal? Close observers had to be impressed by the Republicans' resolve and party discipline. They did what they said they would do. Although no one expected the Senate to move as quickly, its initial attempts to act on Contract items were disappointing. In addition to defeating the Balanced Budget Amendment by a single vote, the Senate generally formulated narrower versions of many of the Contract proposals. The House leadership has had difficulty building cross-chamber coalitions for the legislation in its pure form. Nevertheless, by fall the Senate was moving ahead steadily as Majority Leader Dole (KS) was making good on his pledge to bring every Contract item to a vote.

Congress is judged by the politically aware public by the extent to which it can pass legislation.[22] Perhaps because passage has been slow, the public's assessment of the legislative branch had warmed only slightly by April, 1995. Only 38 percent reported having read or heard anything about the Contract with America.[23] Congressional approval ratings increased from the high teens to the low forties in January when the new Congress convened. By the end of the 100 days, though, approval had dropped slightly (see Figure 10-1).[24] Forty percent approval was still a solid improvement over the pathetic ratings of 18–19 percent the year before. Democrats, however, had successfully shortened the Republican honeymoon by conveying the fear that impending program cuts would be too deep.[25] In a March poll by *ABC News/Washington Post,* people expressed more confidence in President Clinton's ability to protect the environment, America's children, and Social Security while doubting Republican commitment in these areas. According to solid majorities, Republicans still outperformed the president in areas such as reforming welfare, controlling crime, cutting taxes, and reducing the deficit.[26] Perot voters were reportedly disappointed about the failure of term limits and the balanced budget amendment—issues that Perot's grassroots groups had heavily promoted.[27] Two-thirds of

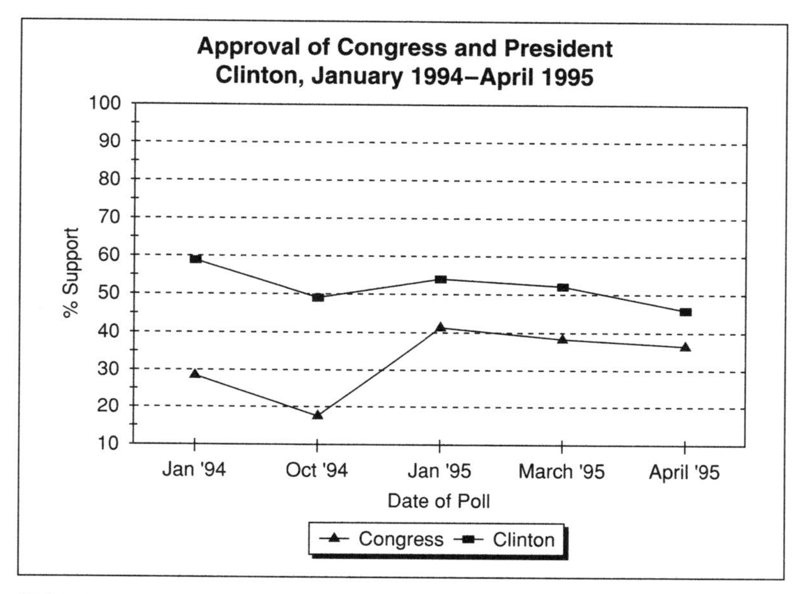

FIGURE 10-1 **Presidential and Congressional Approval Ratings through the First 100 Days**

Source: ABC News/*Washington Post* Monthly Polls.

Perot supporters voted Republican in 1994, but they may not stay in the Republican camp if they remain dissatisfied with the pace of change.

LOOKING TO THE 1996 ELECTIONS

Following the first 100 days, House Republicans were left with a full 630 days in the 104th Congress (not including the recesses) and much could be accomplished in that time. The Contract will be back in 1996 as a major campaign theme. Republican members will campaign on congressional reform and accountability, welfare reform, and other Contract items that did pass while promising to build momentum toward victory on issues that did not. But Republicans will also have to defend their spending cuts. The months between April, 1995, and November, 1996, would determine whether people would be willing to accept program cuts to solve the deficit problem. If the House leadership did not present deficit reduction as a positive in people's lives, they would face certain defeat in 1996. The short-run impact of the Contract also depended upon the President's actions. Most of the Contract's themes remained popular with the public. The Republicans would have to blame President Clinton for the Contract's failures to enhance the likelihood of a Republican President and a Republican Speaker in 1996.

THE CONTRACT AND THE SHIFT IN THE POLICY AGENDA

Perhaps the most lasting impression the Contract will leave on American politics is the agenda change that it has wrought. As Chapters 4 through 9 indicate, new proposals emerged in the policy debate that had never been given a hearing before. This shift is no trivial matter since agendas eventually shape what passes into law. While the policy change likely to come from the 1994 elections may not be on the scale of the New Deal legislation that followed the 1932 and 1934 elections, it signals a significant step away from the legacy of government centralization left by that New Deal revolution.

The public may never come to understand or appreciate the policy redirection brought about by the Republican capture of the U.S. House. This text has documented a few of the steps toward policy change in the space allotted for a book of average length. Some may say that this book is premature, that I should have waited to see how much of the Contract would pass into law before writing, that the Contract was little more than a cloud of dust—by the time it settles, nothing will have changed. But already things have changed. Welfare is no longer a federal entitlement. The criticism that, because the Senate has been slow to act, change has not occurred implies that the only changes that matter are the ones that alter the U.S. Code and do so quickly and radically. This "legicentric" view strikes me as naïve and shortsighted given the complexity of policymaking in a decentralized political system. The 435 House members that now have records on the Contract with America's proposals will have to defend those records regardless of whether all the proposals become law. In addition, the Republican leadership has set new standards for what party leadership is capable of doing in Congress. No matter how long Republicans maintain their majority status in the House, students of politics will look back on the first 100 days of the 104th Congress with fascination at the will and initiative that established some important new precedents while redirecting the policy debate for years to come.

▶Endnotes

Chapter 1

1. This would increase to 231 with the April, 1995, switch of Georgia Democrat Nathan Deal to the Republican party; 232 with the June, 1995, switch of Texas Democrat Greg Laughlin; and 233 with the July switch of Louisiana Democrat Billy Tauzin.
2. Cited in: "Clinton: A Group Portrait," *The American Enterprise* 5:6 (November–December 1994) pp. 112–113.
3. Jon Healey, "Jubilant GOP Strives to Keep Legislative Feet on Ground," *Congressional Quarterly Weekly Report,* 11/12/94, p. 3215.
4. Steve Langdon, "Clinton's High Victory Rate Conceals Disappointments," *Congressional Quarterly Weekly Report,* 12/31/94, p. 3620.
5. Langdon, *Congressional Quarterly Weekly Report,* 12/31/94, p. 3619–3620.
6. Cited in: "Clinton: A Group Portrait," p. 112.
7. Eric M. Uslaner has detailed this long term decline in confidence. See: *The Decline of Comity in Congress* (Ann Arbor, MI: University of Michigan Press, 1994).
8. Everett Carll Ladd, ed., *America at the Polls 1994* (Storrs, CT: The Roper Center for Public Opinion Research, 1995).
9. Robert Merry, "Voters' Demand for Change Puts Clinton on Defensive," *Congressional Quarterly Weekly Report,* 11/12/94, p. 3207.
10. *The Washington Post,* 11/10/94, p. A1, A28.
11. Interview with Congressman Charles Canady (FL), 2/2/95.
12. American Political Science Association Committee on Political Parties, "Toward a More Responsible Two-Party System," supplement to the *American Political Science Review* 44:3 (September 1950).
13. V. O. Key, Jr., *Politics, Parties and Pressure Groups,* 5th edition (New York: Thomas Y. Crowell, 1964) p. 675.
14. Paul S. Herrnson, "Why the United States Does Not Have Responsible Parties," *Perspectives on Political Science* 21:2 (Spring 1992) pp. 91–99.
15. Merry, *Congressional Quarterly Weekly Report,* 11/12/94, p. 3208.
16. Interview with Republican Pollster Frank Luntz, 3/24/95.
17. Newt Gingrich, Richard K. Armey and the House Republican Conference. *Contract with America* (New York: Times Books, 1994).
18. Interview with Scott Reed, RNC Executive Director, 1/31/95.
19. Stephen Ansolabehere, David Brady and Morris Fiorina, "The Vanishing Marginals and Electoral Responsiveness," *British Journal of Political Science* 22 (1992) pp. 21–38, quote on p. 36.
20. William F. Connelly and John J. Pitney, *Congress' Permanent Minority?* (Lanham, MD: Rowman and Littlefield, 1994) Chapter 6.

21. Connelly and Pitney (1994) p. 140.
22. Paul S. Herrnson, *Congressional Elections: Campaigning at Home and in Washington.* (Washington, DC: Congressional Quarterly Press, 1995).
23. Herrnson (1994).
24. Jonathan Krasno and Donald Philip Green, "Preempting Quality Challengers in House Elections," *Journal of Politics* 50 (1988) pp. 920–36; Alan Ehrenhalt, *The United States of Ambition: Politicians, Power and the Pursuit of Office.* (New York: Random House, 1991); Gary Jacobson, *The Electoral Origins of Divided Government* (Boulder, CO: Westview Press, 1990); Gary Jacobson, *The Politics of Congressional Elections,* 3rd ed. (New York: Harper Collins, 1992).
25. Linda Fowler, *Candidates, Congress and the American Democracy* (Ann Arbor, MI: University of Michigan Press, 1993) p. 112.
26. David Canon argues that there are certain electoral climates that favor amateurs, as when a candidate can claim to be "above politics," or run as a "citizen politician." See his *Actors, Athletes and Astronauts* (Chicago: University of Chicago Press, 1990) p. 35.
27. Herrnson (1995). Jacobson (1992). Gary Jacobson, "The Effects of Campaign Spending in Congressional Elections," in *American Political Science Review* 72 (1978) pp. 469–491.
28. Jacobson (1978).
29. Herrnson (1995) p. 213.
30. Interview with Tony Blankley, Press Secretary for Speaker Newt Gingrich, 2/17/95.
31. Interview with Congressman Dana Rohrabacher (CA), 3/30/95.
32. Interview with Congressman Bob Inglis (SC), 4/5/95.
33. Interview with Congressman John Boehner (OH), 4/4/95.
34. Herrnson (1995).
35. Herrnson (1995) reports that scandal has the second largest impact (first is the presence of a minor party candidate) on incumbent vote shares in the 1992 House elections. See Table 9-1, p. 207 and Appendix A-2, p. 273.
36. Philip Klinkner, *The Losing Parties* (New Haven, CT: Yale University Press, 1994).
37. See also the post-election analysis by David Brady, John F. Cogan and Douglas Rivers, "How the Republicans Captured the House," Hoover Institution Essays in Public Policy, Stanford University, 1995.
38. Robert Marshall Wells, "A Longtime Voting Bloc Falls with Southern Democrats," *Congressional Quarterly Weekly Report,* 12/31/94, p. 3627–3628.
39. David Rohde, *Parties and Leaders in the Post-Reform House* (Chicago: University of Chicago Press, 1991) pp. 166–167.
40. Janet Hook, "Conservative Freshman Class Eager to Seize the Moment," *Congressional Quarterly Weekly Report,* 1/7/95, p. 47.
41. James Q. Wilson, *The Amateur Democrat* (Chicago: University of Chicago Press, 1962) pp. 18–21. For a more refined typology of the amateur politician, see David Canon, *Actors, Athletes and Astronauts* (Chicago: University of Chicago Press, 1990). Wilson's amateur is closest to what Canon calls the "policy amateur."
42. David Brady, *Critical Elections and Congressional Policy Making* (Stanford, CA: Stanford University Press, 1988). David Brady and John Ettling, "The Electoral Connection and the Decline of Partisanship in the 20th Century House of Representatives," in *Congress and the Presidency* 11:1 (Spring 1984) pp. 19–36; David Brady, Joseph Cooper and Patricia Hurley, "The Decline of Party in the U.S. House of Representatives, 1887–1968," in *Legislative Studies Quarterly* 4:3 (August 1979) pp. 381–407.
43. Connelly and Pitney (1994).

Chapter 2

1. Interview with Congressman Philip Crane (IL), 3/20/95.
2. Interview with Congressman Joel Hefley (CO), 3/29/95.

3. Interview with Congressman Bill Goodling (PA), 4/5/95.
4. Interview with Congresswoman Barbara Cubin (WY), 3/29/95.
5. Interview with Congressman Philip Crane (IL), 3/20/95.
6. Interview with Ed Gillespie, Press Secretary for Richard K. Armey (TX), 2/10/95.
7. Interview with Congressman John Boehner (OH), 4/4/95.
8. Of the dozens of members interviewed for this study, only a few expressed the leadership's optimism. These included Chris Shays (CT) and Bill Emerson (MO).
9. Gingrich, Armey, et al. (1994) p. 4.
10. Gingrich, Armey, et al. (1994) p. vii–ix.
11. Interview with Chuck Greener, RNC Communications Director, 2/15/95.
12. Interview with Brian Gaston, House Republican Conference Committee, 2/17/95.
13. Interview with Brian Gaston, House Republican Conference Committee, 2/17/95.
14. Interview with Tony Blankley, Press Secretary for House Speaker Newt Gingrich, 2/17/95.
15. Interview with Congressman Amo Houghton (NY), 2/24/95.
16. Interview with Congressman Bill Goodling (PA), 4/5/95.
17. Interview with Congressman Christopher Shays (CT), 4/5/95.
18. Interview with Congressman Dana Rohrabacher (CA), 3/30/95.
19. Interview with Congressman Carlos Moorhead (CA), 2/15/95.
20. *New York Times,* October 9, 1994, A26.
21. Interview with Congressman Charles Canady (FL), 2/2/95.
22. Interview with Congressman Mark Souder (IN), 2/2/95.
23. Interview with Congressman Jerry Weller (IL), 2/15/95.
24. Interview with Congressman John Tanner (TN), 4/5/95.
25. Interview with Congressman Glen Browder (D-AL), 3/31/95.
26. Interview with Congressman Scotty Baesler (KY), 6/9/95.
27. Interview with Congressman Jerry Weller (IL), 2/15/95.
28. Interview with Congressman Jerry Weller (IL), 2/15/95.
29. Interview with Congressman Dick Chrysler (MI), 2/14/95.
30. Interview with Congresswoman Enid Waldholtz (UT), 2/10/95.
31. Interview with Congresswoman Enid Waldholtz (UT), 2/10/95.
32. Interview with Congressman Peter Hoekstra (MI), 3/1/95.
33. Interview with Congressman Bob Inglis (SC), 4/5/95.
34. Interview with Congressman Bob Ney (OH), 2/22/95.
35. Interview with Congressman Bob Ehrlich (MD), 1/26/95.
36. Interview with Congressman Mark Souder (IN), 2/2/95.
37. Interview with Barry Jackson, Staff Director, House Republican Conference Committee, 3/1/95.
38. Interview with Chuck Greener, RNC Communications Director, 2/15/95.
39. Interview with Congressman Rick White (WA), 1/26/95.
40. James Gimpel, *National Elections and the Autonomy of American State Party Systems* (Pittsburgh, PA: University of Pittsburgh Press, 1996). Chapter 5.
41. David R. Mayhew, *Congress: The Electoral Connection* (New Haven, CT: Yale University Press, 1975). John Kingdon, *Candidates for Office: Beliefs and Strategies* (New York: Random House, 1968). John Kingdon, "Politicians' Beliefs About Voters," in *American Political Science Review* 61 (1967) pp. 137–145.
42. Kingdon (1967; 1968).
43. Interview with Lincoln Diaz-Balart (FL), 2/10/95.
44. Interview with Ileana Ros-Lehtinen (FL), 2/22/95.
45. R. Douglas Arnold, *The Logic of Congressional Action* (New Haven, CT: Yale University Press, 1990).
46. Interview with Congressman Ray LaHood (IL), 2/22/95.
47. Interview with Congressman Ray LaHood (IL), 2/22/95.

48. Interview with Congressman Jim Bunn (OR), 3/17/95.
49. Interview with Congressman Ray LaHood (IL), 2/22/95.
50. Interview with Congressman Ileana Ros-Lehtinen (FL) 2/22/95.
51. Barbara Sinclair, *Majority Leadership in the U.S. House* (Baltimore, MD: Johns Hopkins University Press, 1983).
52. Sinclair (1981) p. 28.
53. For a pictorial history with a description of Kennedy's first 100 days, see Martin Agronsky (ed.) *Let Us Begin* (New York: Simon and Schuster, 1961).
54. I am indebted for my knowledge of this fact to John J. Pitney of Claremont McKenna College.
55. Steven S. Smith, *Call to Order: Floor Politics in the House and Senate* (Washington, D.C.: Brookings, 1989). William Connelly and John J. Pitney, *Congress' Permanent Minority?* (Lanham, MD: Rowman and Littlefield, 1994).
56. Interview with Congressman Rick White (WA) 1/26/95.
57. Interview with Congresswoman Lynn Rivers (MI) 2/22/95.

Chapter 3

1. Barbara Sinclair, *Majority Leadership in the U.S. House* (Baltimore, MD: Johns Hopkins University Press, 1983).
2. John R. Petrocik, "Realignment: New Party Coalitions and the Nationalization of the South," *Journal of Politics* 49 (1987) pp. 347–375; Dorothy Davidson Nesbit, "Changing Partisanship Among Southern Party Activists," in *Journal of Politics* 50 (1988) pp. 322–334; Bruce A. Campbell, "Patterns of Change in the Partisan Loyalties of Native Southerners: 1952–1972," in *Journal of Politics* 39 (1977) pp. 730–761; Paul Allen Beck, "Partisan Dealignment in the Postwar South," in *American Political Science Review* 71 (1977) pp. 477–496.
3. Linda Fowler, *Candidates, Congress and the American Democracy* (Ann Arbor, MI: University of Michigan Press, 1993) p. 144.
4. Michael Barone and Grant Ujifusa, *The Almanac of American Politics* (Washington, D.C.: National Journal, 1984) p. 291.
5. Catalina Camia, "Texans Top List of Aides Picked to Help Gingrich," *Congressional Quarterly Weekly Report,* 12/10/94, p. 3492.
6. Roger H. Davidson and Walter J. Oleszek, *Congress and Its Members,* 4th edition (Washington, D.C.: Congressional Quarterly Press, 1994).
7. Interview with Tony Blankley, Press Secretary for Speaker Newt Gingrich, 2/17/95.
8. Interview with Tony Blankley, Press Secretary for Speaker Newt Gingrich, 2/17/95.
9. Interview with Robert Livingston (LA), 4/13/95.
10. Interview with Congressman Robert Livingston (LA), 4/13/95.
11. Interview with Congressman Chris Cox (CA), 4/5/95.
12. David W. Rohde, *Parties and Leaders in the Post-Reform House* (Chicago: University of Chicago Press, 1991); Paul S. Herrnson and James G. Gimpel, "District Conditions and Primary Divisiveness in Congressional Elections," in *Political Research Quarterly* (March 1995) 48:1:117–134.
13. David W. Brady, *Critical Elections and Congressional Policy Making* (Stanford, CA: Stanford University Press, 1988).
14. "New Chairman Swing to Right; Freshmen Get Choice Posts," *Congressional Quarterly Weekly Report,* 12/10/95, p. 3494.
15. Interview with Congressman Paul Kanjorski (PA), 3/29/95.
16. Interview with Congressman Paul Kanjorski (PA), 3/29/95.
17. Interview with Congressman Ben Cardin (MD), 3/1/95.
18. Interview with Congressman Ben Cardin (MD), 3/1/95.
19. Interview with Congressman Rick White (WA), 1/25/95.

20. David S. Cloud, "GOP, To Its Own Great Delight, Enacts House Rules Changes," *Congressional Quarterly Weekly Report,* 1/7/95, pp. 13–16.
21. Cloud, *Congressional Quarterly Weekly Report,* 1/7/95, pp. 13–15.
22. David S. Cloud, "GOP's House-Cleaning Sweep Changes Rules, Cuts Groups," *Congressional Quarterly Weekly Report,* 12/10/94, p. 3488.
23. *Roll Call,* 1/23/95, p. A10.
24. *Roll Call,* 2/2/95, pp. A1, A15.
25. Interview with Congressman Albert Wynn (MD), 2/28/95.
26. Interview with Congressman David Dreier (CA), 3/10/95.
27. Leroy N. Rieselbach, *Congressional Reform* (Washington, D.C.: CQ Press, 1986).
28. On the importance of traceability to accountability, see: R. Douglas Arnold, *The Logic of Congressional Action* (New Haven, CT: Yale University Press, 1990).

Chapter 4

1. *Gallup Poll Monthly,* 2/1/94, p. 11.
2. James D. Savage, *Balanced Budgets and American Politics* (Ithaca: Cornell University Press, 1988).
3. Gary Jacobson, *The Electoral Origins of Divided Government* (Boulder, CO: Westview Press, 1990).
4. R. Douglas Arnold, *The Logic of Congressional Action* (New Haven: Yale University Press, 1990) p. 111.
5. Jacobson (1990) p. 111.
6. R. Douglas Arnold (1990) p. 73.
7. Donald Kettl, *Deficit Politics: Public Budgeting in Its Institutional and Historical Context* (New York: Macmillan, 1992); James M. Buchanan, "Public Debt and Capital Formation," in D.R. Lee (ed.) *Taxation and the Deficit Economy* (San Franscisco: Pacific Research Institute for Public Policy, 1986) Chapter 6. For a general treatment of budgetary control issues, see: Alan Schick, *The Federal Budget: Politics, Policy, Process* (Washington, DC: The Brookings Institution, 1995) Chapter 10.
8. Quoted in Kettl (1992) p. 31.
9. Buchanan (1986) p. 185. Schick (1995) Chapter 10.
10. Kettl (1992) p. 32.
11. Arnold (1990) p. 101.
12. Gingrich, Armey, et al. (1994).
13. For historical background on proposed balanced budget amendments, I have relied upon the discussion in James V. Saturno, "A Balanced Budget Amendment: Procedural Issues." *Congressional Research Service Issue Brief.* Washington, D.C.: Library of Congress, January 17, 1995. Also: James D. Savage, "Thomas Jefferson's Balanced Budget Amendment: An Introduction to the Symposium on the Federal Budget," in *Journal of Law and Politics* 9:1 (Fall 1992) pp. 1–7.
14. Sondra J. Nixon, "Budget Amendments: An Idea that Never Goes Out of Style," *Congressional Quarterly Weekly Report,* 1/14/95, pp. 143–145.
15. Alan J. Auerbach, "Taxes and Spending in the Age of Deficits: A View from Washington and Academe," in *National Tax Journal* 45:3 (September 1992) pp. 239–241; Neal Devins, "A Symbolic Balanced Budget Amendment," in *Journal of Law and Politics,* 9:1 (Fall 1992) pp. 61–88. Also: Louis Fisher, "The Effects of a Balanced Budget Amendment on Political Institutions," in *Journal of Law and Politics,* 9:1 (Fall 1992) pp. 89–104.
16. Schick (1995) p. 196.
17. *Washington Times,* 1/7/95, p. A1, A7.
18. Nixon, *Congressional Quarterly Weekly Report,* 1/14/95, pp. 142–144.
19. Arnold (1990) p. 111.

20. Andrew Taylor, "Amendment Remains a Gamble Despite Its Popularity," *Congressional Quarterly Weekly Report,* 1/14/95, p. 147.
21. *Washington Times,* 1/18/95, A1, A9.
22. Interview with Ed Gillespie, Press Secretary for Majority Leader Richard K. Armey (TX), 2/10/95.
23. William T. Bianco, *Trust: Representatives and Constituents* (Ann Arbor, MI: University of Michigan Press, 1994).
24. Bianco (1994) p. 158.
25. David R. Mayhew, *Congress: The Electoral Connection* (New Haven, CT: Yale University Press, 1975).
26. David W. Brady, *Critical Elections and Congressional Policy-Making* (Stanford, CA: Stanford University Press, 1988).
27. Ideally we would want data on a representative's true reelection constituency rather than Census data on the entire constituency. Unfortunately, however, such refined data collection would be a costly undertaking and is far beyond the budgetary scope of this project.
28. John Mark Hansen, "Public Constituencies for Deficit Finance," Paper presented at the annual meeting of the American Political Science Association, New York, September 1994. pp. 11–13.
29. Lewis Froman, *Congressmen and Their Constituencies* (Skokie, IL: Rand McNally, 1963). David W. Rohde, *Parties and Leaders in the Post Reform House* (Chicago: University of Chicago Press, 1991).
30. David J. Lanoue, "Partisan Schemas and Economic Voting: The Federal Budget Deficit and the 1988 Presidential Election," *Political Behavior* 13:4 (1991) pp. 285–302; Hansen (1994).
31. Mayhew (1974) p. 57.
32. Roger Davidson and Walter Oleszek, *Congress and Its Members,* 4th edition (Washington, DC: Congressional Quarterly, 1994) pp. 375–377.
33. D. Roderick Kiewiet and Mathew D. McCubbins, "Presidential Influence on Congressional Appropriations Decisions," in *American Journal of Political Science* 32:4 (1988) pp. 713–735.
34. Antony R. Petrilla, "The Role of the Line-Item Veto in the Federal Balance of Power," in *Harvard Journal of Legislation* 31:2 (Summer 1994) pp. 469–509.
35. Neil Berch, "The Item Veto in the States: An Analysis of the Effects Over Time," in *Social Science Journal* 29:3 (1992) pp. 335–346.
36. Thomas E. Cronin and Jeffrey J. Weill, "An Item Veto for the President?" in *Congress and the Presidency* 12:2 (Autumn 1985) pp. 127–149.
37. For a general treatment of the impoundment issue, see Virginia McMurtry, "The President and the Budget Process: Expanded Impoundment and Item Veto Proposals," Washington, DC: Library of Congress, Congressional Research Service, November 28, 1994.
38. Here I have drawn on the discussion by McMurtry (1994, 2).
39. Gingrich, Armey, et al. (1994).
40. House Republican Conference Committee, *Legislative Digest,* 1/28/95, p. 28.
41. Douglas Holtz-Eakin, "The Line-Item Veto and Public Sector Budgets," *Journal of Public Economics* 36 (1988) pp. 269–292; Glenn Abney and Thomas P. Lauth, "The Line-Item Veto in the States: An Instrument for Fiscal Restraint or an Instrument for Partisanship?" in *Public Administration Review* 45 (1985) pp. 372–377.
42. Quoted in *The New York Times,* 2/3/95, p. B8.
43. David C. Nice, "The Item Veto and Expenditure Restraint," in *Journal of Politics* 50:2 (June 1988) p. 489.
44. A survey of 118 governors and former governors by the Cato Institute, a libertarian think tank, showed that 92 percent favored a federal line-item veto provision. Reported in the *Washington Times* 1/27/95, p. A1.

45. Nice (1988). Holtz-Eakin (1988). Also: Burton Abrams and William R. Dougan, "The Effects of Constitutional Restraints on Governmental Spending," in *Public Choice* 49 (1986) pp. 101–116.
46. Berch (1992) p. 343.
47. John R. Carter and David Schap, "Line-Item Veto: Where is Thy Sting?" in *Journal of Economic Perspectives* 4:2 (Spring 1990) pp. 103–118.
48. Interview with Congressman Bob Ney (OH), 2/22/95.
49. *Washington Times,* 2/7/92, p. A9.
50. Lanoue (1991).
51. The standard error for the party variable is inflated in the model for the Stenholm version of the line-item veto because of collinearity with other variables in the model.
52. The low significance of the Perot vote variable in the Contract model in Table A2 is due to its collinear relationship with related variables.
53. *The Hill,* July 19, 1995, p. 46.

Chapter 5

1. William J. Chambliss, "Policing the Ghetto Underclass: The Politics of Law and Law Enforcement," in *Social Problems* 41:2 (May 1994) pp. 177–193.
2. John J. DiIulio, Jr., "The Question of Black Crime," *Public Interest* 117 (1994) 3–32. Also: "White Lies About Black Crime," *Public Interest* 118 (1995) 31–44.
3. DiIulio (1995). Keith D. Harries, "Black Crime and Criminal Victimization," in D. Georges-Abeyie (ed.), *The Criminal Justice System and Blacks* (New York: Clark Boardman, 1984); Coramae Richey Mann, *Unequal Justice: A Question of Color* (Bloomington, IN: Indiana University Press, 1993) pp. 46–52.
4. Wesley G. Skogan, *Disorder and Decline* (New York: The Free Press, 1990), Chapter 1. James Q. Wilson, "Crime and American Culture," *Public Interest* 70 (1983) pp. 22–48. Robert J. Sampson and John H. Laub, *Crime in the Making* (Cambridge: Harvard University Press, 1993). Judith Blau and Peter Blau, "The Cost of Inequality: Metropolitan Structure and Violent Crime," in *American Sociological Review* 47 (1982) pp. 114–129. Jonathan Simon, *Poor Discipline: Parole and the Social Control of the Underclass, 1890–1990* (Chicago: University of Chicago Press, 1993). Miles D. Harer and Darrell Steffensmeier, "The Differing Effects of Economic Inequality on Black and White Rates of Violence," *Social Forces* 70:4 (June 1992) pp. 1035–1054.
5. Wilson (1983). Of course few legislators would take the position that only one strategy will do. Crime control policy is usually a mix of the two, with some favoring traditional law enforcement while others favor prevention.
6. DiIulio (1994).
7. Joan Petersilia, "Racial Disparities in the Criminal Justice System: Executive Summary of Rand Institute Study, 1983," in Daniel Georges-Abeyie (ed.), *The Criminal Justice System and Blacks* (New York: Clark Boardman, 1984) pp. 225–253.
8. DiIulio (1994).
9. David C. Baldus, George Woodworth and Charles A. Pulaski, Jr., *Equal Justice and the Death Penalty* (Boston: Northeastern University Press, 1990).
10. Lawrence M. Mead, *The New Politics of Poverty* (New York: Basic Books, 1992) p. 40.
11. Mead (1992) p. 41.
12. *Gallup Poll Monthly,* August 1994, p. 16. The poll revealed that 52 percent thought the Republicans could best deal with crime, compared to a minuscule 11 percent who thought the Democrats could best handle the issue.
13. The funding for this provision was more than doubled to provide an estimated 100,000 new police.
14. Holly Idelson, "More Cops, Jails: House Takes a $28 Billion Aim at Crime," *Congressional Quarterly Weekly Report,* 4/23/94, pp. 1001–1004.

15. Holly Idelson, "In Surprising Turnaround, House Ok's Weapons Ban," *Congressional Quarterly Weekly Report,* 5/7/94, pp. 1119–1123.
16. *Roll Call* 8/15/94, p. 1, 16.
17. Holly Idelson and Richard Sammon, "Marathon Talks Produce New Anti-Crime Bill," *Congressional Quarterly Weekly Report,* 8/20/94, p. 2453.
18. For additional details on the contents of the Violent Crime Control and Law Enforcement Act of 1994, see: Elizabeth Bazan, Keith Bea, Suzanne Cavanagh, David Teasley and Charles Doyle, "Crime Control: Summary of the Violent Crime Control and Law Enforcement Act of 1994," (Washington, D.C.: Library of Congress, Congressional Research Service, November 11, 1994).
19. David Masci, "$30 Billion Anti-Crime Bill Heads to Clinton's Desk," *Congressional Quarterly Weekly Report,* 8/27/95, p. 2493.
20. *Gallup Poll Monthly,* August 1994, p. 15.
21. Interview with Paul McNulty, Chief Counsel, House Subcommittee on Crime, 2/24/95.
22. Filing an appeal in Court to request a review of a conviction is known technically as "filing a writ of habeas corpus." *Habeas corpus* is Latin for "you have the body." In filing a writ of habeas corpus, an inmate is asking the Court to determine whether (s)he has been lawfully imprisoned.
23. House Republican Conference Committee, "Legislative Digest," January 11, 1995, p. 12.
24. Vivian Berger, "Justice Delayed or Justice Denied? A Comment on Recent Proposals to Reform Death Penalty Habeas Corpus," in *Columbia Law Review* 90 (1990) pp. 1665–1714.
25. John J. DiIulio et al., "Crime Solutions: Eighteen Things We Can Now Do To Fight Back," *The American Enterprise,* May/June 1991, pp. 32–51. See especially pp. 40–41.
26. House Republican Conference Committee, "Legislative Digest," January 11, 1995, p. 13.
27. Merlo and Benekos (1994).
28. Keith Krehbiel, *Information and Legislative Organization* (Ann Arbor: University of Michigan Press, 1992) Chapter 5.
29. Interview with Congressman Barney Frank (MA), 3/10/95.
30. On members' desire to advance policy goals, see: Richard F. Fenno, Jr., *Congressmen in Committees* (Boston: Little Brown and Co., 1973) p. 77.
31. Interview with Paul McNulty, Chief Counsel, House Subcommittee on Crime, 2/24/95.
32. On the floor, the Berman provision was amended to cap the amount the Federal government would have to pay border states but the cap was set at a higher level than in the 1994 legislation.
33. Holly Idelson, "GOP Splits Up Crime Bill; Panel OK's First Pieces," *Congressional Quarterly Weekly Report,* 1/28/95, p. 290. *The Washington Post,* 2/10/95, p. A11.
34. Holly Idelson, "House GOP Crime Bills Win Easy Passage," *Congressional Quarterly Weekly Report,* 2/11/95, pp. 456–457.
35. Quoted in *The Washington Times,* 2/9/95, p. A1.
36. Interview with Paul McNulty, Chief Counsel, Subcommittee on Crime, 2/24/95.
37. Interview with Congressman Owen Pickett (VA), 3/3/95.
38. Interview with Congressman Barney Frank (MA), 3/10/95.
39. R. Douglas Arnold, *The Logic of Congressional Action* (New Haven, CT: Yale University Press, 1990) p. 68.

Chapter 6

1. Quoted in *The Washington Post,* 1/28/95, p. A1.
2. James M. Lindsay, *Congress and the Politics of U.S. Foreign Policy* (Baltimore: Johns Hopkins University Press, 1994) pp. 12–14; James M. Lindsay and Randall Ripley, "How Congress Influences Foreign and Defense Policy," in James M. Lindsay and Randall Ripley

(eds.), *Congress Resurgent: Foreign and Defense Policy on Capitol Hill* (Ann Arbor: University of Michigan Press, 1993) Chapter 2; Barry M. Blechman, *The Politics of National Security: Congress and U.S. Defense Policy* (New York: Oxford University Press, 1990).
3. Christopher J. Deering, "National Security Policy and Congress," Chapter 14 in Christopher J. Deering, ed., *Congressional Politics* (Pacific Grove, CA: Brooks-Cole, 1989) p. 286.
4. Paul E. Peterson and Jay P. Greene, "Questioning by the Foreign Policy Committees," in Paul E. Peterson, ed., *The President, The Congress and the Making of Foreign Policy* (Norman, OK: University of Oklahoma Press, 1994) pp. 74–100.
5. Thomas Hartley and Bruce Russett, "Public Opinion and the Common Defense: Who Governs Military Spending in the United States?" in *American Political Science Review* 86:4 (December 1992) pp. 905–915; George H. Quester, *The Future of Nuclear Deterrence* (Lexington, MA: Lexington Books, 1986).
6. Larry Bartels, "Constituency Opinion and Congressional Policy Making: The Reagan Defense Buildup," in *American Political Science Review,* 85:2 (June 1991) pp. 457–474.
7. John J. Weltman, "The Setting for American National Security in the 1990s," in John J. Weltman, Michael Nacht, and George H. Quester, eds., *Challenges to American National Security in the 1990s* (New York: Plenum Press, 1991) pp. 1–24.
8. Randall B. Ripley and Grace A. Franklin, *Congress, the Bureaucracy and Public Policy,* 5th edition (Pacific Grove, CA: Brooks Cole, 1991) pp. 173–174.
9. For excellent discussions of issues relating to NATO's expansion, see: Howard E. Frost, "Eastern Europe's Search for Security," in *Orbis* (Winter 1993) pp. 37–53. Also: Jeffrey Simon, "Does Eastern Europe Belong in NATO?" in *Orbis* (Winter 1993) pp. 21–35.
10. Caroll S. Doherty, "The High Costs and Faint Hopes of Peace," *Congressional Quarterly Weekly Report,* 2/18/95, p. 536.
11. Quoted in Dick Kirschten, "A Contract's Out on U.N. Policing," *National Journal,* 1/28/95, p. 231.
12. Paul Bracken and Stuart E. Johnson, "Beyond NATO: Complementary Militaries," in *Orbis* (Spring 1993) pp. 205–221.
13. Interview with Congressman Joel Hefley (CO), 3/29/95.
14. Lindsay (1994) p. 51.
15. Colin L. Powell, "U.S. Forces: Challenges Ahead," in *Foreign Affairs,* 71:5 (Winter 1992) pp. 32–45.
16. Interview with Congressman Floyd Spence (SC), 2/10/95.
17. Bruce A. Ray, "Military Committee Membership in the House of Representatives and the Allocation of Defense Department Outlays," in *Western Political Quarterly* 34 (June 1981) pp. 222–234. Also: Leonard G. Ritt, "Committee Position, Seniority and the Distribution of Government Expenditures," *Public Policy* 24 (Fall 1976) pp. 453–489.
18. Ripley and Franklin (1991).
19. Interview with Congressman Floyd Spence (SC), 2/10/95.
20. This provision was later amended in the National Security Committee to give the Defense Department additional leeway by stating that the deployment should be as early as is practical.
21. Lindsay (1994) Chapter 5; Lindsay and Ripley (1993) p. 28.
22. Lindsay and Ripley (1993) p. 30.
23. Caroll Doherty and Pat Towell, "GOP Retreats on Boosting Spending, Clamps Down on Peacekeeping," *Congressional Quarterly Weekly Report,* 2/4/95, pp. 376–377.
24. A similar provision later came up on the floor debate, introduced by Congressman Jim Leach (IA), a moderate Republican. It was defeated 158–267 with Sisisky himself voting against it.
25. Lindsay (1994).

26. Interview with Congresswoman Ileana Ros-Lehtinen (FL), 2/22/95.
27. Interview with Congressman Dana Rohrabacher (CA), 3/30/95.
28. Interview with Congressman Albert Wynn (MD), 2/28/95.
29. Congressional Record, 2/15/95, p. H1776.
30. Interview with Congressman Barney Frank (MA), 3/10/95.
31. Interview with Congresswoman Lynn Rivers (MI), 2/22/95.
32. Interview with Congressman David Dreier (CA), Vice Chair of the Rules Committee, 3/10/95.
33. See the remarks by Congressman Eliot Engel (NY), *Congressional Record,* 2/15/95, p. H1785. Also: Pat Towell, "House Votes to Sharply Rein in U.S. Peacekeeping Expenses," *Congressional Quarterly Weekly Report,* 2/18/95, pp. 535–538.
34. See the remarks by Congresswoman Rosa DeLauro (CT), *Congressional Record,* 2/15/95, p. H1790.
35. See the remarks by Congressman John Spratt (SC), *Congressional Record,* 2/15/95, p. H1816–1817.
36. Lindsay (1994) p. 45.
37. These figures are contained in *Congressional Districts in the 1990s* (Washington, D.C.: Congressional Quarterly Press, 1993).
38. Interview with Congressman Owen Pickett (VA), 3/3/95.
39. Interview with Congressman Mike Parker (MS), 5/3/95.
40. Interview with Congressman Bob Ney (OH), 2/22/95.
41. Pat Towell, "Senate Bill Boosts ABM Effort, Draws Line on Nuclear Cuts," *Congressional Quarterly Weekly Report,* July 29, 1995, pp. 2285–2291.
42. Carroll Doherty, "In Stinging Rebuff To President, Senate Votes to Lift Arms Ban," *Congressional Quarterly Weekly Report,* July 29, 1995, pp. 2282–2284.

Chapter 7

1. Lawrence M. Mead, *The New Politics of Poverty* (New York: Basic Books, 1992) pp. 43–45, 186–192; Christopher Jencks, *Rethinking Social Policy* (New York: HarperPerennial, 1993) pp. 8–9.
2. Mead (1992) pp. 43–45. Judith M. Gueron, "Work and Welfare: Lessons on Employment Programs," *Journal of Economic Perspectives* 4:1 (1990): 79–98, see especially pp. 80–81.
3. William Julius Wilson, *The Truly Disadvantaged: The Inner City, the Underclass and Public Policy* (Chicago: University of Chicago Press, 1987); Douglas Glasgow, *The Black Underclass: Poverty, Unemployment and the Entrapment of Ghetto Youth* (New York: Random House, 1980); June O'Neill et al., *An Analysis of Time on Welfare* (Washington, DC: Urban Institute, 1984); Richard Nathan, "Will the Underclass Always Be With Us?" *Society* 24 (March-April, 1987): 57–62; Charles Murray, *Losing Ground: American Social Policy 1950–1980* (New York: Basic Books, 1984); David T. Ellwood, "Targeting 'Would-be' Long-Term Recipients of AFDC," (Princeton, NJ: Mathematica Policy Research, 1986). For a good overview of this literature, see: Michael B. Katz, *The Undeserving Poor: From the War on Poverty to the War on Welfare* (New York: Pantheon Books, 1989) Chapter 5. More recently, see Mead (1992) Chapter 9.
4. Phillips Cutright, "AFDC, Family Allowances and Illegitimacy," *Family Planning Perspectives* 2:4 (October 1970): 4–9; Winegarden, C. R. "AFDC and Illegitimacy Ratios: A Vector Autoregressive Model," *Applied Economics* 20 (1988) pp. 1589–1601; Shelly Lundberg and Robert D. Plotnick, "Adolescent Premarital Childbearing: Do Opportunity Costs Matter?" Discussion Paper no. 90-23. (Seattle: University of Washington, Institute for Economic Research, 1990).
5. Lee Rainwater, "Class, Culture, Poverty and Welfare," (Ann Arbor: Center for Human Resources, Heller Graduate School, 1987). Sara McLanahan, "Family Structure and the Reproduction of Poverty," *American Journal of Sociology* 90 (1985): 873–901; Sara

McLanahan, "Family Structure and Dependency: Early Transitions to Female Household Headship," *Demography* 25:1 (1988): 1–16; Peter Gottschalk, "The Intergenerational Transmission of Welfare Participation: Facts and Possible Causes," *Journal of Policy Analysis and Management* 11:2 (1992): 254–272.

6. Michael T. Hannan and Nancy Brandon Tuma, "A Reassessment of the Effect of Income Maintenance on Marital Dissolution in the Seattle-Denver Experiment." *American Journal of Sociology* 95 (March 1990): 1270–98; Marjorie Honig, "AFDC Income, Recipient Rates and Family Dissolution," *The Journal of Human Resources* 9:3 (Summer 1974): 303–322; Robert Rector, "Welfare Reform, Dependency Reduction and Labor Market Entry," *Journal of Labor Research* 14:3 (Summer 1993): 283–297.

7. Jencks (1992) p. 204.

8. Jencks (1992) p. 222.

9. Ron Haskins, "Congress Writes a Law: Research and Welfare Reform," *Journal of Policy Analysis and Management* 10:4 (1991): 616–632.

10. Hugh Heclo, "The Political Foundations of Anti-Poverty Policy," in Sheldon H. Danziger and Daniel H. Weinberg, eds., *Fighting Poverty: What Works and What Doesn't* (Cambridge, MA: Harvard University Press, 1986). pp. 312–340. Katz (1990).

11. Katz (1990) pp. 185–186. Also: Fay Cook and Edith Barrett, *Support for the American Welfare State: The Views of Congress and the Public* (New York: Columbia University Press, 1992).

12. Interview with Congressman Floyd Spence (SC), 2/10/95.

13. Interview with Congresswoman Rosa DeLauro (CT), 3/29/95.

14. As introduced in the 102nd Congress, Weber's bill, H.R. 5501, set a four-year time limit on welfare benefits.

15. Jeffrey L. Katz, "GOP Moderates Central to Welfare Overhaul," *Congressional Quarterly Weekly Report,* 3/18/95, p. 814.

16. *Congressional Quarterly Almanac,* "Jobless Benefits Get Two Extensions," (Washington, D.C.: CQ Press, 1994) pp. 392–393.

17. For details on the framing of the Clinton welfare proposal see: *Congressional Quarterly Almanac,* 1993. "Clinton, Congress Talk of Welfare Reform," (Washington, D.C.: CQ Press, 1994) pp. 373–375.

18. Santorum was elected to serve in the U.S. Senate in 1994.

19. Interview with Congressman Tim Hutchinson (AR), 6/22/95.

20. Interview with Congressman Tim Hutchinson (AR), 6/22/95.

21. Before the issue of funding orphanages was so highly politicized by Gingrich's statements, they were being seriously considered as an alternative to foster care for some children. See: Penelope Lemov, "The Return of the Orphanage," *Governing* Vol. 4; No. 8 (May 1991) pp. 31–35. Also: David Van Biema, "The Storm Over Orphanages," *Time* Vol. 144; No. 50 (December 12, 1994) pp. 58–62. The orphanage flap is a fine example of how politics can suffocate an idea worth considering.

22. House Republican Conference, "Legislative Digest," March 23, 1995.

23. House Republican Conference, "Legislative Digest," March 23, 1995.

24. Interview with Congressman Bill Emerson (MO), 3/17/95.

25. Interview with Congressman Philip Crane (IL), 3/20/95.

26. Interview with Congressman Bill Goodling (PA), 4/5/95.

27. Interview with Congressman Bill Emerson (MO), 3/17/95.

28. Jeffrey L. Katz, "Members Pushing to Retain Welfare System Control," *Congressional Quarterly Weekly Report,* 1/28/95, p. 280.

29. Interview with Congressman E. Clay Shaw (FL), 5/12/95.

30. Quoted in Jeffrey L. Katz, "Concerns over House Bill," *Congressional Quarterly Weekly Report,* 1/28/95, p. 282.

31. See dissenting views in the Hearing Report on the "Welfare Transformation Act of 1995," Report 104-81, 104th Congress, 1st Session, p. 363.
32. Interview with Congressman Dave Camp (MI), 4/10/95.
33. Interview with Congressman Phil Crane (IL), 3/20/95.
34. Interview with Congressman Andy Jacobs (IN), 3/30/95.
35. Interview with Congressman Andy Jacobs (IN), 3/30/95.
36. Interview with Congressman E. Clay Shaw (FL), 4/12/95.
37. Interview with Congressman Andy Jacobs (IN), 3/30/95.
38. Jeffrey L. Katz and Alissa J. Rubin, "House Panel Poised to Approve GOP Welfare Overhaul Bill," *Congressional Quarterly Weekly Report,* 3/4/95, p. 692.
39. Interview with Congressman Bill Goodling (PA), 4/5/95.
40. Quoted in *The Washington Post,* 2/23/95, p. A16.
41. David Hosansky, "Bill to Set Food Stamp Cuts, Work Rules, Ok'd by Panel," *Congressional Quarterly Weekly Report,* 3/11/95, p. 758.
42. *The Washington Post,* 3/2/95, p. A4.
43. Katz and Rubin, *Congressional Quarterly Weekly Report,* 3/4/95, pp. 690, 757.
44. *New York Times,* 3/8/95, p. A16.
45. *New York Times,* 3/6/95, p. B7.
46. Hosansky, *Congressional Quarterly Weekly Report,* 3/11/93, p. 758.
47. Interview with Congressman Bill Emerson (MO), 3/17/95.
48. Interview with Congressman Scotty Baesler (KY), 6/9/95.
49. Jeffrey L. Katz, "House Passes Welfare Bill; Senate Likely to Alter It," *Congressional Quarterly Weekly Report,* 3/25/93, pp. 872–875.
50. *Congressional Record,* 3/21/95, p. H3358.
51. *Congressional Record,* 3/21/95, p. H3359.
52. *Congressional Record,* 3/21/95, p. H3360.
53. See, for example, the remarks of Congressman Frank Riggs (CA), *Congressional Record,* 3/21/95, p. H3383.
54. Interview with Congressman Dave Camp (MI), 5/10/95.
55. *Congressional Record,* 3/22/95, p. H3500.
56. *Congressional Record,* 3/22/95, p. H3500.
57. *Congressional Record,* 3/22/95, p. H3510.
58. See remarks by Congressman Bill Clay (MO), *Congressional Record,* 3/22/95, p. H3512, and remarks by Congresswoman Patsy Mink (HI), *Congressional Record,* 3/22/95, p. H3513.
59. When party is dropped from the model, the income variable is statistically significant in all instances.
60. Interview with Congressman E. Clay Shaw (FL), 5/12/95.
61. Interview with Congressman Mike Parker (MS), 4/3/95.
62. Interview with Congressman Jim Talent (MO), 6/16/95.

Chapter 8

1. Interview with Congressman Paul Kanjorski (PA), 3/29/95.
2. Richard F. Fenno, *Congressmen in Committees* (Boston: Little Brown and Co., 1973) pp. 54–55.
3. Interview with Congressman Bob Inglis (SC), 4/5/95.
4. On reelection rates in the U.S. House, see James C. Garand, Kenneth Wink and Bryan Vincent, "Changing Meanings of Electoral Marginality in U.S. House Elections, 1824–1978," *Political Research Quarterly,* 45:1 (1993) 55–66. See generally the essays in Edward H. Crane and Roger Pilon, eds., *The Politics and Law of Term Limits* (Washington, D.C.: Cato Institute, 1994); Mark Petracca, "Initiative 553—Yes: Should Lawmakers' Terms be Limited?" *Seattle Times,* October 6, 1991, A15.

5. Thomas Mann, "Is the House of Representatives Unresponsive to Policy Change?" in A. James Reichley, ed., *Elections American Style* (Washington, DC: Brookings, 1987) pp. 263–264.
6. Norman J. Ornstein, Thomas E. Mann, and Michael J. Malbin, *Vital Statistics on Congress, 1991–1992* (Washington, D.C.: CQ Press, 1993).
7. James L. Payne, "Limiting Government by Limiting Congressional Terms," *The Public Interest,* 103 (Spring 1991) 106–117.
8. Rebekah Herrick, Michael K. Moore and John R. Hibbing, "Unfastening the Electoral Connection: The Behavior of U.S. Representatives when Reelection is No Longer a Factor," *Journal of Politics,* 56:1 (1994) 214–227; David R. Mayhew, *Congress: The Electoral Connection* (New Haven, CT: Yale University Press, 1974).
9. Herrick, Moore and Hibbing (1994) p. 216.
10. Payne (1991) p. 109.
11. Sula Richardson, "Term Limits for Federal and State Legislators," (Washington, D.C.: Library of Congress, Congressional Research Service, March 28, 1994) pp. 21–26; Newt Gingrich, Richard K. Armey and the House Republican Conference, *Contract with America* (New York: Times Books, 1994), pp. 158–159.
12. One state, Utah, passed term limits through legislation, not through a ballot initiative.
13. Richardson (1991) pp. 47–48.
14. Interview with Congressman Bill Emerson (MO), 3/17/95.
15. Interview with Congressman Bill Emerson (MO), 3/17/95.
16. Quoted in *The Washington Post,* 5/23/95, p. A6.
17. See also: Sula Richardson, "Congressional Terms of Office and Tenure: Historical Background and Contemporary Issues," (Washington, D.C.: Library of Congress, Congressional Research Service, December 9, 1991) p. 2; Lloyd N. Cutler, "The Constitutionality of State-Imposed Term Limits for Federal Office," in Crane and Pilon, eds. *The Politics of Law and Term Limits* (1994) pp. 99–108; Troy Eid and Jim Kolbe, "The New Anti-Federalism: The Constitutionality of State-Imposed Limits on Congressional Term of Office," *Denver University Law Review* 69 (1992) pp. 1–56, see especially pp. 7–22.
18. See the summary of Justice Stevens' ruling in *The Washington Post,* 5/23/95, p. A6. See also: Joshua Levy, "Can They Throw The Bums Out? The Constitutionality of State-Imposed Congressional Term Limits," *Georgetown Law Journal* 80 (1992) pp. 1912–1940.
19. Interview with David Mason, The Heritage Foundation, 4/13/95.
20. Interview with Congressman Joel Hefley (CO), 3/29/95.
21. These members included Bob Ehrlich (MD), Rick White (WA), Enid Waldholtz (UT), Mark Souder (IN), and Dick Chrysler (MI).
22. *Roll Call,* 2/2/95, p. 1, 17.
23. Interview with Congressman Dave Camp (MI), 5/10/95.
24. Interview with Congressman Barney Frank (MA), 3/10/95.
25. Interview with Congressman Bob Inglis (SC), 4/5/95.
26. Interview with Congressman Bob Inglis (SC), 4/5/95.
27. Interview with Katherine Hazeem, Staff Director, Subcommittee on the Constitution, 3/10/95.
28. Interview with David Mason, The Heritage Foundation, 4/13/95.
29. Jennifer Babson, "House Rejects Term Limits; GOP Blames Democrats," *Congressional Quarterly Weekly Report,* 4/1/95, p. 919.
30. Alan Greenblatt, "Four Versions of Term Limits," *Congressional Quarterly Weekly Report,* 3/25/95, p. 848.
31. Interview with Congressman John Boehner (OH), 4/4/95.
32. *Congressional Record,* 3/29/95, pp. H3905–H3906.
33. *Congressional Record,* 3/29/95, p. H3898.

34. See the remarks by Congressman Bill McCollum (FL), *Congressional Record,* 3/29/95, p. H3938.
35. See the remarks by Congressman Bob Inglis (SC), *Congressional Record,* 3/29/95, p. H3941.
36. See remarks by Jose Serrano (NY), *Congressional Record,* 3/39/95, pp. H3953–H3954.
37. See remarks by Speaker Newt Gingrich (GA), *Congressional Record,* 3/29/95, p. H3964.
38. John W. Kingdon, *Congressmen's Voting Decisions* (Ann Arbor: University of Michigan Press, 1989) pp. 64–65.

Chapter 9

1. Interview with Congressman Ray LaHood (IL), 2/22/95.
2. The President's plan also imposed higher taxes on gasoline and exposed a larger portion of senior citizens' social security payments to tax liability.
3. House Republican Conference Committee, *Legislative Digest,* 4/4/95, p. 13.
4. See the essays in the volume by Henry Aaron and Joseph Pechman, eds., *How Taxes Affect Economic Behavior* (Washington, D.C.: Brookings Institution, 1981); R. Hall and Dale W. Jorgenson, "Tax Policy and Investment Behavior," *American Economic Review,* 58:3 (1968) pp. 391–414.
5. For an excellent and readable summary and critique of the supply-side argument and the rationale behind tax reduction, see Paul Krugman, *Peddling Prosperity: Economic Sense and Nonsense in the Age of Diminished Expectations* (New York: W. W. Norton, 1994). Quote on page 94.
6. Alan Reynolds, "Irrelevant Measures of Americans' Hostility to Taxes," *Challenge,* September-October (1991) pp. 48–50.
7. Krugman (1994) pp. 94–95.
8. R. Douglas Arnold, *The Logic of Congressional Action* (New Haven: Yale University Press, 1990) p. 207.
9. Michael B. Berkman, *The State Roots of National Politics: Congress and the Tax Agenda, 1978–1986* (Pittsburgh, PA: University of Pittsburgh Press, 1993).
10. John E. Chapoton, "The Tortuous Route to Tax Rate Reduction," in Marvin H. Kosters, ed., *Personal Saving, Consumption and Tax Policy* (Washington, D.C.: American Enterprise Institute, 1992) pp. 27–33.
11. Chapoton (1992) p. 31.
12. J. Gregory Ballentine, "Tax Policy and Revenue Sufficiency in the 1980s," in Kosters, ed., (1992) pp. 34–38. William A. Niskanen, *Reaganomics: An Insider's Account of the Policies and the People* (New York: Oxford University Press, 1988); Henry Aaron and Harvey Galper, *Assessing Tax Reform* (Washington, D.C.: The Brookings Institution, 1985).
13. Niskanen (1988) p. 27.
14. John F. Witte, *The Politics and Development of the Federal Income Tax* (Madison, WI: The University of Wisconsin Press, 1985) pp. 339–352.
15. William F. Connelly, Jr. and John J. Pitney, Jr., *Congress' Permanent Minority?* (Lanham, MD: Rowman and Littlefield, 1994) Chapter 5.
16. Republicans also proposed an inflation adjustment or "indexation" for capital gains. The profit taxed is defined as the sale price of an asset minus its purchase price. The Contract's legislation changed this measurement by adjusting the purchase price to reflect inflation between the time of purchase and the time of sale. The effect of this is to reduce the amount of profit subject to taxation.
17. Martin Feldstein, Joel Slemrod, and Shlomo Yitzhaki, "The Effects of Taxation on the Selling of Corporate Stock and the Realization of Capital Gains," *Quarterly Journal of Economics* 94 (June 1980) pp. 777–791; Joseph J. Minarik "Federal Tax Policy for the 1990's: The Prospect from the Hill," *American Economic Review* 82:2 (1992) pp. 268–273.

18. Interview with Congresswoman Enid Waldholtz (UT), 2/10/95.
19. The Budget and Commerce Committees also had jurisdiction over certain titles in the bill. The Budget Committee reported Title I limiting discretionary spending on March 16, 1995 by a vote of 24–11.The Commerce Committee ordered Titles II, III, and V reported out on March 15, 1995. The Commerce Committee's titles were relatively noncontroversial and unrelated to taxation so they will not be discussed here.
20. *The Washington Times,* 1/6/95, p. A1.
21. Interview with Congressman Paul Kanjorski (PA), 3/29/95.
22. As early as June 1993, as President Clinton turned away from his promise to deliver a middle-class tax cut. A CBS News/*New York Times* poll suggested that 75 percent of the respondents were willing to postpone the cut to achieve deficit reduction.
23. *The Washington Times,* 2/22/95, p. A1.
24. Interview with Congressman Philip Crane (IL), 3/20/95.
25. Interview with Congressman E. Clay Shaw (FL), 5/12/95.
26. Interview with Congressman Dave Camp (MI), 5/10/95.
27. Interview with Congressman Andy Jacobs (IN), 3/30/95.
28. Alissa J. Rubin, "Tax Cuts Cruise to House Floor, But Face Dissent Within GOP," *Congressional Quarterly Weekly Report,* 3/18/95, pp. 799–800.
29. Carroll J. Doherty, "Time and Tax Cuts Will Test GOP Freshman Solidarity," *Congressional Quarterly Weekly Report,* 4/1/95, p. 916, 927.
30. See, for example, the remarks of Congressman Robert Matsui (CA), *Congressional Record,* 4/5/95, p. H4214. Also, remarks of Jim McDermott (WA), *Congressional Record,* 4/5/95, p. H4218.
31. *Congressional Record,* 4/5/95, p. H4220.
32. See, for example, the remarks of Congresswoman Nancy Johnson (CT), *Congressional Record,* 4/5/95, p. H4218 and the remarks of Congresswoman Jennifer Dunn (WA), *Congressional Record,* 4/5/95, p. H4219.
33. Remarks by Congressman Charles Rangel (NY), *Congressional Record,* 4/5/95, p. H4221.
34. Remarks by Congresswoman Lynn Woolsey (CA), *Congressional Record,* 4/5/95, p. H4234.
35. Remarks by Congressman James Traficant (OH), *Congressional Record,* 4/5/95, p. H4246.
36. Remarks of Congressman Scott Klug (WI), *Congressional Record,* 4/5/95, p. H4250.
37. Interview with Congressman Christopher Shays (CT), 4/5/95.
38. David Broder, "At 6 Months, House GOP Juggernaut Still Cohesive," *The Washington Post,* July 17, 1995, p. A1.
39. Interview with Congressman Mike Parker (MI), 5/3/95.
40. Among the Democrats voting for the legislation were several prominent members of The Coalition, including Gary Condit (CA), John Tanner (TN), Glen Browder (AL), Tom Bevill (AL), Nathan Deal (GA), and Billy Tauzin (LA).
41. Interview with Congressman Bill Goodling (PA), 4/5/95.
42. Interview with Congressman Dan Frisa (NY), 3/30/95.
43. This was a compromise with the House's Contract legislation that sought $345 billion in cuts and the original Senate legislation that contained only $170 billion in tax relief.

Chapter 10

1. Steven S. Smith, *Call to Order: Floor Politics in the House and Senate* (Washington, D.C.: The Brookings Institution, 1989) p. 41.
2. Stanley Bach and Steven S. Smith, *Managing Uncertainty in the House of Representatives: Adaptation and Innovation in Special Rules* (Washington, DC: The

Brookings Institution, 1988). Keith Krehbiel, *Information and Legislative Organization* (Ann Arbor: University of Michigan Press, 1992) p. 181.
3. Interview with Congressman Mark Souder (IN), 2/2/95.
4. David E. Price, "Policymaking in Congressional Committees: The Impact of Environmental Factors," *American Political Science Review* 72:2 (June 1978), pp. 268–269.
5. C. Lawrence Evans, "Influence in Congressional Committees: Participation, Manipulation and Anticipation," in Christopher J. Deering, ed. (1989) pp. 155–175.
6. To derive a score for all members, the Contract rating counts only the number of yes votes cast as a percentage of all Contract votes up to April 7, 1995. Excluding the votes cast on the opening day reforms, twenty-four votes were included in the rating.
7. Interview with Congresswoman Lynn Rivers (MI), 2/22/95.
8. Interview with Congressman Dan Frisa (NY), 3/30/95.
9. Interview with Congressman Steny Hoyer (MD), 2/28/95.
10. Interview with Congressman Ben Cardin (MD), 3/1/95.
11. Interview with Congressman Philip Crane (IL), 3/10/95.
12. The member interviewed requested anonymity.
13. Interview with Congressman Peter Hoekstra (MI), 3/1/95.
14. Interview with Congressman Ron Coleman (TX), 3/30/95.
15. Interview with Congressman Albert Wynn (MD), 2/28/95.
16. Interview with Congressman Mike Parker (MS), 5/3/95.
17. Interview with Congressman John Tanner (TN), 4/5/95.
18. Here I am drawing upon the discussion of House and Senate differences in Walter J. Oleszek, "House-Senate Relations: A Perspective on Bicameralism," in Roger H. Davidson (ed.), *The Postreform Congress* (New York: St. Martin's Press, 1992) pp. 193–208.
19. *The Washington Post,* 7/20/95, p. A25.
20. Interview with Dan Meyer, Chief-of-Staff, House Speaker Newt Gingrich (GA), 3/1/95.
21. Interview with Dan Meyer, Chief-of-Staff, House Speaker Newt Gingrich (GA), 3/1/95.
22. Barbara Sinclair, "Leadership Strategies in the Modern Congress," in Christopher Deering, ed., *Congressional Politics* (Pacific Grove, CA: Brooks-Cole, 1989) pp. 135–154.
23. *New York Times,* 4/6/95, p. A1.
24. *New York Times,* 4/6/95, pp. A1, B11.
25. *Washington Post,* 3/21/95, pp. A1, A6.
26. *Washington Post,* 3/21/95, p. A6.
27. *New York Times,* 4/9/95, pp. A1, A24.

Appendix

Table A1 Determinants of the Floor Division on Two Versions of the Balanced Budget Amendment, 104th Congress

Variable	Contract	Stenholm
Party	5.16***	5.13***
(0 = D, 1 = R)	(.49)	(.74)
Effect	82.1	59.6
South	1.54***	1.90***
	(.47)	(.43)
Effect	26.5	12.9
% Elderly	–.09*	–.02
	(.045)	(.05)
Effect	–69.0	–8.4
Income	–.00002	.00004
	(.00003)	(.00003)
Effect	–17.6	12.3
% African-American	–.03*	–.01
	(.017)	(.01)
Effect	–48.5	–12.2
% Rural	.02*	.02*
	(.009)	(.009)
Effect	26.1	13.5
% Perot	.04	.05
	(.04)	(.04)
Effect	21.7	14.7
Constant	–6.47	–8.48
Predicted	90.1%	87.0%
$-211X^2$	361.6	295.7
Significance	$p < .0001$	$p < .0001$
Cases	426	432

***$p < .01$
**$p < .05$
*$p < .10$

Logit regression; MLE Estimation; standard errors in parentheses. Effect = change in the probability of voting in favor of the legislation by moving the variable from its lowest to highest value while all other variables are held constant at their means.

Table A2 Determinants of the Floor Division on Two Versions of the Line-Item Veto Legislation, 104th Congress

Variable	Stenholm	Contract
Party	–13.38	4.33***
(0 = D, 1 = R)	(17.68)	(.54)
Effect	–85.6	58.6
South	1.09***	.81***
	(.50)	(.38)
Effect	.66	8.5
% Elderly	.01	–.02
	(.07)	(.05)
Effect	.21	–8.9
Income	.00005	–.000002
	(.00003)	(.00002)
Effect	1.6	–1.0
% African-American	–.01	–.02*
	(.01)	(.01)
Effect	–.28	–24.0
% Rural	–.006	.005
	(.01)	(.008)
Effect	–.23	5.4
% Perot	.08*	.05
	(.04)	(.03)
Effect	1.4	17.0
Constant	11.94	–5.48
Predicted	90.3%	82.7%
$-211X^2$	370.0	252.3
Significance	$p < .0001$	$p < .0001$
Cases	422	428

***$p < .01$
**$p < .05$
*$p < .10$

Logit regression; MLE Estimation; standard errors in parentheses. Effect = Change in the probability of voting in favor of the legislation by moving the variable from its lowest to highest value while all other variables are held constant at their means.

Table A3 Determinants of the Floor Division on Crime Legislation, 104th Congress

Variable	Search & Seizure H.R. 666	Death penalty appeals H.R. 729	Prison construction grants H.R. 667	Crime block grants H.R. 728
Party	4.10***	5.44***	3.20***	6.14***
(0 = D, 1 = R)	(.47)	(.77)	(.32)	(.59)
Effect	61.2	59.4	60.8	80.3
South	1.50***	1.85***	1.75***	1.34***
	(.41)	(.46)	(.38)	(.55)
Effect	17.9	10.9	30.7	14.1
% African-American	–.05***	–.06***	–.03***	–.03
	(.01)	(.01)	(.01)	(.02)
Effect	–69.0	–73.9	–50.3	–41.4
Income	.00002	–.00004	–.000009	–.00004
	(.00003)	(.00003)	(.00002)	(.00003)
Effect	1.2	–15.4	–8.3	–2.3
% Rural	.02***	.02***	.00005	.03***
	(.007)	(.01)	(.008)	(.01)
Effect	19.5	9.8	.10	14.8
Constant	–5.16	–5.00	–3.93	–8.04
Predicted	86.8%	87.2%	83.9%	94.0%
$-211X^2$	280.3	309.8	215.2	420.9
Significance	$p < .0001$	$p < .0001$	$p < .0001$	$p < .0001$
Cases	432	429	421	430

***$p < .01$
**$p < .05$
*$p < .10$

Logit regression; MLE Estimation; standard errors in parentheses. Effect = Change in the probability of voting in favor of the legislation by moving the variable from its lowest to highest value while all other variables are held constant at their means.

Table A4 Determinants of the Floor Division on Defense Legislation, 104th Congress

Variable	Spratt amendment	Final passage
Party	–5.75***	6.78***
	(.50)	(.64)
Effect	–88.7	91.2
South	–1.13**	1.09**
	(.49)	(.52)
Effect	–24.2	18.7
% Rural	–.01	.03**
	(.01)	(.01)
Effect	–13.1	37.0
Defense employees	–.00006	.00008*
	(.00005)	(.00004)
Effect	–55.1	7.8
Constant	9.97	–10.6
Predicted	92.8%	95.0%
$-211X^2$	390.1	434.8
Significance	$p < .0001$	$p < .0001$
Cases	430	422

***$p < .01$
**$p < .05$
*$p < .10$
Logit regression; MLE Estimation; standard errors in parentheses. Effect = Change in the probability of voting in favor of the legislation by moving the variable from its lowest to highest value while all other variables are held constant at their means.

Table A5 Determinants of the Floor Division on Welfare Reform Legislation, 104th Congress

Variable	En bloc amendments	Talent amendment	Mink substitute	Final passage
Party	7.74***	1.78***	–10.42	7.06***
(0 = D, 1 = R)	(1.13)	(.32)	(17.38)	(.68)
Effect	89.8	23.6	–39.6	94.1
% Black	–.05**	–.02	–.04***	.001
	(.02)	(.01)	(.01)	(.02)
Effect	–69.5	–14.2	2.9	1.7
Income	–.00008*	–.000009	–.00004	–.00001
	(.00004)	(.00002)	(.00003)	(.00005)
Effect	–51.8	–5.0	–.41	9.9
% Rural	.002	.01*	–.03***	.03*
	(.01)	(.007)	(.009)	(.015)
Effect	1.9	13.2	–.51	47.4
South	.05	.66**	–1.16***	.54
	(.54)	(.29)	(.44)	(.69)
Effect	.57	9.6	–.26	12.27
Constant	–6.97	–4.33	11.87	–11.53
Predicted	94.1%	78.8%	86.1%	96.8%
$-211X^2$	433.4	68.3	234.5	482.4
Significance	$p < .0001$	$p < .0001$	$p < .0001$	$p < .0001$
Cases	426	433	432	433

***$p < .01$
**$p < .05$
*$p < .10$

Logit regression; MLE Estimation; standard errors in parentheses. Effect = Change in the probability of voting in favor of the legislation by moving the variable from its lowest to highest value while all other variables are held constant at their means.

Table A6 Determinants of the Floor Division on Four Alternative Term Limits Measures, 104th Congress

Variable	Peterson/ Dingell substitute	Inglis substitute	Hilleary substitute	Final passage
Party (0 = D, 1 = R)	–1.15***	1.62***	2.04***	2.85***
	(.24)	(.30)	(.28)	(.28)
Effect	–26.8	21.1	31.3	59.9
% Perot	.04*	.07***	.10*	.10***
	(.02)	(.02)	(.03)	(.03)
Effect	28.3	28.4	46.8	63.8
Year elected	.07***	.10	.13***	.11***
	(.02)	(.02)	(.02)	(.02)
Effect	46.4	28.1	40.0	75.2
South	.67***	.48*	.68***	.70**
	(.25)	(.29)	(.30)	(.33)
Effect	16.1	6.7	11.6	16.0
% Rural	.002	.007	.01*	.02**
	(.005)	(.006)	(.006)	(.006)
Effect	4.2	7.0	15.3	33.6
Constant	–5.75	–14.37	–18.04	–15.92
Predicted	72.5%	77.7%	80.2%	82.8%
$-211X^2$	42.3	102.3	182.9	250.4
Significance	$p < .0001$	$p < .0001$	$p < .0001$	$p < .0001$
Cases	432	430	432	431

***$p < .01$
**$p < .05$
*$p < .10$
Logit regression; MLE Estimation; standard errors in parentheses. Effect = Change in the probability of voting in favor of the legislation by moving the variable from its lowest to highest value while all other variables are held constant at their means.

Table A7 Determinants of the Floor Division on Tax Cut Legislation, 104th Congress

Variable	Gephardt substitute	Final passage
Party (0 = D, 1 = R)	−11.77 (17.31)	5.08*** (.45)
Effect	−60.3	84.0
% Perot	−.11*** (.04)	.03 (.04)
Effect	−1.7	21.0
Income	.00006** (.00003)	−.00002 (.00003)
Effect	1.2	−19.6
% African-American	−.004 (.01)	−.02 (.02)
Effect	−.08	−28.4
South	−.78** (.38)	1.35*** (.46)
Effect	−.21	27.4
% Rural	.01 (.01)	.01 (.01)
Effect	.32	18.3
Constant	12.53	−7.56
Predicted	84.0%	91.2%
$-211X^2$	254.6	367.9
Significance	$p < .0001$	$p < .0001$
Cases	432	434

***$p < .01$
**$p < .05$
*$p < .10$

Logit regression; MLE Estimation; standard errors in parentheses. Effect = Change in the probability of voting in favor of the legislation by moving the variable from its lowest to highest value while all other variables are held constant at their means.

Table A8 Votes on the Contract with America

Contract measures	Principal committee	House vote
OPENING DAY REFORMS		
Congressional Accountability Act (HR 1)	none	429–0
Cutting Committees and Staff	none	416–12
Budget Reform	none	421–6
Term Limits for Speaker, Committee Chairs	none	355–74
Ban Proxy Voting	none	418–13
Open Meetings for Public and Press	none	431–0
3/5 Vote for Tax Increases	none	279–152
Audit of House Books	none	430–1
THE FISCAL RESPONSIBILITY ACT		
Balanced Budget Amendment (HJRes 1)	Gov't Reform	300–132
Line-Item Veto Act (HR 2)	Gov't Reform	294–134
THE TAKING BACK OUR STREETS ACT (HR 3)		
Victim Restitution Act (HR 665)	Judiciary	431–0
Exclusionary Rule Reform Act (HR 666)	Judiciary	289–142
Effective Death Penalty Act (HR 729)	Judiciary	297–132
Violent Criminal Incarceration Act (HR 667)	Judiciary	265–156
Criminal Alien Deportation Act (HR 668)	Judiciary	380–20
Local Law Enforcement Block Grant Act (HR 728)	Judiciary	238–192
THE NATIONAL SECURITY REVITALIZATION ACT (HR 7)	Nat. Sec Int. Rels.	241–181
THE JOB CREATION & WAGE ENHANCEMENT ACT (HR 9)		
Unfunded Mandate Reform Act (HR 5)	Gov't Reform	394–28
Paperwork Reduction Act (HR 830)	Gov't Reform	418–0**
Risk Assessment and Cost-Benefit Act (HR 1022)	Judiciary	286–141**
Regulatory Reform and Relief Act (HR 926)	Commerce	415–15**
Private Property Protection Act (HR 925)	Judiciary	277–148**
Tax Incentives for Job Creation (HR 1215)	Ways & Means	246–188
COMMON SENSE LEGAL REFORM ACT (HR 10)		
The Attorney Accountability Act (HR 988)	Judiciary	232–193
Securities Litigation Reform Act (HR 1058)	Judiciary	325–99
Product Liability and Legal Reform Act (HR 956)	Judiciary	265–161

Table A8 Votes on the Contract with America (*continued*)

Contract measures	Principal committee	House vote
THE PERSONAL RESPONSIBILITY ACT (HR 4)	Ways & Means Educ & Econ Agriculture	234–199
THE CITIZEN LEGISLATURE ACT (HJRes 2&3)	Judiciary	227–204*
THE AMERICAN DREAM RESTORATION ACT (HR 6)	Ways & Means	246–188
THE SENIOR CITIZENS' EQUITY ACT (HR 8)		
Senior Citizen Tax Relief (HR 1215)	Ways & Means	246–188
Housing for Older Persons Act (HR 660)	Judiciary	424–5
THE FAMILY REINFORCEMENT ACT (HR 11)		
Family Reinforcement Tax Relief (HR 1215)	Ways & Means	246–188
Family Privacy Protection Act (HR 1271)	Gov't Reform	418–7

Source: Congressional Quarterly Weekly Report, various issues, 1995.
*Measure failed
**These measures were ultimately combined into H.R. 9 and passed the House 277–141 on March 3, 1995.

Index